WOMEN, BIOLOGY, AND PUBLIC POLICY

Volume 10
Sage Yearbooks in WOMEN'S POLICY STUDIES

WOMEN, BIOLOGY, AND PUBLIC POLICY

Edited by

VIRGINIA SAPIRO

 SAGE PUBLICATIONS
Beverly Hills London New Delhi

For information address:

SAGE Publications, Inc.
275 South Beverly Drive
Beverly Hills, California 90212

SAGE Publications India Pvt. Ltd.
M-32 Market
Greater Kailash I
New Delhi 110 048 India

SAGE Publications Ltd
28 Banner Street
London EC1Y 8QE
England

Printed in the United States of America

Library of Congress Cataloging in Publication Data

Main entry under title:

Women, biology, and public policy.

(Sage yearbooks in women's policy studies ; v. 10)
Contents: Biology and women's policy, a view from the biological sciences / Ruth Bleier—Biology and women's policy, a view from the social sciences / Virginia Sapiro—Male and female hormones / Marianne H. Whatley—[etc.]
   1. Sociobiology—Addresses, essays, lectures.
2. Social policy—United States—Addresses, essays, lectures.   3. Women—Health and hygiene—Addresses, essays, lectures.   4. Women—Government policy—United States—Addresses, essays, lectures.   I. Sapiro, Virginia.
II. Series.
GN365.9.B55   1985   304.5   85-1935
ISBN 0-8039-2452-6
ISBN 0-8039-2453-4 (pbk.)

FIRST PRINTING

CONTENTS

*To the Women's Studies Program
University of Wisconsin—Madison*

INTRODUCTION

Virginia Sapiro

This book is intended to stand at the crossroads of a number of avenues of inquiry that have been developing over the past decade. First, of course, is the growth of the interdisciplinary field of women's studies, and especially that part of it that is concerned with understanding the contemporary issues and problems that affect women's—and men's—day-to-day lives. This focus has been boosted by awareness and interest on the part of academics, activists, and laypeople of the political situation of women and the prominence of news about Reagan era retrenchment and the "gender gap" in political response.

During the same time period academic and popular inquiries into the relationship between our physical and social natures have caught our attention. Numerous books, articles, journals, and societies have been devoted to what has variously been called sociobiology, biopolitics, or biosocial phenomena. These inquiries spark immense controversy not just from the point of view of intellectual or scientific concerns, but also because they touch some of the most profound political and social questions of our day. Hardly a policy area has remained apart from debates based in part on questions that concern the relationship between our social and political life and biology. Policymakers are now forced to make decisions defining when life begins, when it ends, when and under what circumstances we may begin a life and when and under what circumstances we may end a life—or at least allow a life to end.

A final line of inquiry underlying this book is a growing trend within the policy sciences to integrate a concern for theory, including normative theory, with the study of public policy. Here again, recent years have witnessed the generation of books, articles, journals, and professional associations devoted to such themes as policy evaluation and political argument. A journal entitled *Ethics* is often quite frankly devoted to isses of current policy concern. An understanding of public policy is not—cannot be—limited to investigating policy description or even empirical analytical knowledge of the causes and "practical" impacts of alternative policy formulations.

Women, Biology, and Public Policy, therefore, represents the attempts of scholars based in political science, sociology, law, the biological sciences, and women's studies to grapple with implications of the issues raised by these different themes for women's policy. These chapters move well beyond the agenda raised most often by contemporary sociobiology, which often seems limited to exploring the ways in which differences between male and female biological makeup places women at a disadvantage in competition for highly valued social, economic, and political resources. Our approach is more sophisticated and varied, and encompasses the effects of both human biology and our understanding of human biology on policy formulation, implementation, and impact, and the effects of public policy on both human biology and our understanding of human biology.

We begin with two theoretical and historical treatments of the links between biology and women's policy. One by Ruth

Bleier (Chapter 1), offers the perspective of a biological scientist; the other, by Virginia Sapiro (Chapter 2), offers the perspectives of a social scientist. These two essays focus especially on the relationship between the biological sciences and policy science, on the relationship between human understanding of our "nature" and our making. They provide a context in which specific policy problems may be considered.

The remaining essays focus on specific policy areas and problems. Chapters 4 through 8 look at issues raised through the life course of birth, learning, working, and aging. Mariamne Whatley (Chapter 3) considers the content of school curricula, textbooks, and teacher training in health and sex education, particularly with regard to what children and young people are taught about hormones and their link to sex and gender differences in human beings. She shows that a considerable degree of error and sexist bias is present in the education young people receive and suggests some of the dangers involved in not addressing their problems in education policy.

Janet Gallagher (Chapter 4) and Barbara Katz Rothman (Chapter 5) investigate two different areas of law and policy relating to women's rights and control in reproduction and childbirth. Gallagher looks at recent developments in the concept of "fetal personhood" that, in part because of new technological and medical advances, has increasingly resulted in the "interests" of the fetus and mother being pitted against each other during pregnancy and labor. She points out that the famous 1973 abortion cases that are often hailed by feminists as the major supports for freedom of choice in reproduction have been used by medical and legal practitioners to sanction such practices as court-ordered cesarean sections. Gallagher suggests that a combination of political climate, legal precedent, and medical technology may mean that women's legal rights during childbirth are shrinking and more vulnerable than they have been.

Barbara Katz Rothman looks at women and childbirth policies from another angle. She looks at the implications of medical training and licensing practices as they shape the kind of treatment women receive during childbirth. She contrasts the "medical model" of childbirth used primarily by doctors with alternatives that are more likely to be used by midwives. Her essay underscores the significance of different perspectives on childbirth as a medical, psychological, and social event, and shows how policies can favor one or another with resulting differences in how childbirth actually works and is experienced.

Women as well as men now spend major portions of their adult lives in the workforce. As Graham K. Wilson and Virginia Sapiro point out (Chapter 6), although the phrase "protective labor legislation" most often calls to mind policies aimed specifically at women, women's health and safety have actually received less protection in the workplace than have men's, and the "protection" they have received has often placed them at an economic disadvantage compared with man. Their analysis focuses on two reasons: gender-specific policies based on patriarchal gender ideology, and gender-specific effects on apparently gender-neutral policies.

Whereas policy studies of women once concentrated nearly exclusively on issues most directly affecting women in the early and middle portions of their lives, recent years have witnessed increased attention to the problems and needs of women in later adulthood. This research is especially important not just because women constitute the vast majority of the aged but also because, as at other ages, older women's social, economic, and personal situation is somewhat different from that of men at the same age. Some of these differences are due to the cumulative effects of the lifelong influence of gender norms and roles whereas some are due specifically to the interaction of gender and aging. Laura Katz Olson (Chapter 7) focuses on the implications of these different norms in shaping policy as it affects older women.

The final three chapters turn to another set of policy concerns—those that fall under themes expressed by the Constitution writers as the head for government to provide for "domestic tranquility and the common defense." Susette Talarico (Chapter 8) focuses on criminal justice, and analyzes the politics of biosocial approaches to criminology. Judith Stiehm (Chapter 9) concentrates on one of the most controversial questions raised in recent discussions of equal rights: the assumptions underlying integration of women into the military and the personnel policies that differentially affect female and male members of the armed forces. Jane Jaquette and Kathleen Staudt (Chapter 10) remind us that the policy influences of biological assumptions about sex and gender are not merely domestic but extend in their impact to populations around the world. Their analysis of the Agency for International Development (AID) underscores the degree to which American foreign policy can be and has been used to maintain or change the condition of people's lives on a gender basis in Third World nations.

A number of unifying themes and conclusions can be drawn from these very diverse specific themes and case studies. First, a common gender ideology that is based on certain assumptions about the different biological natures of males and females affects policies as apparently disparate as those that shape education, childbirth, criminal justice, and foreign policy. Second, gender ideology shapes not just the relatively uninformed layperson's views of gender issues in politics, but also the development, interpretation, and application of scientific research as it is linked to public policy. Third, gender-based policies have real, tangible, and differential effects on the biological condition of women and

men in both direct and indirect ways. Fourth, these effects
are not limited to cases in which policy was specifically and
intentionally designed to target women or men or
"women's" or "men's" problems; rather, they can also be
found in cases in which gender was never considered as a relevant issue or concern. Indeed, given a particular structure of
gender ideology, these are precisely some of the cases in
which we are likely to find profoundly gender-related effects
of policy.

The two final conclusions have more to do with the way we
need to think about the policy sciences and feminist approaches to this as well as related areas. Many of the most
powerful conclusions that can be drawn from this volume are
illuminated by allowing comparison of very different policy
issues by the combination of theoretical and more empirical
treatments and by the coordinated efforts of scholars in different disciplines. We can learn much from a case study of a
particular policy or policy problem, but, as we hope this
volume shows, we can learn much more from that case study
if it is placed in theoretical and historical context as we have
done here by providing a framing discussion of the historical
links among gender ideology, biological science, and politics.

Last but not least, if anyone should still suspect that
feminist scholars are necessarily dedicated to expunging
"biology" from our vocabulary, this volume should dispel
those suspicions for a number of reasons. Biology is the
theme, and there are even professional biologists in our
midst. Even on a personal level, the obvious influence of our
constitution as mortal creatures is most apparent; during the
genesis of this book many of the contributors directly confronted our biological selves in the experiences of birth and
death. Despite our confrontation with the ultimate "facts of
life," including the most sex-specific one, we would all probably agree that the significance of these events, how they are

experienced, what impact they have on our lives, the vast proportion of the choices we make regarding them, and even, in many cases, the fact that they occurred when and how they did, was in large part determined by social and personal forces and choices. As for the "debilitating" effects of women's biology, three pregnancies and births among the authors, including the editor, did not keep the book from being delivered on time as scheduled to the publisher.

I would like to offer a special thanks to the two editors at Sage who worked with us. This book is dedicated to the Women's Studies Program at the University of Wisconsin—Madison, which is now a decade old and has provided a supportive and stimulating home to many feminist scholars from many different fields, and has taught me, if I did not know it before, how personally and intellectually exciting it is for people with such diverse interests and skills to work together on common questions.

I

THEMES AND THEORIES

1

BIOLOGY AND WOMEN'S POLICY: A VIEW FROM THE BIOLOGICAL SCIENCES

Ruth Bleier

The influences of biology and policy on each other as they affect the lives of women are manifold and complex, ranging from the obvious, as in the issue of abortion, to the obscure, as in the ideologies of inferiority and subordinance. In this chapter, I shall develop the theme that biological theories have provided the scientific justification for ideologies that support, explain, mystify, and obfuscate patriarchal relationships of power, domination, and control—a role similar to the one science has played with respect to race. Since government, like other social institutions, has come to rely on science and technology as objective and rational means toward desired ends, a publicly shared view, the power of science to reinforce ideology has been enhanced immeasurably.

If science, however, simply uncovers "truths," can we criticize its theories for their unavoidable political and social implications? That is a question that does not require tortured analysis because science does not simply uncover truths. Rather, science, a "system of cognitive production," constitutes a "plurality of socially constructed ways of comprehending natural and social phenomena" (Mendelsohn, Weingart, & Whitley, 1977). A cultural product and institution, like literature, film, and political science, it is a body of interpretations and language used by persons who together create and discover meaning in what they study. And those persons, born into, reared, and situated within a particular class, gender, race, ethnic, and national context, have—like all other human beings—a world view. That view and life history of experiences and relationships, a scientist's values, beliefs, and biases, help to determine what questions scientists find interesting to ask, what assumptions they make, what language they use to pose questions, what they see and fail to see, how they interpret their data, what they hope, want, need, and believe to be true.

It is probably easier for people to understand subjectivity as an influence on (or as part of) research in the social sciences when the subject is, for example, the history of labor unions in the United States in the 1920s, a period of violence and forced deportation of radicals. Events and people's actions did occur, as real and objective as nature. Yet surely the written history of those events will be very different depending on whether the writer is a communist labor leader, a reformist labor leader, or a grandson of John D. Rockefeller.

Not so easy to understand is that our values, beliefs, and expectations can determine what we actually are able to see or hear with our perfectly functioning senses. For example, leading microscopists of the seventeenth and eighteenth centuries, including the great van Leeuwenhoek, asserted they had seen "exceedingly minute forms of men with arms, heads and legs complete inside sperm" under the microscope (Hillman, 1972, p. 221). Their observations were constrained not by the limited resolving power of the microscopes of the time but rather by the 2,000-year-old concept dating from the time of Aristotle that women, as totally passive beings, contribute nothing to conception but the womb as incubator.

Historians of science have documented the intertwining, interdependence, sharing, and trading of concepts, language, and metaphors between the natural sciences and the dominant social-economic order. The concepts of "struggle for existence" and "survival of the fittest," central to Darwinist theories of natural selection, were also essential for the laissez-faire philosophy of a new, rising, competitive capitalism. The other side of the coin—the implication of the disastrous effects of the weak, the inferior, or "degenerate" on the survival and vigor of the species or, more usually, the "race"—became scientific bases for proposals for eugenics programs in the United States and England in the nineteenth and twentieth centuries and for the ultimate program of extermination of inferior (i.e., non-Aryan) peoples in Europe in the 1930s and 1940s.

Under the influence of the intense technological drive and the ideology of developing capitalism from the mid-fifteenth century onward, a new metaphor of the body as machine emerged, a metaphor extended also to society, nature, and the cosmos (Haraway, 1979; Merchant, 1980). With the mechanistic view, values of order, predictability, power, and control—over machines, nature, the self, people, society—were prized in a capitalist economy and state and could replace older notions of uncertainty, disorder, skepticism, and unknowability. Everything and everyone have their proper places in an ordered universe, and everything is ultimately knowable and, hence, controllable. Merchant (1980) has shown how Francis Bacon (1561-1626), seen as the father of modern science and of the inductive scientific method, made explicit the program for the (male) control of nature for human benefit. Working at the height of the inquisition and murder of witches in England, his writings are replete with sexual imagery that equated the enslavement of women with the scientific probing and exploitation of nature. In Merchant's (1980, p. 172) words,

The interrogation of witches as symbol for the interrogation of nature, the courtroom as model for its inquisition, and torture through mechanical devices as a tool for the subjugation of disorder were fundamental to the scientific method as power. For Bacon, as for Harvey, sexual politics helped to structure the nature of the empirical method that would produce a new form of knowledge and a new ideology of objectivity seemingly devoid of cultural and political assumptions.

Haraway (1978) has described in detail the development, since the turn of the century, of the principle of domination as the important link in the historical and ideological union between the physiological and the political, between the human organism and the body politic, between animal sociology and human social organization. Though a prominent theme in all of the natural sciences that seek to explain the origins and biological bases of human behaviors and social organization, domination became an organizing principle in the field of animal sociology, particularly primatology. Human social relationships (in twentieth-century United States) shaped implicit assumptions for the methods, observations, and interpretations made of primate behaviors that, with circular logic, thus served to reinforce the ideology of the naturalness of domination and hierarchy in human social relations: "Animal sociology has been central in the development of the most thorough naturalization of patriarchal division of authority in the body politic and in reduction of the body politic to sexual physiology" (Haraway, 1978, p. 26).

While science, as a cultural production by social beings, cannot help but be influenced by social beliefs and concerns, it has been during periods of dramatic social unrest that theories of biological determinism become prominent in scientific circles and commonplace in society. The practice of science—the observations and "objective" measurements,

the language and interpretations, and perceptions themselves—becomes skewed and distorted by the investigator's
fears, hopes, and beliefs. The resultant data then are the base
for theories that become part of the public domain, incorporated into the consciousness of individuals and into the
cultural ideology that is reflected in public and social policy.
The effect of such scientific conclusions is that millions of
people can thus suspect "that their social prejudices are scientific facts after all" (Gould, 1981, p. 28).

Gould (1981) has analyzed in detail the work of well-
known scientists in the latter half of the nineteenth and twentieth centuries, a period marked by an obsession with
numbers, quantification, and measurement as signs of scientific rigor and indicators of scientific truths. A popular
science of the day was craniometry, the measure of skulls
(and, by deduction, of the brains therein, and, by further
deduction, of intelligence). Leaders in the science of
craniometry generated copious measurements that "confirmed all the common prejudices of comfortable white males—
that blacks, women, and poor people occupy their subordinate roles by the harsh dictates of nature." They used
numbers "not to generate new theories but to illustrate a
priori conclusion" (Gould, 1981, p. 74). The scientists included the well-known cousin of Darwin, Francis Galton, in
England, the Virginian Robert Bean, and, the most eminent
of them all, Paul Broca of Paris and Carl Vogt of Berlin.
Each in his own way was able to assemble figures and make
calculations that proved the inferiority of the brains of
"Negroes" or of women. In all of their work, when uncom-
fortable contradictions and exceptions arose in their
measurements, each scientist was able to find ample explanation that would leave the a priori conclusion intact. Even
when Bean found (and noted only in an addendum) that the
weights of the brains of blacks and whites he measured were

the same, he concluded that weight is not worth discussing or considering. He contributed to scientific and popular journals, and one medical journal editorial, written in 1907 on the basis of Bean's work on the inferiority of the "Negro" brain, suggested that "leaders in all political parties now acknowledge the error of human equality. ... It may be practicable to rectify the error and remove a menace to our prosperity—a large electorate without brains" (Gould, 1981, p. 80). Bean's mentor at Johns Hopkins Medical School repeated Bean's work but without prior knowledge of which brains were from blacks and which from whites, and found none of the differences reported by Bean.

It was also important in this period, wracked not only by antislavery but also by suffragist movements and sentiments, to document by copious measurements the similar inferiority of the female brain. The renowned neuroanatomist Carl Vogt wrote in 1864:

> By its rounded apex and less developed posterior lobe the Negro brain resembles that of our children, and by the protuberance of the parietal lobe, that of our females.... The grown-up Negro partakes, as regards, his intellectual faculties, of the nature of the child, the female, and the senile white. (Gould, 1981, p. 103)

Gould (1981, p. 80) notes, "Prior prejudice, not copious numerical documentation, dictates conclusions."

While the eminent Parisian scientist Paul Broca used body size difference as a correction factor to account for the larger brain size he found in Germans compared with Frenchmen in order to discount any idea of German superiority, he did not find it necessary to make any correction for the body size difference between the women and men whose brains he compared. He wrote in 1861:

We might ask if the small size of the female brain depends exclusively upon the small size of her body. Tiedemann has proposed this explanation. But we must not forget that women are, on the average, a little less intelligent than men, a difference which we should not exaggerate but which is, nonetheless, real. (Gould, 1981, p. 104)

Lest we try to find comfort in the fact, however, that this was a science of over 100 years ago, less technically and conceptually sophisticated than science today, it is necessary to note that Broca's circular logic is characteristic of studies appearing today that attempt to link presumed sex differences in brain hemispheric asymmetries with presumed sex differences in cognitive functions (see Bleier, 1984; Kimball, 1981). G. Le Bon, whom Gould calls the chief misogynist of Broca's school, wrote in 1879:

In the most intelligent races, as among the Parisians, there are a large number of women whose brains are closer in size to those of gorillas than to the most developed male brains. This inferiority is so obvious that no one can contest it for a moment; only its degree is worth discussion. All ... recognize today that they represent the most inferior forms of human evolution and that they are closer to children and savages than to an adult, civilized man. (Gould, 1981, pp. 104-105)

Because higher education for women was an important issue of the day, Le Bon continued, "A desire to give them the same education, and, as a consequence, to propose the same goals for them, is a dangerous chimera" (Gould, 1981, p. 105). Ten years later the biologist E. D. Cope warned, "Should the nation have an attack of this kind [i.e., a spirit of revolt among women], it would leave its traces in many after-generations" (Gould, 1981, p. 105).

While most people would probably recognize the bias in the writings cited above, it is more difficult to see clearly something that is happening in science today and to believe that today's social values—in particular, resistance to dramatic changes in traditional gender roles, can affect the questions that scientists find interesting to ask, the methods they use, and the interpretations that they make of their data. Another problem is that we tend to see the scientific truths of today as the final valid truths, the culmination of the previous centuries' unavoidable and primitive follies and approximations. Yet today's truths are as relative, as changing, and as certain to be superseded in coming decades as they ever were. Biological facts and concepts have always changed over time and there is every reason to believe that they will continue to do so.

It was a century of chronological time but only a moment of social-intellectual progress from Le Bon and Broca to the sociobiology[1] introduced by E. O. Wilson in 1975 and further popularized by Richard Dawkins, David Barash, and others. We can compare the statement of Le Bon and Cope with those of Barash (1979, p. 114):

> Because men maximize their fitness differently from women, it is perfectly good biology that business and profession taste sweeter to them, while home and child care taste sweeter to women.

But Barash then cautions us about our modern "alternative lifestyles": With our changing child care practices, in the efforts "to 'liberate' the biological parents, particularly the mother, from the social responsibility of child care ... predictably there is a cost in disregarding biology" (p. 114). "Biology's whispers can be denied, but in most cases at a real cost" (p. 115). In the film *Sociobiology: Doing What Comes*

Naturally, the sociobiologist Robert Trivers says, "It's time we started viewing ourselves as having biological, genetic, and natural components to our behavior, and that we start setting up a physical and social world to match those tendencies." When sociobiologists define "those tendencies" to be territoriality, racism, xenophobia, conformity, male aggressivity, female passivity and nurturance, and dominance hierarchies, it takes little imagination to see how scientific theories become the basis for conservative or reactionary political programs and policies. Throughout the sociobiological literature there are the warnings—familiar to us from the writings of Victorian physicians and scientists—that by "tampering" with our natures we risk the biological future of our species.

Sociobiology claims that human behaviors and forms of social organization are explicitly programmed in our genes and have evolved over millions of years because they were adaptive for survival. Consequently they consider that wars, racism, and national chauvinism are genetically determined and, therefore, inevitable. They have taken as their particular subject of interest issues that are direct responses to the concerns and goals of the contemporary women's movement. Barash (1977, p. 283) writes, "Sociobiology relies heavily upon the biology of male-female differences.... Ironically, nature appears to be a sexist." The danger to women of sociobiological theories becomes more explicit in Barash's discussion of rape, which he describes as a phenomenon in flowers, as well as in ducks. He concludes:

> Rape in humans is by no means as simple, influenced as it is by an extremely complex overlay of cultural attitudes. Nevertheless mallard rape and bluebird adultery may have a degree of relevance to human behavior. Perhaps human rapists, in their own criminally misguided way, are doing the best they

can to maximize their fitness [i.e., leave as many offspring as possible]. If so, they are not that different from the sexually excluded bachelor mallards. (1979, p. 55)

Barash's discussion of rape demonstrates both the scientific weakness and the ideological purpose of Wilsonian socio-biology. Through circular logic, Barash uses the word "rape," which has a specific connotation in human terms, to describe behavior of a plant and a bird. He then claims to have proven, through this misuse (anthropomorphism) of language, the naturalness, the inevitability of rape in humans. The effect is to defuse rape as an urgent political issue that has its origins in the social acceptance of violence toward women. Were it not for the women's movement and the extraordinary efforts it has made to force the public, political, and official recognition and punishment of rape and battering as crimes against women, sociobiology would simply have laid a veil of complacency over the mask of in-visibility that has officially protected male violence against women.

The significance of sociobiological theories lies not only in the political implications but in the fact that sociobiology as a science and methodology is deeply flawed. Its basic method-ology is first to claim a large number of human behaviors and characteristics as universals, true of all humans for all times from our earliest evolutionary past: male aggressivity, entre-preneurship, and competitiveness; female passivity, nurtur-ance, and coyness; territoriality; national chauvinism; con-formity, and so on. Sociobiologists then attempt to show how these have been evolutionarily adaptive by making up plaus-ible evolutionary scenarios that would "show" why these characteristics would have been adaptive. But because there are no fossil remains for female coyness, for example, they carefully select animal behaviors to show that human behavior exists "in nature," assuming that animals are "un-contaminated" by the cultural effects that obscure the biological core of behavior in humans. Central problems are the selective use of animal models, anthropomorphism of concepts and language (rape in plants, machismo in insects, prostitution in apes and birds, homosexuality in worms), and distortions and misrepresentations in the use of data.

The basic premises in sociobiology are flawed. The universal behaviors and characteristics that they presume to explain as biological and innate are not universal either within or between cultures. Furthermore, the behaviors of animals cannot be seen as "uncontaminated" by culture because animals learn and have cultures; even such seemingly instinctual behaviors as specific bird songs are learned. The newly hatched duckling does not follow its own mother from instinct, but rather as the result of a learning process while still inside the shell that requires hearing its mother's and siblings' vocalizations and responding to them (Brown, 1975). Finally, the basic dichotomy that sociobiology resurrects, the gene-environment, nature-nurture dichotomy, is a false issue and an anachronism. It is not possible to tease apart genetic and other biological factors from environmental and learning factors in human development and to measure the proportions of each. From the point of view of science, this is a meaningless way to view the problem because from conception the relationships between genes and genes' actions and the fetus's maternal (and external) environment are inextricable (see Bleier, 1984; Lappé, 1979).

This is dramatically true for the brain, of particular relevance here because the brain is the organ of mind and behavior. In all mammals, the major proportion of brain growth occurs postnatally, and the human brain is the most immature of all mammalian brains at birth. It doubles in size by the end of the first year of life and doubles again by the end of the fourth year. A major part of the brain's growth is due to the growth in size and complexity of the nerve cells, or neurons, which have long cytoplasmic processes (axons and dendrites) that normally communicate with between 1,000 and 5,000 other neurons (Holloway, 1968). Thus the major neuronal and brain growth and development occur precisely when the immature and growing neurons are exposed to a massive increase in sensory input from the external world. Research on developing animals has shown that these processes of growth and formation of functional connections (synapses) between neurons require input from the external world for normal brain development and function to occur. If a cat or monkey is deprived of vision or hearing from the time of birth, its neurons that process vision or hearing are reduced in number and size, in the complexity of their axons and dendrites, and, therefore, in the number and complexity of synaptic connections with other neurons. Such changes were also found in the brain of a child born with neural deafness (Hirsch & Leventhal, 1978; Hubel & Wiesel, 1970; Trune, 1982; Webster & Webster, 1977, 1979; Wiesel & Hubel, 1963).

Whatever the genetic and hormonal influences are on the development of our fetal and newborn brains, they are inextricable from the influence of the environmental milieu, from sensory input, and from learning. The biology, the structure and functioning of the brain, reflect environmental influences. If it is not possible to separate biological from cultural factors in the structure itself of the brain, it is not possible to separate them in the products of the brain's activity—mind and behavior.

If we conclude, then, that the basic issues sociobiology raises are useless as scientific issues, we must seek elsewhere for their usefulness. These lie in the comfortable message that injustices and inequalities, sexism and racism, oppression and wars are natural and inevitable consequences and accomplices of human evolution. The same forces that have driven "man" to construct cultures and civilizations are also the sources of "his" drives to violence and domination. Although Wilson and other sociobiologists deny that their theories have a reactionary political message, there are innumerable examples of the explicitly sociological and political content of sociobiological writings. It is a political statement to claim that conformity and indoctrinability, national chauvinism and racism, aggressivity, dominance, and hierarchies are innate human traits. Ignoring political and social factors in analyzing the origins of political and social relationships is in fact taking a specific political position under the guise of science. The position is that it is not only useless but biologically hazardous to do social "tampering" and to have political programs that fly in the face of our genetically programmed natures. Not only do sociobiological theories obviate the necessity—even the wisdom—of taking social and political responsibility or action for changing unjust and oppressive conditions, but they provide self-confirmation for those who find comfort in the status quo and in its legitimization by science. In the following chapter, Virginia Sapiro explores in more detail the political and policy implications of biology and science.

The levels at which science—so clearly influenced by cultural norms and language—affects our cultural norms and social policy are multiple, often obscure and conjectural, and probably ultimately unmeasurable. It seems likely that science becomes, in this arena, a handmaiden to other forces. It provides the final word, the justification, the legitimization for policies that are based on a combination of ideological and material forces.

Starting at the level of individuals, any theory of biological determinism that reduces a person to, confines her within, and defines her in terms of her biological capacity to reproduce makes her less than fully human and, therefore, inferior. The absolute concordance between this scientific view of women and their assigned roles within any patriarchal social order is striking. Despite more than a decade of affirmative action regulations and policies, the worlds of politics, industry, and academe have undergone little change in gender composition or attitudes. Women, however well trained and qualified, are not hired or promoted at anywhere near the numbers of well-qualified and ill-qualified men. This is a logical consequence of the patriarchal structuring of society into public and private spheres that requires—is based upon—the assignment of women to the sphere of home and family or to the helping, nurturing, and domestic professions.

This historically and culturally specific division of labor has been supported by an ideology that views it as based in biological necessity—the reproductive and mothering functions of women. The sciences provide ever more refined explanations for this situation. The Victorians warned that the intellectual activities of the mind would drain vital energies from the womb and thus endanger the species; modern biologists have postulated a lack of drive, ambition, and aggressiveness (i.e., intelligence, imagination, creativity) in women because of their low levels of testosterone. Sociobiologists ground these differences between women and men in our genes. Central to sociobiological theory is the observation that the egg is 85,000 times larger that the sperm and that women produce on the average only about 400 eggs in a lifetime, whereas men can produce millions of sperm a day. This is the biological case for women's greater "investment" in their offspring and, therefore, their greater attachment to home, family, nursery, and monogamy. There is little doubt that such "scientific" theories about women's intellectual passivity and lack of creativity and ambition (taken together with personal attitudes and prejudices about a particular woman's appearance, behavior, or lifestyle) serves to obscure from the consciousness of "liberal" men, or to validate in minds of others, their private opinions about proper roles for women. Such theories make it possible to justify their hesitations or unwillingness to hire, promote, pay, or recognize women as equals. As I noted previously, such theories make it possible for people to believe, in Stephen Gould's (1981) words, "that their social prejudices are scientific facts after all."

Barthes has noted that the "voice of the natural" has always been a voice for the status quo (Sturrock & Barthes, 1979, p. 60). It is inevitable that that voice will become incorporated into more or less official political philosophies, as it has into the vacuously clever popular philosophy of George Gilder, savant of the New Right. To him sexism is "based on the exaltation of women, acknowledgment of the supremacy of domestic values" (Gilden, 1973, p. 247). "The woman's place *is* in the home.... The fact is that there is no way that women can escape their supreme responsibilities in civilized society without endangering civilization itself" (pp. 248-249). For him the enemy is the technocratic marketplace and state. The only institutions remaining as obstacles to this "totalitarian usurpation" are the home and family, to which women and her values of love and sexuality, "natural and inevitable" (p. 261), are central. Women's liberation is thus "the fifth column of the technocracy" (p. 262). It is not a far leap from this purple prose to the political program of the New Right in the United States today that is expressed in its efforts to reinforce the patriarchal family and reinstate it as women's exclusive sphere by withdrawing programs for social welfare and removing women from the labor force (Eisenstein, 1982).

I have previously discussed the sociobiological theory on rape and its possible effect on popular and legal tolerance of this violent crime. In a similar way medicine and science have been complicit with ideologies, practices, and official policies that are based on the view of women as dependent and incomplete as persons and, with their children, the property of men. The goal of traditional psychotherapy has been to enforce the conformity of women to their "natural" roles as wives and mothers. Until the insistence of the women's movement, the battering and rape of wives and other women and the physical and sexual abuse of children went virtually unrecognized and unreported as the major epidemics they have been. Like the law, medical practice has often considered the integrity of the family to be more important than the safety—or even the lives—of women and children. In their study of emergency room practices and records on the treatment of battered women, Stark et al. (1979, p. 464) indicated the extent to which the social services, including education, religion, medicine, law, the police, and welfare, "function today as a reconstituted or extended patriarchy, defending the family form 'by any means necessary', including violence, against both its internal contradictions and women's struggles."

At the international level, the debt of the political right to sociobiology is overt. The British sociobiologist Hamilton (1975, p. 134) wrote:

> I hope to produce evidence that some things which are often treated as purely cultural in man—say racial discrimination— have deep roots in our animal past and thus are quite likely to rest on direct genetic foundations.

It did not require any distortion of Hamilton's meaning for Verrall (1979, p. 11), spokesperson for the extreme right National Front in England, to say:

> Of a far greater significance is the basic instinct common to all species to identify only with one's like group; to in-breed

and to shun out-breeding. In human society this instinct is *racial* and it—above all else—operates to ensure genetic survival.

In attacking " 'feminist' talk of sexual roles," Verrall (1979, p. 10) writes:

Sexual and other behavior differs between man and woman simply because of differences in male and female hormone secretions. . . . This is why men and women think and behave differently.

And finally, Verrall (1979, p. 10) locates his program in science:

The theory that behavior and social organization are deter- mined to a crucial extent by genetic inheritance is central to that most progressive branch of the biological sciences called "sociobiology."

Finally, I would like to suggest a connection between the ethnocentrism of biological determinism and the programs and policies of Western industrialized countries toward the Third World. It seems unlikely that sociobiologists are as lacking in knowledge or awareness of the existence of other cultures as their writings suggest. One begins to suspect that the ethnocentrism of their description rests on an important unspoken ideological bias: Western industrial "man" is the ultimate embodiment of human evolution, and Western in- dustrial cultures are the endpoint of human civilization. All the other types of human actions and forms of social organization that they know to exist in other cultures and that do not conform on the surface to the universals that sociobio- logists have described must be viewed, then, as intermediate, transitional, and (though it cannot be said aloud) imperfect forms of human and cultural evolution. If other cultures and peoples do not manifest hierarchies, aggressivity, competitiveness, and entrepreneurship, it is due to their still primitive and undeveloped state of civilization. We can be sure that the predispositions for such behaviors exist and will become manifest under appropriate social and environmental conditions (for example, under our civilizing, industrializing influences).

One can perhaps only wonder if this constitutes the philosophical justification for the drive to "develop" "underdeveloped" countries, granted that the drive is impelled by the need to protect, if not maximize, profits for the colonizing nations. Although in some Third World countries some people benefit from increased economic opportunities provided by the large-scale commercialization of agriculture and by multinational export industries, by and large this importation of foreign capital has resulted in the increased economic dependence of the Third World countries, increased proletarianization of workers, and increased impoverishment of women, who are displaced from their central roles in agricultural production, commerce, and trade and are marginalized as producers (Safa & Leacock, 1981). Western industrial (patriarchal) concepts of women's dependence and inferiority join with ethnocentric assumptions to justify the economic exploitations of the people of Third World countries and the particular economic and social subordination of women in those countries. This theme is developed by Jane Jaquette and Kathleen Staudt in their chapter in this book.

One is led to wonder what accounts for the current intense interest in biological explanations for human behavior and social relationships. It is clear that myriad worldwide crises confront us: nuclear annihilation, civil wars and revolutions, devastating and unnecessary poverty, disease, and starvation.

Most of these seem beyond the control or even comprehension of any ordinary individual. Alongside this, women in the United States, as in many other countries, are threatening by their words and actions a system of dominance and exploitation that touches every home, shop, office, and factory. This is a system, however, in which ordinary people have had some control, however unconscious they may have been of that control or of their complicity. Systems of exploitation or dominance are seldom acknowledged voluntarily by the exploiters, and they are generally protected by belief systems and ideologies that render them invisible or make them appear acceptable and natural. When the system of exploitation is forced—usually by the exploited or oppressed—onto the public stage for analysis, definition, and explanation, elaborate justifications become necessary, particularly in liberal democracies such as ours where all men, it is said, are born free and equal. It seems that science traditionally plays an important role—however unintentionally—at such critical moments. In the late 1960s and early 1970s in the wake of the powerful civil rights movement, the issue of race, IQ, and the heredity of intelligence again became a raging scientific controversy. Yet it was an issue, like that of sex differences, with no possible scientific solution in a society that is severely stratified and segregated by race, class, and sex in its cultural, educational, job training, and employment opportunities. That is, almost none of the relevant variables can be controlled.

Today, almost any scientific study or theory, however flimsy the evidence, that offers a biological and hence "natural" explanation for troublesome social phenomena, is avidly featured by the press and, one assumes, incorporated into popular thought, if not actually welcomed by the populace. Thus there are headlined stories about the genetic basis for property crimes, the innateness of male superiority in mathematical ability, the hormonal basis for rape or homosexuality, and so on. And for each such theory, there is an appropriate implication for social/political policy and biological manipulation.

It is important that we recognize that science will not provide easy and value-free solutions because scientists have the same range of beliefs, commitments, and social investments as the rest of humanity. Although the issue of differences in achievement between the sexes or races is an important, useful, and interesting question, the significance lies in how these differences are interpreted. The differences between groups—women and men or blacks and whites—are trivial compared to the enormous range of differences (for example, in intelligence, verbal skills, or mathematical ability) that exists within any group. There are girls and boys, blacks and whites at the lowest end of the scale and at the highest. What are usually measured are differences in mean scores between groups, and those differences are small and sometimes (depending on how the groups were selected) nonexistent. The more significant and useful question for a science responsible to its society to answer is why there is so dramatic a range *among people* in the realization of their individual and cultural potential. It is ignoring the obvious (and the alterable) to look for biological explanations when such enormous inequalities exist among people in access to educational, training, and employment opportunities.

Biology and culture together have provided us with a brain that has enormous potential for flexibility, learning, and creativity. Rather than biology, it is the culture we have created that limits, by its institutions, ideologies, and expectations, the full expression of that potential. One of the most important political problems we need to face is what role public policy, as the authoritative enforcer of cultural values, will play in the development or limitation of that potential.

NOTES

1. Sociobiology has been an important science concerned with the social behaviors of animals. In this chapter, I discuss the particular body of theories introduced by E.O. Wilson in 1975.

2. I have presented a more detailed description and criticism of sociobiology elsewhere (Bleier, 1984).

RESOURCES

Barash, D. (1979). *The whisperings within.* New York: Harper & Row.

Bleier, R. (1984). *Science and gender: A critique of biology and its theories on women.* New York: Pergamon.

Brown, J. L. (1975). *The evolution of behavior.* New York: W. W. Norton.

Eisenstein, Z. (1982). "The sexual politics of the new right: Understanding the crisis of liberalism for the 1980s. *Signs, 7,* 567-588.

Gilder, G. (1973). *Sexual suicide.* New York: Quadrangle.

Gould, S. J. (1981). *The mismeasure of man.* New York: Norton.

Hamilton, W. (1975). Innate social aptitudes of man: An approach from evolutionary genetics. In R. Fox (Ed.), *Biosocial anthropology.* New York: Wiley.

Haraway, D. (1978). Animal sociology and a natural economy of the body politic. Part 1: A political physiology of dominance. *Signs, 4,* 21-36.

Haraway, D. (1979). The biological enterprise: Sex, mind, and profit from human engineering to sociobiology. *Radical History Review, 20,* 206-237.

Hillman, J. (1972). *The myth of analysis.* Evanston, IL: Northwestern University Press.

Hirsch, H.V.B., & Leventhal, A. G. (1978). Functional modification of the developing visual system. In M. Jacobson (Ed.), *Handbook of sensory physiology, 9, development of sensory systems.* New York: Springer-Verlag.

Holloway, R. (1968). The evolution of the primate brain: Some aspects of quantitative relations. *Brain Research, 7,* 121-172.

Hubel, D., & Wiesel, T. (1970). The period of susceptibility to the physiological effects of unilateral eye closure in kittens. *Journal of Physiology 206,* 419-436.

Kimball, M. M. (1981). Women and science: A critique of biological theories. *International Journal of Women's Studies, 4,* 318-338.

Lappé, M. (1979). *Genetic politics.* New York: Simon & Schuster.

Mendelsohn, E., Weingart, P., & Whitley, R. (1977). *The social production of scientific knowledge.* Boston: Reidel.

Merchant, C. (1980). *The death of nature. Women, ecology and the scientific revolution.* New York: Harper & Row.

Safa, H., & Leacock, E. (Eds.). (1981). Development and the sexual division of labor. *Signs, 7,* 2.

Stark, E., Flitcraft, A., & Frazier, W. (1979). Medicine and partriarchial violence: The social construction of a "private" event. *International Journal of Health Services, 9*, 461-493.

Sturrock, J., & Barthes, R. (1979). In J. Sturrock (Ed.), *Structuralism and since.* Oxford: Oxford University Press.

Trune, D. (1982). Influence of neonatal cochlear removal on the development of mouse cochlear nucleus. I. Number, size and density of its neurons. *Journal of Comparative Neurology, 209*, 409-424.

Verrall, R. (1979). Sociobiology: The instincts in our genes. *Spearhead, 127*, 10-11.

Webster, D., & Webster, M. (1974). Effects of neonatal conductive hearing loss on brain stem auditory nuclei. *Annals of Otolaryngology, 88*, 684-688.

Webster, D., & Webster, M. (1977). Neonatal sound deprivation affects brain stem auditory nuclei. *Archives of Otolaryngology, 103*, 392-396.

Weisel, T., & Hubel, D. (1963). Effects of visual deprivation on morphology and physiology of cells in the cat's lateral geniculate body. *Journal of Neurophysiology, 26*, 978-993.

Wilson, E. O. (1975). *Sociobiology: The new synthesis.* Cambridge: Harvard University Press.

2

BIOLOGY AND WOMEN'S POLICY: A VIEW FROM THE SOCIAL SCIENCES

Virginia Sapiro

One of the most curious sentences in the literature on the links between biology and human social behavior is David Barash's (1979, p. 230) claim: "My own feeling is that sociobiology has very few political, ethical, or moral implications." It is curious for a number of reasons. First, the book in which the sentence is found, *Sociobiology: The Whisperings Within,* is a popularized treatment of sociobiology that has been the center of tremendous controversy, much of it political, since its publication. But even more, this sentence appears at the end of a book that claims to demonstrate that human biology and the natural sexual differentiation within it assures that males will tend to dominate over females (and, even, that males have a natural tendency to rape), that women's lives will revolve around the home and children and that monogamous, patriarchal families are in their best interest, whereas men will prefer promiscuity, and that only "unfeminine" women will tend to succeed in the male world. If politics is the art of the possible, then Barash's book suggests that pursuing an equal distribution of resources and opportunities for men and women is beyond the reasonable goals of policy.

Barash's "feeling" is ill-founded, and not just because he is unaware of the implications of his own book. Biology, meaning both the field of inquiry and, to a lesser degree, the phenomena that constitute its subject, does have political, ethical, and moral implications. The implications of biology are not that the structure of our nature somehow determines in any direct fashion what policy alternatives we should or must choose, as some sociobiologists seem to suggest. Rather, our understanding of biology can influence what we define as political problems that might be solved, and it shapes the solutions regarded as feasible and appropriate at particular times. The biological sciences play important roles in the process of policymaking and implementation. This has been particularly true in the case of women's policy. Unfortunately, a large proportion of the work that attempts to identify the significance of biology for the social world—but by no means all—tends to argue that women's opportunities or status will or must remain limited in comparison with men's.

This chapter focuses on alternative views of the significance of biology for public policy. Its emphasis is on some of the theoretical and conceptual problems social scientists and policy analysts must consider in exploring the links between biology and public policy. It begins with an outline of some of the different ways one might understand the phrase, "policy implications of biology"; in other words, some of the propositions that might be implied by this phrase. It then turns to a discussion of the politics of understanding biology, and argues that anti-feminists and feminists have tended to understand the links between biology and politics and policy in very different ways. The essay concludes with a brief discussion of the role of different policy actors in forging the links between biology and policy, as well as the possibilities for change.

THE MEANINGS OF
"POLICY IMPLICATIONS OF BIOLOGY"

What are the political and policy implications of biology? In order to answer this question it is necessary to specify further what we mean by both "biology" and "policy implications." "Biology" has two different meanings that have been used in the context of politics. On the one hand, "biology" refers to a field of study, its methods, theories, and its current state of knowledge, in other words, both the biological sciences and conventional wisdom about human biology. On the other hand, it refers to the phenomena investigated by that field of study, or the object of that body of knowledge. The political significance of biology depends on which meaning is intended. As I shall discuss in more detail later, the former meaning has been a particularly central concern of feminist scholarship; the latter has been the special focus of sociobiology.

"Implication" offers an even wider range of alternative interpretations and, therefore, potential answers to the original question. When discussing the policy implications of biology we are really asking what is or should be the relationship between human biology or biological knowledge on the one hand and public policy on the other. "Relationship" (and the related term, "causality") raises the question of directionality, reminding us that we cannot speculate only about the effects biology or biological knowledge may have on policy formulation or implementation, but the effects public policy may have on biological knowledge and on human biology and biological processes themselves.

Figure 2.1 presents a schematic drawing of the points I have raised thus far, suggesting in brief form the different meanings we might intend when investigating the relationship between biology and public policy. On the left-hand side it indicates the two different meanings of "biology" we have been using: biological phenomena and biological knowledge, including biological science. The arrows indicate the four different logical possibilities of linkage to public policy.

Arrow A suggests the proposition that biological phenomena shape the formulation and/or impact of public policy. There are numerous suggestions of this sort in the literature on biology and politics including those that hypothesize that human hunger or sexual needs shape the policy choices societies make or shape the potential impact and success of relevant policies.

Arrow B suggests that public policies have an impact on biological phenomena. Included among these propositions are many of the arguments made by health or environmental specialists.

Arrow C suggests that biological knowledge or science helps to shape the formulation and impact of public policies. The case in favor of this proposition has become increasingly obvious as more members of the "expert" science community take a formal role in governmental agencies and policy-oriented organizations. This proposition, however, implies more than the formal policy role of scientists; it also encompasses the suggestion that the current state of biological knowledge and research methodology helps to determine policy choices that can and will be made.

Arrow D suggests that public policy helps to determine the state of biological knowledge. This proposition, again, would appear to be self-evident given the substantial dependence of contemporary science funding on public agencies and money.

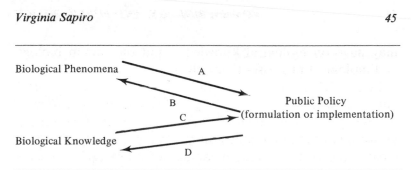

Figure 2.1:   The Policy Implications of Biology: An Outline of Linkages

The important point is that public policy can determine not just how much research is undertaken, and with what investment of resources, but that it can also determine what kind of science and knowledge will receive support.

In order to offer further illustration of the meanings of the policy implications of biology, there follows an expanded outline of the points raised above that corresponds to the schematic diagram presented in Figure 2.1. The outline includes the four major categories of propositions, including those that refer to "biology" as biological phenomena themselves and those that refer to the biological sciences and knowledge about biology; those in which biology or biological science is posed as a shaper of policy and those in which policy is posed as a shaper of biology or biological science.

In each category of the outline examples are provided, in some cases to clarify meaning and, in cases in which the meaning is self-evident, to offer an illustration directly relevant to current women's policy questions. The examples are by no means offered as statements that are true; in some cases research has offered clear evidence that they are false. Rather, they are statements of policy implications that have been suggested by literature in the field or that have, at one time or another, gained wide acceptance.

A. BIOLOGICAL PHENOMENA AS
DETERMINANTS OF POLICY

(1) Biology determines human responses to environmental stimuli (possibly through "instincts") and therefore determines what policy choices people will make.

[e.g.] A threatening situation will lead to a policy that embodies the principles of "fight or flight."

(2) Biology determines human responses to environmental stimuli (possibly through "instincts") and therefore determines the potential effectiveness and impact of a given policy

[e.g.] The "selfish gene" drives men to try to impregnate as many women as possible and supports aggressive and promiscuous male sexuality; therefore, policies designed to make men less sexually exploitative of women or to deter rape of unprotected women will be relatively ineffective (e.g., Barash, 1979; Dawkins, 1976).

(3) Biology determines human traits or capabilities and therefore the potential effectiveness of any given policy.

[e.g.] Women are relatively passive and noncompetitive compared with men and men have a "bonding instinct" that women lack; therefore, regardless of public policies aimed at increasing equity, men will maintain the predominant hold over valued resources and positions (e.g., Tiger, 1969).

[e.g.] Men have superior natural mathematical skills as well as field independence in perception; therefore, no policy aimed at employment or educational equity will create gender equality in the fields of science, engineering, or architecture.

(4) Biology determines the rules of social organization and, particularly, it tends toward principles of parsimony, order, and functionality and therefore determines the potential effectiveness of policies designed to affect social organization.

[e.g.] A sexual division of labor in which women specialize in production related labor is, for biological reasons, a highly efficient strategy toward preservation of the species; it will therefore defy attempts at alteration.

[e.g.] See also point 3.

B. BIOLOGICAL PHENOMENA AS EFFECTS OF PUBLIC POLICY

(5) Public policy may affect the biological conditions of human beings.

[e.g.] Policy has an impact on fertility rates or the conditions of reproduction by affecting nutrition, education, availability of contraceptive devices, health care, and child birth practices, or through direct incentives for bearing or not bearing children.

C. BIOLOGICAL SCIENCE, KNOWLEDGE, AND ASSUMPTIONS AS DETERMINANTS OF POLICY

(6) The biological sciences determine what are regarded as the facts of biology, and therefore determine what we understand as the limits and possibilities of policy.

[e.g.] Whether or not women are naturally more nurturant and child oriented than men are, if policymakers believe this is true, policies will treat women and men as though it is true, and therefore will emphasize reproductive roles for women and others for men.

[e.g.] If a patriarchal division of labor is understood to be a biologically determined, efficient mode of social organization, policy will encourage maintenance of that division of labor.

(7) To the degree that biological scientists and others employ value judgments in their understanding of biological phenomena, biological models and assumptions will help

determine what is regarded as a "policy problem" and what solutions should be investigated and considered.

[e.g.] Population policies do not just depend on how large a population is, but on whether that size is regarded as a "good" or "bad" thing, a judgment made in part by biological scientists. If the size is determined to be a problem, the strategies investigated and pursued with the help of biological research will be determined in part by moral and ethical values: Would we use eugenics if we had a better knowledge of how to do so? Should we investigate possibilities that would require limiting women's roles other than reproduction (e.g., Jaquette and Staudt, 1985)?

[e.g.] Educational and other policies relating to sports have not emphasized fitness and athletics for women in part because medical scientists have accepted the traditional view that sports and the values associated with them are not only more important for males but are contradictory to the norms of femininity and feminine beauty such as softness and weakness.

(8) The biological sciences and related applied fields develop new technology and skills that can, in turn, create policy problems.

[e.g.] The possibility of creating life in test tubes or engaging in genetic or fetal manipulation creates the policy problem of determining when and under what circumstances to do so (e.g., Gallagher, 1985).

[e.g.] Development of "high technology" birthing practices has opened the possibility of its abuse, which in turn creates policy questions about the appropriate use of these practices (e.g., Rothman, 1985).

[e.g.] The development of more precise methods of determining the cause of specific health problems creates a greater possibility for policy-based solutions to health problems (e.g., Wilson and Sapiro, 1985).

[e.g.] The invention of the birth control pill greatly changed the politics of contraception and reproduction.

D. BIOLOGICAL SCIENCE, KNOWLEDGE, AND ASSUMPTIONS AS EFFECTS OF PUBLIC POLICY

(9) Education policy determines the state of knowledge about biology in the general population (e.g., Whatley, 1985).

[e.g.] Young Americans have less understanding of human sexuality and human reproduction than do young people in countries with more and better sex education in schools (Goldman and Goldman, 1982).

[e.g.] School boards determine the curricular balance between the teaching of "creation science" and evolution, as well what textbooks will be used, and therefore affect not only what people learn about biology, but how they understand the nature of knowledge about biology.

(10) Public policy determines what biological skills, technology, and knowledge are developed because of the dependence of science on public funding.

[e.g.] Knowledge about rape, incest, and related forms of violence has increased in recent years because research has been encouraged and stimulated by the actions of agencies such as the National Institute of Mental Health (NIMH), which have responded to policy and political demands.

(11) Public policy determines the nature of the relationship between the biological sciences and governmental action, and especially what role scientists will play in policymaking, which scientists will play a role, and which scientific theories and conclusions will be employed in public policy.

[e.g.] Feminist and nonfeminist scientists often use different assumptions and models and come to conflicting conclusions about the same phenomena. On which will public policy be based? On which should it be based?

These alternatives are obviously not mutually exclusive. It is certainly possible to construct a model of the relationship be-

tween biology and policy that includes features of both
biology and biological knowledge as shapers of policy (including its effectiveness) and features of policy that affect
biological conditions and knowledge. It is also possible to
hypothesize that biology or biological knowledge affect
policy in a variety of ways and that policy affects biological
conditions and knowledge in a variety of ways. One of the
important tasks of the policy sciences is to test these alternative hypotheses. Unfortunately, rigorous investigation of
theses alternatives has been inhibited in large part because the
alternative perspectives have been politically charged and
discussion of them has taken place largely in the spirit of
politcal commitment and partisanship.

The historical political debate between left and right,
feminist and nonfeminist over the relationship between
biology and politics and policy has turned on differences in
emphasis and acceptance of the alternative propositions
outlined above. The first and most persistent object of
disagreement concerns the question of biological determinism
of human motivation, thought, and behavior, and therefore
the biologically determined impact of public policies. The
second, and related, disagreement is over the politics of
science and, especially, the possibility of an "objective
science," particularly as science is increasingly called on to
make a contribution to policymaking and implementation.
The history of these debates illustrates clearly how interwined
have been questions of scholarly and especially scientific
knowledge on the one hand and politics and policy on the
other. Let us turn to this to illustrate further the political
significance of the propositions outlined above.

THE POLITICS OF BIOLOGICAL
MODELS OF POLITICS

By the last third of the nineteenth century arguments over
the power of biology in explaining the conditions and poten-

tial of male and female life became important not just in scholarly discussion but in political debate as well. The differences are well illustrated by the Englishmen Herbert Spencer and Walter Bagehot, who attacked feminism by using evidence drawn from contemporary theories of biology and especially evolution, and John Stuart Mill, whose arguments in favor of feminism rested largely on his attack on biological determinism through the evidence of environmentalism and cultural variability. As Janet Sayers (1982) points out, the case of Spencer is particularly interesting because he seemed to turn against his own earlier sympathy for equality of the sexes as he came to adopt a biological perspective and "social Darwinism."

The dominant strain of biopolitical analysis of gender has tended to emphasize the success and functionality of gender divisions of labor and the enevitability of at least some of these divisions. With regard to the alternative propositions about "policy implications" outlined above, this strain has argued or implied the propositions that biology affects the effectiveness and impact of policy (especially propositions 2-4). As Okin (1979) and Rifkin (1980) argue, political thought, law, and policy as they specifically concern women have long been based on the principle that a division of labor between male and female, and especially a patriarchal division of labor and power, is the most appropriate, efficient, and "natural" mode of social organization. It has also generally been regarded as a permanent fact of life because the division of labor is organized around the biological roles of reproduction. The proposition that has been most central, therefore, is listed above as point 4: Social divisions between the sexes are not only natural, but should be encouraged in order to make sure that society is developed to its best advantage.

Biology has offered political thinkers and policymakers a powerful justification for maintaining and, at times, extending divisions of roles and inequality between women and men. This is not simply because political theorists and policymakers have made selective use (or misuse) of biological research or even current conventional wisdom about biology. As Ruth Bleier explains in this volume, scientists' observations and conclusions have often been biased by what they expect to find, and their expectations are shaped and tempered by the political and social views of the society in which they live. When scientists thought that men had the primary reproductive role of transferring tiny versions of the unborn being into the female womb, they looked through their microscopes at sperm and saw tiny people, horses, or whatever species they happened to be investigating. When they expected women to be less intelligent than men or to lack skills necessary for fulfilling key social roles other than reproductive ones, they found not only that women were less intelligent or skilled, but also a succession of biological reasons to explain women's relative stupidity. In these ways biological science has contributed to the principle of social division between the sexes as well as what we might regard as the corollary propositions—that the traits and characteristics of males and females are different in such a way as to serve the principle of social division (proposition 3) and that the natural mechanisms of human response and behavior serve the same end (proposition 2).

Many critics have suggested that it is the theme of inevitability that gives biological determinism its conservative, antiegalitarian bent. Those who argue, for example, that biology determines that women are inevitably less competent than men at mathematical and other abstract skills or that they are inevitably more emotional or more tied to their children must logically accept the idea that policies intended to create social equality in relevant social roles and positions will enevitably fail in their purpose. In fact, the concept of inevitability is related to policy thinking in an even more complex way.

Biological thinking tends to be based in an understanding of systems, or ecologically related phenomena. One can therefore believe that biology supports divisions of labor and inequality between the sexes and, at the same time, that human intervention through policy can eliminate these divisions of labor or inequality in social roles and practices—but at the cost of creating dysfunctional imbalances in human social systems and, more generally, mediocrity (or worse) in human performance. Talcott Parsons (1954), for example, thought that many of the social problems and instabilities he observed in working-class life were attributable to the tendency for working-class wives not just to seek employment, but to take in earnings that were not as far below their husbands' as was true of middle-class women. His reasoning was based on a psychoanalytic, biologically based set of assumptions. Many other social commentators, at least earlier in this century, suggested that one of the factors that kept "backward" societies in their retarded condition was the relatively low level of sexual specialization in social and economic roles. In a classic example of confusing species evolution with human history, many of these writers attempted to prove their point by showing how, in the animal world, the higher the species, the greater the degree of differentiation and specialization between the sexes.

These and other examples show that conservative theories of biological determinism need not depend on any simple concept of biological determinism; social constructionist theorists score few winning points merely by showing that the world contains a considerable degree of variation in social structure and roles. Rather, biological determinism probably finds its most powerful political form precisely by accepting the possibility of social and policy intervention but arguing that such intervention is bound to have negative consequences of which societies may only become aware when it is too late.

FEMINISM AND THE POLITICS
OF BIOLOGICAL SCIENCE

It is commonly believed, and many conservative sociobiologists often assert, that feminist scholars reject out of hand any idea that biology might influence human roles and characteristics. Feminists tend to be wary of theories that smack of biological determinism—for good reason, as we have seen—and there is certainly a branch of feminist thinking that argues that biological (as opposed to social) causation plays such a minor role in social life as to make it unworthy of observation. But as Janet Sayers (1982) shows, the claims are exaggerated. Even functionalist-evolutionary theory, which has tended to be a mainstay of conservative antifeminist argument, has a long tradition within feminist theory.

Antoinette Brown Blackwell published a critique of Spencer and Darwin in 1875 that is notable not only as one of the first feminist works on the sociology of knowledge and science, but also as a first use of evolutionary theory to justify freeing women to take on a wider range of social roles and responsibilities (see Rossi, 1973). Her argument, quite simply, was that if human males and females, as partners in an advanced species, have developed a high degree of differentiation and specialization in characteristics, one sex or the other should not be artificially repressed but rather, must be freed to make distinctive and complementary contributions in all walks of life. John Stuart Mill contributed to this same line of thinking when he wrote that if biology does shape sex-distinct characteristics and capabilities, social intervention designed to sort people out into male and female roles is, at minimum, unnecessary, but more often harmful. In a free society, he believed, people will not do what they are incapable of doing, but in an unfree society the powerful will take all advantages to make themselves more dominant. In Blackwell's direct and Mill's indirect way, evolutionary theory was drawn to the service of liberalism by becoming a buttress for a case for a free market of roles.

Even more influential in American feminist social and political theory is the work of the progressive sociologist Charlotte Perkins Gilman (1966) who originally published, in 1898, her most well-known book, *Women and Economics*. She argued that the gender division of labor current in her society—and, to an only slightly lesser degree, ours—is dysfunctional to the development of human society and life. She was willing to accept the idea that a certain degree of sexual specialization was necessary when it took most of women's life energy merely to replace the current population. In contrast, the advances in health, industry, and education that shape the modern world mean that if women were regarded only as reproducers, they would be turned into parasitic dependents who would be a drag on further progress. She did not simply argue for ending discriminatory policy to create a free market of roles as, in effect, Blackwell and Mill had done. She went further and argued explicitly for policies that would reshape the structure of society by replacing gender divisions of roles with more rational and modern divisions based on training. When she looked at the way women cooked, kept their houses, or cared for their children, or the way men ran industry and politics, she saw no evidence that either sex was specially and naturally fitted to "its" tasks. She believed all of these tasks should be done by specialists, so designated by their training and development of expertise and not by the irrationalities of ascriptive characteristics.

The study of biological influences on males and females in social life takes on a very different character when it is influenced by feminism compared to when feminist influence is absent. One of the primary reasons is that, beginning with people like Blackwell, those working in this field have taken not just the study of biological phenomena, but an understanding of the sociology and politics of biological science as central to their work. As Ruth Bleier (Chapter 1) correctly observes, people generally seem better able to understand that the social sciences are informed and shaped by the political and cultural perspectives of the researcher than they are to accept this of the "harder sciences." As feminists in the biological sciences review the literature in their fields, they are repeatedly shocked by the degree of bias, or androcentrism as Gilman called it, that they find. (See also Bleier, 1984.) A major policy problem, therefore, is the probability that some of these biological models and assumptions will remain unquestioned components of policymaking. Historians and social scientists point out how these biases and often empirically incorrect views have persistently served as the basis of policy and policy argument that, in turn, affects the real life conditions of women and men.

Feminist research, therefore, has been particularly likely to focus on the genesis of biological thinking and research, the influences of biological knowledge and models on society and policy (propositions 6-8), and, in turn, the impact of these on biological conditions of women (proposition 5). It is generally based on the view that the significance of human biology for politics and public policy depends largely on cultural values and interpretation of biological phenomena and perceptions of the potential for human management of their own biological conditions.

Feminist research places emphasis on what Ruth Bleier calls the "symbol system" of biological thinking and its links to political values and action. As a result, this kind of research is particularly sensitive to the language of scientific and political debate and justification. Consider the following three examples.

In her chapter in this volume, Mariamne Whatley points out that there is no biological rationale for labeling androgen and estrogen (or progesterone), respectively, "male" and "female" hormones, but this is exactly what scientists and laypeople alike do. Whatley shows that far from being a trivial semantic quibble, this labeling stands at the core of an understanding of a biological model of sex differences that is not only seriously misleading, but also has negative consequences for how people understand themselves. For a second example, it is common for people to talk about male and female "biological roles" in the family. "Biological role" generally refers to a wide variety of behaviors encompassing sexual and reproductive behavior as well as the tendency for women to do the bulk of childraising and to deemphasize other economic roles, and the tendency for men to specialize in other economic roles and do comparatively little childcare. In fact, the only strictly biological portion of this entire system is that only women can bear children and lactate. All of the rest are at least largely social conventions and institutional arrangements that are determined primarily by social factors and constitute not a biological role, but elaborations on what nature provided. In labeling social roles and activities "biological," they appear to be relatively inflexible.

A third and most telling example of the symbol system of biosocial knowledge concerns what is generally known as "field dependence" and "field independence." Studies of perception have generally found that men are more likely to be able to discern embedded figures in a surrounding design (and are therefore labeled as "field independent") compared with women, who are more likely to perceive the design as a totality (and are therefore labeled "field dependent"). The most popular explanations, now called into question by recent research, point to differences in the functioning of male and female brains. The social significance of this work is that it has served as the basis for arguing that women cannot, by nature, become as skilled as men in architecture or engineering; "field dependence" is one of women's physiological drawbacks. Some feminist critics have argued that if these differences actually do exist they can be seen just as easily in a very different light, with very different significance. The same studies might be said to show that women have greater field sensitivity while men are more field insensitive. This might suggest that men will never be as competent as women at, for example, urban planning, because a woman, more able to discern how an object will look in context, would never throw up buildings that blight the landscape or stick out like a sore thumb.

Feminist approaches to understanding the policy significance of biology are unique in two ways. First, I have argued that feminists interpret biology in a way that is different from the more conventional approaches and they look at different kinds of evidence. Second, because they reject the model that sees women primarily as functional social units defined by their reproductive capacities, they understand women's rights, roles, and problems in a different way. They are concerned not just with the impact of women on other people's lives (such as their children or husbands) or on social institutions (such as "the" family), but also with the quality of women's lives per se; their approach is "woman centered." A considerable amount of research shows the negative and sometimes dangerous effects on women of policies that see women as merely functional instruments of reproduction (see chapters by Gallagher, Rothman, and Jaquette and Staudt in this volume). Woman-centered approaches allow analysis of the nonobvious impacts of policy on women, as in Wilson and Sapiro's study (Chapter 6) of how women fall through the cracks in occupational safety and health policy.

BIOLOGY AND WOMEN'S POLICY:
POLICYMAKING AND CHANGE

Thus far I have discussed the policy implications of biology in a relatively abstract way. To conclude, let us focus briefly on policy actors and the problems of forging links between politics and science to create more woman-centered policy.

If, as argued above, the policy relevance of biology depends upon cultural interpretation and values, it is important to understand whose interpretation and values influence policy and how. Of special importance are three overlapping groups of people: the public, biological scientists, and public officials.

By "public" interpretation I am referring to the basic configuration of human experience and understanding of "human nature": conventional wisdom. Anthropologists and historians offer sometimes remarkable evidence of how widely the experiences and impact of nature in different cultures diverge. Such apparently physiological phenomena as hunger, pain, pregnancy, and death are not experienced in the same way universally; rather, they vary not only individually but systematically across cultures. People in different societies take discrete biological cues such as skin color or secondary sex characteristics, and build around them large and complex edifices of social and political significance that are, in turn, accepted as part of nature. People are then treated as though they conform to "nature" as defined by the prevailing ideology. One of the problems that confounds attempts by scientists to strip away culture and examine "nature" is that when people are expected to have specified characteristics and are treated as though they do, they often begin to develop those characteristics, thus reinforcing the conventional wisdom.

The public interpretation of biology plays a role in policymaking and impact in two ways. First, decision makers, including scientists and politicians, are themselves a part of this public culture and reflect it in their decisions, a point discussed below. Second, the public is loathe to accept governmental decisions that appear to them to contravene the "laws of nature." Some of the clearest illustrations may be found in the history of law and policy on racial equality, gender inequality, and sexuality. Antagonists of policies pursuing racial integration have often used the argument that the mixing of the races is "unnatural." Likewise because conventional wisdom has tended to assume that interaction between the sexes is based on biological imperatives rather than rigorously inculcated social values and customs, objections to increased gender integration in, for example, schools and workplaces have often emphasized the dire "natural" outcomes of too much contact between males and females. The history of debate over equalization policy is marked by repeated claims that these policies are intended to turn nature on its head, in part by pushing people beyond their natural capacities, or eliminating natural race or sex distinctions, and therefore that these psychological, social, and moral effects of these policies can only be disastrous.

The policy relevance of biology also depends on the perspectives offered by biological scientists. In her essay in this volume, Ruth Bleier shows how biological science has historically been an important part of and contributor to political discourse and, further, how the political character of the biological sciences determines, sometimes to an astounding degree, how we see the "truths" (or, as television commercials say, the "scientific facts") of the natural world.

Biological and medical scientists have long played a direct role in offering assistance to those who make and implement public policy; their involvement precedes the later twentieth-century development of vast governmental bureaucracies in which these scientists are employed formally in policy relevant jobs. Even in the nineteenth century the scientists raised their voices and provided evidence in the debates over women's education, employment, and political rights. Their influence is evident in late nineteenth- and early twentieth-century family policies, especially as they concerned child welfare, abortion, and contraception policy.

Scientists and scientific evidence also contributed to debates over protective labor legislation and, particularly, criminal justice and penal reform (for discussion, see the chapters by Wilson and Sapiro and by Talarico in this volume). Their impact and that of their colleagues in more applied practice has often been particularly great at the stage of implementation. Elizabeth Anne Mills (1982) offers a shocking illustration of this informal but nevertheless crucial role in her study of treatments of rage in professional medical journals from 1860 to 1960. She discovered a virtually uniform stream of advice to doctors to be deeply skeptical of any woman who claims she has been raped and, further, to be careful to break through what is likely to be a pack of lies based on women's tendency to be irrational, hysterical, and vengeful.

The formal policy role of biological scientists and related personnel has increased substantially over the twentieth century with the growth of government and the importance attached to experts and expert advice in policymaking and implementation. In 1981 the federal government employed nearly 135,000 full-time white collar workers in medical, hospital, dental, and public health jobs, another 58,700 biological scientists, and an additional 60,600 in the social sciences, psychology, and welfare. These figures do not include people employed part time or those employed by the military or state or local government, or those employed privately but working under government contract, as is the case with private university or research institute personnel holding government research grants. Throughout this volume are numerous examples of the current contribution of biological science and scientists to policies with special impact on women.

These formal roles have created close links between scientists and the third group involved in drawing the policy relevance of biology, the public officials and policymakers themselves. Indeed, as the figures presented above demonstrate, the scientists and public officials are not distinct but rather are overlapping groups of policy actors. The public officials with the authority to make policy decisions, of course, have the final power to determine the policy relevance of biology. Because of the considerable reliance of scientists on government funding, government officials have substantial control over what kinds of research may be pursued, whose hypotheses are worth testing, and with what research strategies. Scientists may tell the government which problems, in their perspective, need solving and which are theoretically possible to solve, but policy-makers will balance their scientists' views against those of other economic and political advisors.

Public officials are increasingly called upon to make decisions that would seem to require a substantial amount of scientific expertise and knowledge but that go as far as defining life and death itself. Although in 1973 the Supreme Court explicitly denied that it had the ability or need to define when life begins during its deliberation in *Roe v. Wade,* judges, legislators, and bureaucrats alike have found it necessary time and time again to define, for practical purposes, when and under what circumstances life begins and ends. Some politicians, such as those who have proposed legislation or constitutional amendments that would define the beginning of life, have sought out this role eagerly. It is now a "fact of life" that human beings can create life, alter its biological character, and end life in a way once reserved for the gods. These new "facts of life" have created policy problems we need to solve.

The important question to ask from the point of view of women's policy is how to promote change in the applications of biological models and knowledge to policy questions in such a way as to create public policies that are more responsive to women's needs. It is clear that the answer is not the standard argument that "more research is indicated." More is not enough; there are competing views and perspectives within the sciences that are based in and support different societal and political views of women and men. The choice of which of these perspectives will be accepted is, itself, a result of the policy process and political decision making.

Unfortunately there does not seem to be any one point at which political pressure and debate would appear to be most effective. As this chapter has emphasized, the power of biological models is that they are not issue specific; rather, they provide a framework that offers a certain coherence, for example, of patriarchal principles, across policies. The existence of a common framework does not make the potential for change any easier. Public policy is not made comprehensively and the policy process is not designed to be amenable to comprehensive policymaking. Much as advocates of reform in many different areas have been attracted to the idea of going back to and reconstructing basic principles on which to base new sets of policies, this virtually never happens. Although there are special offices throughout the federal and state bureaucracy that are designated to deal with "women's issues," most policies that affect women in special ways are constructed and implemented through other offices, and the women's offices do not have the resources, formal procedures, or authority needed even to play watchdog and influence most of these. Indeed, feminist policy specialists are only now becoming aware of just how many apparently "neutral" policies need to be understood as women's issues. The conclusion for feminists who are interested in tangible and immediate change (in addition to or instead of the eventual revolution) seems to be to continue to place pressure where they can or, in the catch phrase of policy studies, to "muddle through" while, at the same time, they attempt more thoroughgoing tranformations of our understanding of women and public policy.

RESOURCES

Barash, D. (1979). *The whisperings within.* New York: Harper & Row.
Bleier, R. (1984). *Science and gender: A critique of biology and its theories on women.* New York: Pergamon.
Dawkins, R. (1976). *The selfish gene.* New York: Oxford.
Gilman, C. (1966). *Women and economics.* New York: Harper & Row.
Goldman, R. & Goldman, J. (1982). *Children's sexual thinking.* Boston: Routledge and Kegan Paul.
Mills, E. A. (1982). One hundred years of fear: Rape and the medical profession." In N. H. Rafter & E. A. Stanko (Eds.), *Judge, lawyer, victim, thief: Women, gender roles, and criminal Justice* (pp. 29-62). Boston: Northeastern.
Okin, S. M. (1979). *Women in Western political thoughts.* Princeton: Princeton University Press.
Parsons, T. (1954). Age and sex in the social structure of the United States. In T. Parsons (Ed.), *Essays in sociological theory* (pp. 89-103). New York: Free Press.
Rifkin, J. (1980). Toward a theory of law and patriarchy. *Harvard Women's Law Journal 3* (Spring), 83-96.
Rossi, A. (Ed.). (1973). *The feminist papers.* New York: Bantam.
Rothman, B. K. (1985). Childbirth management and medical monopoly. In V. Sapiro (Ed.), *Biology and women's policy.* Beverly Hills, CA: Sage.
Sayers, J. (1982). *Biological politics: Feminist and anti-feminist perspectives.* New York: Methuen.
Tiger, L. (1969). *Men in groups.* New York: Random House.

II

BIOSOCIAL POLICY QUESTIONS THROUGH THE LIFE COURSE

3

MALE AND FEMALE HORMONES: MISINTERPRETATIONS OF BIOLOGY IN SCHOOL HEALTH AND SEX EDUCATION

Mariamne H. Whatley

In identifying sexism in education and its impact on students, many educators have put a great deal of serious thought into identifying sex-biased language and examples in texts, as well as examining differential treatment of boys and girls in the classroom. However, one area that is left untouched because it is often considered not subject to bias is the presentation of biological or scientific "facts." Scientific research, far from being "pure" and unbiased, can be shaped by the social values of both the scientist and the surrounding society; the views of scientists (whatever their scholarly merits) can be used by the larger society for a variety of social purposes. This is particularly true in a society that claims to value "science" and "rationality."

Feminist scientists have, in recent years, been examining the ways biological research has been used to maintain the status quo in society, supporting racism and sexism by attributing biological causation to social behavior. The use of science to restrict women is by no means new, and the current backlash against feminism creates a climate in which the anti-feminist implications of sociobiology and other biological determinist theories are readily accepted. In response to the growing body of literature in the field of sociobiology and the extensive work attempting to support biological determinism, feminist scientists have produced excellent critiques of biological research involving sex/gender issues (Bleier, this volume, Chapter 1; Bleier, 1984; Fee, 1983; Hubbard & Lowe, 1979; Sayers, 1982). However, these critiques have not filtered down to the textbooks and curricula in the schools, particularly in health and sex education, areas in which there are great possibilities for both bias and impact on students. Nor has any priority been given to consciously changing education in these areas in response to these critiques. Indeed, at the very suggestion that curricula be reviewed for sexism, conservative forces were activated to combat the possiblity of change. The proposed "Family Protection Act" was intended in part to "preserve traditional family values" in the schools.

Health and sex educators in the schools are rarely trained in the evaluation of primary biological and physiological research. Therefore, they are likely to accept and teach a simplified and inaccurate version of biological findings. It is particularly important that the textbooks used to train future teachers and those used by teachers in the classroom be clear, accurate, and as free from bias as possible. Unfortunately, sexism in the fields of health and sex education is as common as it is in other areas.

An examination of health and sex education school curricular materials and teacher education texts reveals the often subtle misinterpretations of biology that can have a serious impact on both female and male students in terms of their perceptions of themselves and others. Often the implication is that the norm is biologically determined and that anything else is clearly deviation. The behaviors seen as part of a biologically determined natural path of development often reflect a sexist and heterosexist bias. From the scientifically incorrect use of the terms "male" and "female" hormones to the explanation of the roles of these hormones in growth and development to the implication of the inevitability of heterosexual dating, marriage, and childbearing, misinterpretation of biology helps teach teenagers to accept the status quo in sex roles. An educational policy at the level of schools of education in which teachers learn to view biological issues more critically and to identify sexism, as well as racism, in science is essential for combating sexism in the classroom, as well as influencing attitudes and patterns of behavior at a crucial stage of development.

In order to evaluate the materials teachers would be exposed to during their training, I examined 25 texts that were commonly used either in health and sex education classes at the college level or were education methods texts and curricular guides in these areas. These texts ranged in publishing dates from 1975 to 1984. In examining these texts, I was particularly looking for errors in facts, oversimplification to the point of innaccuracy, important information missing, and unwarranted social implications. In this chapter, I present several content areas in which flaws in texts have sexist implications.

"MALE" AND "FEMALE" HORMONES

The sex hormones that play a major role in changes occurring at puberty—estrogens and androgens, produced by the ovaries, testes, and adrenals—are present both in males and females. They can also be easily interconverted in different body tissues, often confounding experiments that look at the effects of hormones that are introduced into experimental

animals. Though the average female tends to have higher
levels of estrogens than androgens and the average male the
reverse, there is a great deal of individual variation in the
ratio of these hormones. As with most sex differences, there
is significant overlap between the sexes in hormone levels. It
is, therefore, not possible to determine biological sex based
on hormone levels alone. In addition, these hormones are
necessary for normal development in both sexes, and an increase in both hormones occurs in males and females at
puberty.[1]

In most texts surveyed, there are discussions in which these
hormones are consistently referred to as "male" (androgens)
and "female" (estrogens) hormones. The majority of texts do
not mention that both sexes produce these hormones and that
their role is important in both sexes, though several of the
most recent texts do point this out (Allgeier & Allgeier, 1984;
Kilmann, 1984). It is rarely stated that androgens play a role
in female development, though this has been presented occasionally (Sommer, 1978). Androgen plays an important role
in the development of the female at puberty, in terms of
growth, muscle and bone development, and hair distribution,
yet it is called the "hormone of maleness" in one text (Hafen,
Thygerson, & Rhodes, 1979, p. 259). The unstated implication is that such androgen-controlled aspects of development
as muscle growth are essentially male. One of the texts illustrates this view in its explanation of the possible problems
associated with a female having too much "male" hormone:

> Too much androgen in a woman may enhance her sex drive
> and may cause her to become hirsute or abnormally hairy.
> (McCary & McCary, 1984, p. 31)

It is not clear whether hirsuteness is a price to pay for enhanced sex drive or whether they are both unhealthy and

unfeminine effects of an overdose of the "hormone of maleness" in a female.

Science and science-based education are and should be based on precision and rigor. The imprecision of the preceding terminology is a serious problem because, by avoiding the subtleties of the roles of these hormones, the concepts of "male" and "female" and accompanying behavioral roles become fixed as if caused by the "male" and "female" hormones. After reading repeatedly that the androgens are male hormones and the estrogens are female hormones, one can easily forget that these terms are shorthand for hormones that are found predominantly but not exclusively in one sex or the other. From there it is easy to accept a rather broad role for these hormones in determining sex roles, though these are more likely to be culturally constructed than biologically determined.

THE ROLE OF SEX HORMONES

All texts recognize that these hormones play an important role, either by themselves or interacting, in major pubertal changes, such as those in hair and fat distribution and the development and growth of breasts, genitals, muscles, and bones. Some texts expand beyond these well-established effects:

> The onset of adolescence is triggered by the pituitary, which stimulates the secretion of the sex hormones that have important effects on various tissues of the body, including the brain. These hormonal changes are responsible not only for some of the physical changes that may greatly affect adolescent body image, but also changes in sexual, aggressive, and emotional behavior. (Hafen, Burgener, Hurley, & Peterson, 1978, p. 178)

Other texts support this idea of a biological basis for adolescent behavior. One text lists "Ten Basic Facts of Transescent Physical Development," which includes as a first fact, "Aggressive play and roughness among boys increase because of physiological changes at puberty" (George & Lawrence, 1982, p. 30).

The effects of hormones on the brain are simply not known. The arguments that claim a role for androgens in aggression are very weak, even in terms of the animal models that are generally much easier to study than humans. Biological research on aggression has serious problems relating to the nonrigorous definitions of that term that can range from rough-and-tumble play in nonhuman primates to competition in the business world to wars between nations. The loose definitions allow inappropriate extrapolation from results in animal studies to theories about human behavior. Currently, there is no proof for a causal relationship between physiological changes and aggressive behavior and much stronger arguments have been made for the role of socialization in aggression.[2] Considering the lack of scientific evidence connecting aggression and hormones, it might be wise for a teacher to look for nonbiological explanations of aggressive adolescent male behavior. The preceding passage set up a situation in which "normal" boys are expected to be rough and aggressive because of their hormones, whereas "normal" girls should not be. These expectations of gender-related behavior clearly can help create this socially accepted pattern of behavior without any aid from androgens.

BIOLOGY, SEX ROLES, AND STEREOTYPES

Educators have been making strong pleas to reduce sex role stereotypes and allow full development of the potential of all students, but the misunderstanding of the role of biology in determining sex roles can create confusion. For example, in an article originally published in *Health Education,* Dixie Crase (1978, p. 192) wrote the following:

> In conclusion, whether sexual differences are due to biological and/or sociological factors, the sex of individuals continues to influence their development. It remains as important for a boy or girl to learn his or her sex role as ever. Educators and other adults must begin early to be aware of subtle, unconscious influences in early childhood which limit both boys and girls in terms of future self-concepts and interpersonal relationships. Individuals, families, and society can ill afford to limit the development of human potential.

Although she clearly wishes to avoid forcing constricting sex roles on girls or boys, she seems willing to accept a biological explanation. Earlier in the same article she wrote, "However, recently reported research suggests the newborn human infant is unequivocally a girl or a boy with feminine or masculine predispositions" (p. 187). Although the majority of newborns are unequivocally female or male in terms of external genitalia, the existence of feminine or masculine predispositions is hardly a given. On the contrary, several studies suggest that adults respond as if there were differences in predisposition though there is no objective basis for the described differences. Sex role stereotyping appears to begin at birth; gender "appropriate" descriptions of infants by parents appear not to reflect any real differences among infants (Rubin, Provenzano, & Luria, 1974). In fact, the concept of predispositions that Crase seems to accept serves to place limitations on the possibility of the full development of human potential that she seeks.

Often sex roles are covered as a separate topic in adolescent health and sex education. In texts, the presentation of these roles reflects some of the confusion expressed in the Crase article—that sex roles should not be limiting but that they are necessary, even, perhaps, biologically determined. A good example of these conflicting views can be found in the text, *Creative Teaching in Health* (Read & Greene, 1980, p. 216):

> However, the long-term trend appears to be toward reducing the heretofore sharp distinctions in societal expectations for masculine and feminine patterns of interest and behavior.
>
> Despite the vigorous actions of many feminist groups, certain underlying physiological differences will undoubtedly place limits on this effort and preserve the meaningfulness of sex roles.

It is not clear which underlying physiological differences are being referred to, whether simply to those few clear sex differences—potential to ovulate, gestate, lactate, versus the potential to inseminate—or differences such as those in aggression that are both vaguely defined and unproven as biologically determined. In any case, as with Crase, there is a hope expressed that the "meaningfulness" of sex roles will be preserved.

The lack of clarity about physiological givens versus cultural norms is expressed by Read and Greene (1980, p. 222) in a concept suggested for teaching sex roles:

> 8. *Boys and girls develop typical differences in their personalities, interests, and modes of behavior as they mature.* Physiological differences between men and women have traditionally led to different duties and responsibilities which in turn have produced general personality differences. Although based on physiological factors, this process of role definition is largely a cultural process.

The difference in duties and responsibilities that has a physiological basis is essentially that women can be the ones to give birth and breastfeed and that men cannot. Beyond that there are no roles that can be directly attributable to physiological differences. The token reference to the cultural process at the end of the sentence doesn't clarify at all what roles are attributable to what forces, so that the impression remains that physiology does play a large role in determination of personality differences. The use of the expression "typical differences" clearly indicates that there are specific patterns that are sex-related and, therefore, cannot or should not be altered. This lack of precision leads to the implication that the norm is a biological given and all variations on these sex roles are deviance.

This view is stated much more directly in a list of concepts in a text called *Teaching Secondary Health Science* (Sorochan & Bender, 1978, p. 382):

12. Each person needs to accept his or her sexual-social role.
15. Sexual deviations often stem from unresolved emotional-social conflicts.

Here it is clearly stated that sex roles are given and unalterable; problems arise for individuals when they are unwilling to accept these givens.

The text also expresses the belief that in some cases biology itself might cause a "deviance" in behavior:

Adolescents often manifest extreme reactions to compensate for their size and other physical shortcomings. For instance, a tall girl in junior high may never go to dances because she is certain to be taller than most boys she dances with. Or a large girl may go in for athletics, masculine clothes, and a career because she cannot be "cute" and feminine. (p. 122)

Here what is defined as an "extreme reaction" is for a girl to stray from her sex role, pursuing athletics and a career because of a "physical shortcoming." In this paragraph, it has been clearly established that there is certain normal and healthy behavior for a girl. Instead of merely encouraging the educator to feel sympathetic for a "misfit," the authors could have introduced the idea of valuing individual differences and the possibilities of not fitting into a mold. It would also be an appropriate time to question some accepted standards of adolescent culture, such as girls having the option to dance only with boys who are taller or body size serving as a determinant of femininity. Educators should present athletics and a career as positive possibilities for all students.

Sorochan and Bender (1978, p. 384) even more clearly identify what they see as healthy behavior when they outline "exemplary informational behavioral objectives," some of which are listed below:

The student will be able to:
  6. Date often
 10. Accept sexual-social role
 13. Demonstrate social dating skills
 20. Describe how to select a marriage partner.

The clear core of these objectives is the acceptance of sexual-social roles, with dating and marriage as part of a normal continuum. The importance of dating as part of healthy development is emphasized in other texts as well, and an educator should question these statements. Texts could much better emphasize the importance of developing friendships with members of both sexes, learning to interact with other people in a number of different situations and at different levels of intimacy. Instead, only dating, which often puts extreme social and sexual pressure on an adolescent, becomes the important goal. Although sex educators are always looking for ways to encourage adolescents to say no to unwanted sexual activity, they may be pushing them into the situation that can most easily trap them into saying yes. The impact in terms of self-esteem on those who are not considered datable, the pain of not being invited to a prom or party, the blow to the ego of an invitation rejection, have been well-documented in fiction and nonfiction. For health and sex educators to enforce subtly the status quo in teenage relationships, rather than calling them into question, is to place even more pressure on a group already facing emotional stress.

MALE AND FEMALE SEXUALITY

In an effort to support continued "meaningful" sex roles, health educators often stress differences in sexuality as a basis for these roles:

> Human sexuality refers to all of those qualities that distinguish between maleness and femaleness. The physiological differences are both obvious and important, but in addition there are the equally important differences in attitude, behavior, and responsibilities that define the male and female role in American society. (Read & Greene, 1980, p. 211)

First, it is crucial to note that in this passage human sexuality refers only to those differences and not to similarities between males and females, so that this reinforces the importance of difference between the sexes rather than the similarities of human beings. Sexuality becomes defined in terms of gonads, genitals, and culturally defined sex roles, rather than in any of those areas in which there might be overlap, such as affection, love, and nongenital response.

For example, this passage clearly ignores the fact that the basis physiological mechanisms of the sexual response, vaso-congestion and myotonia, are actually the same in males and females. The well-known research of Masters and Johnson (1966) showed that what may seem to be very different responses, penile erection and vaginal lubrication, are actually controlled by the same mechanism, vaso-congestion or buildup of blood in the genital area, and are indicators of similar levels of arousal. In addition, their classification of the phases of the sexual response, that is, arousal, plateau, orgasm, and resolution, apply to both males and females. After the pioneering research of Masters and Johnson, the overall message was clear that similarities are greater than differences in terms of the sexual response, so that according to the preceding passage, the sexual response would be eliminated from the definition of sexuality.

By maintaining the view of sexuality expressed in the previous passage, all sexually related behaviors become dichotomized into male and female behaviors and there is no longer an area of human sexuality. For example, there is the following discussion:

> Within the male the sex drive is more specific and direct. It tends to be isolated from feelings of love and affection and directed more towards orgasm. Within the female the sex drive is more diffuse and is related to feelings of affection. Indirect stimuli such as sexual fantasies and provocative pictures have a much greater effect on the male than the female. (Read & Greene, 1980, p. 216)

Although it is never stated that the differences in sex drive are biological, it is implied because repeated references are made in the text to the role of physiological differences. (Because it has been shown that androgens play a role in libido, perhaps the suggestion is that the differences in sex drive are attributable to the different levels of androgens in males and females.) However, what makes this statement especially problematic is that it is not clear whether this is a description or prescription or both for "normal" sex drive for both sexes. Is a female who seeks orgasm or a male who seeks affection abnormal? Adolescents are worried and scared by issues of sexuality and want desperately to be "normal." The information from these texts serves to make life worse for them. By making this kind of statement in a book for educators, the authors, perhaps unconsciously, are supporting a common view of sexuality in our society. Texts should not reinforce the double standard. Without any attempt to show alternative approaches to adolescent sexual relations, sex education is often taught with the view that boys have a physiologically uncontrollable sex drive geared toward "doing it" and girls just want affection and a class ring. Therefore, adolescents learn what is "normal" in sexual behavior and try to follow those norms.

In addition to reinforcing certain societal views of sexuality, many health and sex education texts are strongly heterosexist, if not homophobic. A 1978 text (Hafen et al., 1978) reprinted an article from *Journal of School Health* that clearly expresses a negative view:

> Homosexuality, as an enduring sexual pattern, is an illness, no different than any other illness and is a symptom of deep-seated emotional difficulty. Despite propaganda to the contrary, there is no such thing as a well-adjusted, happy homosexual. (Kriegman, 1978, p. 233)

The information provided is often biased and inaccurate, as in the following passage:

> The practice of homosexual behavior leaves much to be desired if one wants to have children. This form of sexual

behavior might prove unsatisfying for some, since mutual
masturbation and oral-anal activity may amount to no more
than impersonal encounters and are frowned upon by society.
(Johns, Sutton, & Cooley, 1975, p. 209)

A number of criticisms of this passage can be made that also
point out common omissions or misinterpretations in texts.
For example, homosexuality does not preclude parenting.
Many lesbians and gay men have had children while they were
in heterosexual relationships and others choose to have
children, often using artificial insemination, after they are in
homosexual relationships. Another problem is that homosexuality is often used as synonymous with male homosexuality, so that descriptions given, accurate or stereotypical, often
apply only to men, leaving lesbians invisible. A third point is
that there is nothing inherently impersonal about homosexual
behavior; it might be suggested that heterosexual intercourse
can as easily lend itself to impersonal encounters as would
mutual masturbation or oral-genital contact.

Returning to the previously discussed area of dating, the
following statement appears as a concept to be taught under
the topic of sex roles: "Adolescent dating activities and other
heterosexual social activities serve important functions in the
process of personality development" (Read & Greene, 1980,
p. 240). Attention should be drawn to the use of the word
"heterosexual" in the preceding passage. It is not clear
whether the authors mean simply that both sexes are present
or that the social activities are truly heterosexual. In the
former case, social activities with both the same sex and op-
posite sex should be considered important for normal
development. In the latter, the approximately 10 percent of
the population that is homosexual is excluded by definition
and those who are not interested in sexual activity at all are
also precluded from the possibility of normal development.

From a simple misuse of the terms "male" and "female" hormones, it is easy to move step by step through the beliefs that certain feminine and masculine behaviors are biologically caused and, therefore, are normal. Deviance from sex roles, including deviance from heterosexuality, is seen as violation of biology. If instead it were clearly indicated that males and females are made up of a mixture of androgens and estrogens, in different proportions, it might be harder to fall into a trap of biological determinism. Flexibility in sex roles might be more easily viewed if it were recognized that there is similarity in hormonal constitution. What may seem a subtle distinction can have a major impact when viewed in terms of how sex roles are taught as part of health education.

"FACTS" IN WOMEN'S HEALTH AND DISEASE

Factual errors appear with surprising frequency in textbook descriptions of women's basic biology and of common diseases and disorders. Even worse than simply providing misinformation, these errors can greatly affect how women, especially adolescents, view their bodies. Providing good, accurate basic health information and demystifying the workings of the female body can help adolescents develop a much more positive view of their bodies and a stronger sense of control over what happens to their bodies at a time in development when changes may seem completely out of control. Through understanding basic physiological mechanisms and disease processes, they can become more active in maintaining their health. These changes can have a positive effect on other areas of their lives, such as enhancing self-esteem.

Textbook treatments of menstruation offer an important illustration of errors and misinterpretations of basic biology with sexist implications. Cramping during menstruation is generally caused by uterine spasms or contractions, which in turn can be caused by high levels of a substance called prostaglandins. Endogenous prostaglandins naturally cause smooth muscle contractions, including of the uterus, and are so powerful in their effect that they can be used as agents in the induction of second-trimester abortions. When it was recognized that high levels of prostaglandins could be causing dysmenorrhea, it was found that the use of inhibitors of prostaglandin synthesis could be potent relievers of menstrual pain. Both clinical and experimental evidence support the prostaglandin theory of causation of dysmenorrhea (Jones & Jones, 1982). Now the existence of such drugs as Motrin, Naprosyn, and Ponstel has eliminated what had been debilitating pain for a number of women.

Discussion of the cause and treatment of dysmenorrhea is particularly important in health education curricula because menstrual pain can be severe among adolescents, who need to understand what is happening to them and what can be done about it. Curiously, this topic leads many authors to minimize biological causation and to emphasize instead the problems of female psychology:

> Painful menstruation or menstrual cramps, called dysmenorrhea, can be caused by a physical abnormality of the reproductive organs. But psychological causes (tense feelings about femininity, sexuality, and menstruation itself) are more common, especially in young women. (Eisenberg & Eisenberg, 1979, p. 428)

Another text agrees with the view that there is a chance that dysmenorrhea may be physiological in origin, but continues, "However, psychological problems, such as those related to tension or self-concept, appear to be the more prevalent cause" (Gay, Wantz, Slobof, Hooper, & Boskin, 1979, p. 117).

Hafen et al. (1979, p. 265) outline possible causes for dysmenorrhea:

1. an inflammation or infection,
2. constipation,
3. poor posture,
4. lack of regular physical activity,
5. psychological factors such as stress or lack of preparation for menstruation,
6. low pain threshold (some can tolerate pain better than others),
7. cysts or fibroid tumors, or
8. positioning of the uterus ("tipped uterus")

Some of these factors may increase the discomfort of dysmenorrhea, but there is no indication that poor posture, lack of preparation for menstruation, or lack of regular physical activity actually cause cramps. This approach is a classic case of blaming the victim. The adolescent girl who suffers severe cramps is seen as being at fault in any of a number of physical or psychological ways, except in extreme instances beyond her control such as having fibroid tumors. The pain of severe dysmenorrhea is stressful enough without also being held responsible for its cause. In addition, this approach helps perpetuate the stereotype of the hypochondriacal female who either imagines or causes her own ailments, a view prevalent in much of medical education.

Some more recent texts do mention the role of prostaglandins (Jones, 1984; Maier, 1984). Others mention no probable cause, which may be better than the blaming the victim policy, though a statement such as the following, while true, does not give much hope to an adolescent suffering cramps: "Cramping sensations, which are probably related to uterine spasms, seem to be less severe among women who have given birth'' (Kilmann, 1984, p. 76). Other new texts ignore the subject of dysmenorrhea altogether (Allgeier & Allgeier, 1984), discussing only premenstrual syndrome (PMS), which is a distinct phenomenon, or confuse the two. One text (McCary & McCary, 1984, p. 31) says that high levels of progesterone cause dysmenorrhea, a theory that is held by a few people but never validated, whereas the prostaglandin theory of dysmenorrhea, which has been well-supported and documented, is not mentioned.

Textbooks should provide more thorough and accurate treatment of a problem that is so common among adolescent females. While nonmedical approaches to reducing cramps, such as exercise and salt reduction, should be discussed, it should also be pointed out that good treatments are available for debilitating cramps. There should never be an issue of a psychological component in dysmenorrhea unless people are willing to explore the subject in enough depth to prevent simplistic interpretations. An educator, especially a health educator who is involved with physical education as is often the case, must be aware that cramps are a real physiological phenomenon and not a rejection of femininity or simply an excuse for skipping gym class. Telling a girl that if she stood up straight, she probably wouldn't have cramps is hardly the answer, especially if she is doubled over from the pain.

It is also interesting to note that two texts that emphasize psychological origins for dysmenorrhea also subscribe to the notion that cystitis, a bladder infection caused by bacteria, may be psychological in origin (Gay et al., 1979, p. 118) and may respond to psychotherapy (Eisenberg & Eisenberg, 1979, p. 428). Cystitis is generally caused when *E. coli*, bacteria that are normal inhabitants of the large intestine, enter the urethra and move into the bladder. Though this infection can occur in males, it is much more common in females, largely due to the much shorter urethra in females. Contamination of the urethra can occur simply by wiping from back to front after defecation, but cystitis is certainly not necessarily the result of poor hygiene. In addition, vaginal intercourse can force bacteria up the urethra and the pressure of the penis can additionally irritate the urethra. However, cystitis can easily occur without any sexual activity.

Though many texts provide accurate medical information on the disease (e.g., Allgeier & Allgeier, 1984; Maier, 1984), another 1984 text describes cystitis as an inflammation of the bladder but never as a bacterial infection. It also adds, "sometimes cystitis is caused or aggravated by emotional factors, usually related to conflict over sexual matters" (McCary & McCary, 1984, p. 303). This view again places the burden of responsibility for causation on the sufferer. Because cystitis is often associated with heterosexual intercourse, it may be seen by a woman with the disease as being very much sexually related and, therefore, hard to discuss if she is also not comfortable discussing her sexual activity or if she is not sexually active at all. It is also important to recognize that it is a bacterial infection because many women suffer through it without seeking treatment and an untreated infection can spread, potentially causing kidney damage. Dysmenorrhea and cystitis are just two of the more obvious examples of the need for evaluating information in texts.

CONCLUSION

While educators who are eager to combat sexism may be carefully changing pronouns and making sure boys cook and girls do woodworking, they may be completely ignoring sexist information appearing in the texts that are used to train teachers. Many of these texts have serious flaws in the presentation of information on such common topics as changes during puberty and menstruation. These problems include oversimplification of information ("male" and "female" hormones), missing information (dysmenorrhea), incorrect information (emotional causes of cystitis and dysmenorrhea), and unwarranted attribution of human behavior to biological causes (aggression, sex roles). Some material carries the implication that, just as certain physical characteristics are biologically determined, so are sex roles. It is implied that variations on specific patterns of male/female behavior violate biological norms and are, therefore, unhealthy. What is stressed as normal and healthy includes a predictable pattern of heterosexual dating, followed inevitably by marriage. The status quo in society is enforced with little room for flexibility.

While stressing a biologically determinist view of sex roles, sexuality, and other behavior such as aggression, many texts offer a psychological explanation for some common problems experienced by females. Texts suggest that females suffering from such conditions as dysmenorrhea or cystitis are largely responsible for their problems due to their "tense feelings about femininity" or other emotional problems.

It is essential to be aware of overt or indirect implications of biological determination in male/female behavior. Sociobiology has become so popularized in its unexamined, simplified form that it can easily find its way into high school texts. Not only should authors of texts be more alert to their use of biology, but also in the training of teachers there must be a much stronger emphasis on a critical analysis of the texts they are using and the subtle ways in which biology can be distorted. In the training of health educators, much more emphasis must be placed on examining the actual biological and physiological information presented. Just as educators have learned to screen history texts for racial bias, we must screen for sexist and racist scientific information. Health and sex education texts must be carefully studied to identify this kind of biological error or misinterpretation. However, with the time delay involved in revising texts, it would certainly be unreasonable to wait for change to occur at that level. It is the health educators who must learn not to accept on faith so-called biological facts. This means that at the level of university schools of education, students must be taught not only content and methodology, but also critical reading of materials.

For those already teaching, workshops, inservices, and continuing education program should be presenting and emphasizing these issues. Local departments of public instruction should take responsibility for providing revised curricular materials and for providing workshops in this area.

Alternative ways to teach these topics can be offered. For example, for an educator who is looking for a way to break out of the biological determinist approach to sex roles, it might be easiest to approach the issue cross-culturally. By examining variations in sex roles in other cultures, the biological argument can be called into question. It may also be easier for students to approach a discussion of sex roles in other cultures rather than to begin by questioning the assumptions and definitions they live with every day. An interesting example that could be used is drawn from Margaret Mead's (1935) *Sex and Temperament in Three Primitive Societies.* She examined a society in which the ideal adult of both sexes is gentle and nurturing, one in which both sexes are raised to be independent and hostile, and one in which the stereotypes of masculinity and femininity in our culture are reversed. Such examples can serve as a starting point to examine assumptions about sex roles in our own society. Biology cannot be viewed as pure unalterable fact by those who teach it, or we will be doing more to enforce sex role stereotypes than we can counter with the simple inclusion of s/he in the text.

NOTES

1. For further reading on these hormones, I recommend Briscoe (1978), who has written a clear informative chapter, accessible to nonscientists.
2. A great deal has been written lately on theories of aggression and the relationship to hormones. Good discussions can be found in Bleier (1984, pp. 94-101) and Sayers (1982, pp. 66-83).

RESOURCES

Allgeier, E. R., & Allgeier, A. R. (1984). *Sexual interactions.* Lexington: MA: D. C. Heath.

Bleier, R. (1984). *Science and gender: A critique of biology and its theories on women.* New York: Pergamon.

Briscoe, A. M. (1978). Hormones and gender. In E. Tobach and B. Rosoff (Eds.), *Genes and gender: I.* New York: Gordian.

Crase, D. R. (1978). Significance of masculinity and femininity. In B. Q. Hafen et al., *Adolescent health: For educators and health personnel.* Salt Lake City: Brighton.

Eisenberg, A., & Eisenberg, H. (1979). *Alive and well: Decisions in health.* New York: McGraw-Hill.

Fee, E. (1983). Women's nature and scientific objectivity. In M. Lowe and R. Hubbard (Eds.), *Woman's nature: Rationalization of inequality.* New York: Pergamon.

Gay, J., Wantz, M., Slobof, H., Hooper, C., & Boskin, W. (1979). *Current health problems.* Philadelphia: W. B. Saunders.

George, P., & Lawrence, G. (1982). *Handbook for middle school teaching.* Glenview IL: Scott, Foresman.

Hafen, B. Q., Burgener, R. O., Hurley, R. D., & Peterson, R. A. (1978). *Adolescent health: For educators and health personnel.* Salt Lake City: Brighton.

Hafen, B. Q., Thygerson, A. L., & Rhodes, R. L. (1979). *Health perspectives.* Provo, UT: Brigham Young University Press.

Hubbard, R., & Lowe, M. (Eds.) (1979). *Genes and gender: II: Pitfalls in re on sex and gender.* New York: Gordian.

Johns, E. B., Sutton, W. C., & Cooley, B. A. (1975). *Health for effective living* (sixth ed.). New York: McGraw-Hill.

Jones, G. S., & Jones, H. W. (1982). *Gynecology* (3rd ed.). Baltimore, MD: Williams and Wilkins.

Jones, R. E. (1984). *Human reproduction and sexual behavior.* Englewood Cliffs, NJ: Prentice-Hall.

Kilmann, P. R. (1984). *Human sexuality in contemporary life.* Boston: Allyn & Bacon.

Kriegman, G. (1978). Homosexuality and the educator. In B. Q. Hafen et al., *Adolescent health: For educators and health personnel.* Salt Lake City: Brighton.

Maier, R. A. (1984). *Human sexuality in perspective.* Chicago: Nelson-Hall.

Masters, W. H., & Johnson, V. E. (1966). *Human sexual response.* Boston: Little, Brown.

McCary, S. P., & McCary, J. L. (1984). *Human sexuality: Third brief edition.* Belmont, CA: Wadsworth.

Mead, M. (1935) *Sex and temperament in three primitive societies.* New York: William Morrow.

Read, D. A., & Greene, W. H. (1980). *Creative teaching in health* (3rd ed.). New York: Macmillan.

Rubin, J. Z., Provenzano, F. J., & Luria, Z. (1974). The eye of the beholder: Parent's views on sex of newborns. *American Journal of Orthopsychiatry, 44,* 512-519.

Sayers, J. (1982). *Biological politics: Feminist and anti-feminist perspectives.* New York: Tavistock.

Shearin, R. B. (1978). Adolescent sexuality. In Hafen, et al.,*Adolescent health: For educators and health personnel.* Salt Lake City: Brighton.

Sommer, B. B. (1978). *Puberty and adolescence.* New York: Oxford University Press.

Sorochan, W. D., & Bender, S. J. (1978). *Teaching secondary health science.* New York: John Wiley.

4

FETAL PERSONHOOD AND WOMEN'S POLICY

Janet Gallagher

The Supreme Court's 1973 ruling in *Roe v. Wade* (1973) invalidated virtually all existing U.S. abortion laws.[1] The decision was grounded in part upon the court's finding that neither English nor American law had ever regarded the unborn as legal persons in "the whole sense" (*Roe v. Wade,* 1973, p. 158). Intensive efforts to overturn that decision through adoption of a constitutional amendment conferring legal personhood upon the fetus have been unsuccessful. The court itself has refused to retreat from its controversial holding despite furious, well-organized, and continuing opposition.

The *Roe* decision has served as a key precedent in the rapid expansion of legal protection for individual rights of personal autonomy and bodily integrity in an increasing number of contexts, especially medical decision making. Yet even as *Roe* has emerged as a guarantor of constitutional protection in gender-neutral, nonabortion contexts, it has been increasingly subjected to a crabbed and mechanical interpretation in cases involving women's reproductive freedom. Indeed, as political and medical preoccupation with the fetus has increased, *Roe* has come to be used as a legal weapon against pregnant women—invoked as authority not only for restrictions on their liberty but even for actual physical invasions such as court-ordered cesarean sections. The new visual accessibility of the fetus through ultrasound and the emergence of new methods of prenatal diagnosis and treatment lend themselves to a transformation of popular perceptions of the fetus and to the reawakening of traditional, indeed classically patriarchal, attitudes toward pregnant women.

While these developments pose a long-term ideological threat to abortion rights, the most immediate and dramatic danger is to women's liberty and choices during pregnancy and childbirth. This chapter will examine a number of recent cases in which legal personhood has been attributed to the fetus, examine the implications of such a trend, and suggest alternative legal and policy solutions.

In its 1973 opinion recognizing a woman's right to choose abortion, the Supreme Court had laid out a three-part scheme of pregnancy. In the first trimester, declared the court, a woman could—in consultation with her doctor—freely choose to terminate her pregnancy. In the constitutional balance established by the court, during the early stage of pregnancy a woman's right to privacy outweighs any possible state interest in regulating abortion. In the second stage of pregnancy, the government could impose certain regulations on abortion, but only those "reasonably related" to the protection of the woman's health. In the third stage of pregnancy, described by the court as following "viability," or the point at which the fetus has the "capability of meaningful life outside the mother's womb," the government is permitted to make regulations protective of its "compelling state interest" in the "potential human life" involved and may even forbid those abortions not necessary to preserve the life or health of the woman (*Roe v. Wade,* 1973, pp. 164-165).

The decision set off a fire storm of opposition. Critics blasted the opinion as an exercise of judicial tyranny, a usurpation of legislative prerogatives (Ely, 1973). The Roman Catholic Bishops urged civil disobedience to any law requiring abortion and reaffirmed that Catholics who underwent an abortion were subject to excommunication (Rubin, 1982). Within two years the Bishops had launched a "Pastoral Plan for Pro-life Activities," establishing antiabortion committees in every parish and congressional district to press for adoption of a constitutional amendment to reverse *Roe* (1973, p. 90).[2]

Right to Life organizations established during the battles over legislative reform moved into action as state lawmakers responded to *Roe*. According to Eva Rubin (1982),

Eighty bills relating to abortion were introduced in state legislatures between January and April, 1973. In October 1973 seven months after the decision, twenty-three states had enacted laws dealing with abortion, and although most of these laws provided for relatively unrestricted first trimester abortions, others had added conditions that made the operation less accessible. These conditions included reporting and record-keeping procedures, requirements of written consent by the woman, consent of husband or parents, waiting periods, counselling, and similar provisions. Nebraska required notification of the grandparents! Many laws contained provisions protecting persons and institutions with religious scruples from being forced to perform abortions.

And, notes Rubin, almost half of the state laws passed in the initial wave of abortion legislation after *Roe* were struck down as unconstitutional by the courts.

The most consistent Right to Life effort has centered on passage of a constitutional amendment that would outlaw abortion by declaring the fetus a person (see Copelon, 1981;

Pilpel, 1976). That amendment drive was defeated in June of 1983 when the Senate refused to pass even a more "moderate" version stating that "a right to abortion is not secured by this constitution." Two weeks earlier the Supreme Court had reaffirmed *Roe v. Wade,* declaring numerous provisions of a model antiabortion ordinance from Akron, Ohio, to be unconstitutional infringements of the abortion right (*City of Akron v. Akron Center for Reproductive Health, Inc., 1983*).

Yet even the dramatic defeat of the constitutional amendment and the firm language of *Akron* left abortion a shrunken, paper right for many of those who had been the chief beneficiaries of *Roe.* The 1980 *McRae* decision upholding the federal ban on Medicaid funding (*McRae v. Califano,* 1980) and the Court's continual unwillingness to strike parental consent and notification statutes cut off meaningful access to abortion for the very women—the poor and the young—generally acknowledged to be most in need of it.[3] And *Roe's* acknowledgment that the state may assert a compelling state interest in the potential life of the fetus at viability is now being invoked not merely to bar abortions, but to force pregnant women to undergo medical procedures and even surgery against their will.

Hospitals in different parts of the country have recently obtained court orders to force individual birthing women to undergo cesarean sections because doctors felt their "fetal patients" required them (*Jefferson v. Griffin Spaulding County Hospital Authority,* 1981; see also Bowes & Selegstad, 1981). The court-ordered surgery seems doubly shocking because the doctors base their claim to such drastic power over pregnant women on *Roe v. Wade* (1973).[4]

While there have been only a handful of reported incidents thus far, the cases are of enormous symbolic and precedential significance. They convey a drastic message about women's moral and legal status, and also serve to legitimize a forceful reassertion of medical control over pregnancy and childbirth.

A 1981 incident of a court-ordered cesarean section in Atlanta, Georgia, arose from a pregnant woman's religious objection to surgery and blood transfusions. The hospital sought court intervention. Doctors testified that the woman had a complete placenta previa, a condition in which the placenta blocks the birth canal. There was, claimed the doctors, a 99 percent certainty that the fetus could not survive vaginal delivery and there was at least a 50 percent chance that the woman herself would die in an attempt at vaginal delivery. A Georgia court, convinced by doctors' presentations, declared that the near term fetus was "a human being fully capable of sustaining life independent of the mother" and that it "lacked proper parental care and subsistence." Citing *Roe v. Wade* as authority for state protection of a viable, unborn child, the Georgia courts granted temporary custody of the fetus to the government social service agencies that had brought the court case, and gave them "full authority to make all decisions, including giving consent to the surgical delivery" (*Jefferson v. Griffin Spaulding County Hospital Authority,* 1981). Their temporary custody ended in an unexpected manner some two weeks later when the woman's placenta shifted and she gave normal birth to a 7 lb., 2 oz. girl (Berg, 1981).

In a Colorado case, even more widely publicized because it was reported in the *American Journal of Obstetrics and Gynecology,* doctors at a Denver hospital called in a psychiatric consultant to examine a woman in labor who refused to undergo a cesarean even after they told her that the monitors showed signs of fetal distress (Bowes & Selegstad, 1981). The woman's refusal was attributed to a fear of surgery. When the psychiatrist declared that the woman was competent to make a rational decision, the hospital attorney was called in and a decision was made to seek a court order for the surgery. A juvenile court judge was asked to take jurisdiction "to protect the interest of an unborn child," and after a hospital room hearing in which the laboring woman and her fetus were represented by separate attorneys, the judge ordered that the cesarean section be performed. Here, as in the Georgia case, the decision was based on the state's "compelling interest to protect the unborn in light of *Roe v. Wade* and *Doe v. Bolton.*" The woman reluctantly submitted, underwent general anesthesia and the baby was delivered. Bowes and Selegstad (1981) note her cooperation with relief: "Had the patient steadfastly refused it might not have been either safe or possible to administer anesthesia to a struggling, resistant woman who weighed in excess of 157.5 gm."

Though less dramatically than in the Georgia case, the Colorado outcome also belied the doctors' drastic predictions. The baby's condition upon birth proved less serious than the doctors had feared. Eight months later the child was described as growing and developing normally (Annas, 1982; Hubbard, 1982).

But the precedent—legal and political—had been set. Doctors throughout the country were being told, in the pages of a nationally respected medical journal, that their duties to the fetus as "patient" might authorize surgery on a pregnant woman even though she refused to consent. And lawyers could point to the Georgia Supreme Court opinion as a precedent for future court orders. It could be cited as authority for other limitations on the decision-making and bodily integrity rights of pregnant women.[5] The *Roe* formula recognizing a state interest in fetal life during the latter stage of pregnancy was being used to override the customary legal rights of the woman.

The use of the courts as "enforcers" for doctors' orders or for the decisions to do cesarean sections is especially startling because it flies in the face of a general legal trend toward honoring individual decision making in the area of medical care (Clarke, 1980). It has long been recognized that touching someone without his or her consent can result in criminal charges or in a civil lawsuit. Doctors may not operate, or carry out medical procedures, without a patient's consent. A doctor who fails to obtain such informed consent can be sued (Prosser, 1971; Annas, Glantz, & Katz, 1981).

In recent years, courts have recognized that individual rights may overrride whatever social interest there may be in forcing a patient to undergo medical teatment. Some of these cases involve fatally ill patients' rights to forego invasive or painful procedures that might prolong but cannot save their lives. Others arise out of treatment refusals motivated by individual religious convictions or other strongly held beliefs.[6] Courts generally conduct a balancing test: weighing the individuals' privacy, the degree of bodily invasion or restriction on liberty, and the impact on third parties (see, e.g., *Superintendent of Belchertown State School v. Saikewicz,* 1977).

Such an ad hoc balancing test approach necessarily results in a range of court opinions, but commentators have noted the increasing trend toward protection of autonomy and bodily integrity (Clarke, 1980; Cantor, 1973). In a recent Massachusetts case, for example, judges of that state's highest court barred the nonemergency use of antipsychotic drugs on institutionalized mental patients who chose to refuse them unless the state had obtained a separate judicial ruling that the patient was incompetent to make such decisions (*Rogers v. Commissioner of the Department of Mental Health,* 1983).

These decisions are based on the tradition of respect for the individual's right to bodily integrity or "the inviolability of his person" and the law's "regard for human dignity and self-determination" (*Saikewicz,* 1977, p. 424). As one court put it, "One of the foundations of the doctrine is that it protects the patient's status as a human being" (*Saikewicz*, 1977, p. 424).

So central, in fact, is this concept of personal autonomy that the courts have labored to develop procedures to protect the treatment refusal rights of children and the retarded and the unconscious by allowing others to assert it on their behalf. In the *Quinlan* (1976) case, for example, the family of a comatose, irreversibly ill woman in New Jersey was allowed to exercise her right to privacy by authorizing removal of artificial life support.

Ironically enough, virtually all of the right to refuse treatment or bodily integrity cases rely on *Roe v. Wade* (1973) as a key precedent. In *Quinlan* (1976), for example, the New Jersey Supreme Court declared:

> The court in *Griswold* found the unwritten constitutional right of privacy to exist in the penumbra of specific guarantees of the Bill of Rights "formed by emanations from those guarantees that help give them life and substance" 381 U.S. at 484, 85 S. Ct. at 1681, 14 L. Ed. 2d at 514. Presumably this right is broad enough to encompass a patient's decision to decline medical treatment under certain circumstances in much the same way it is broad enough to encompass a woman's decision to terminate pregnancy under certain conditions. *Roe v. Wade* 410 U.S. 113, 153, 93 S. Ct. 705, 727, 35 L. Ed. 2d 147, 177 (1973)

And the Massachusetts court's decision (*Rogers*, 1983) involving mental patients' rights had drawn on a previous ruling in which it relied on *Roe:*

> Of even broader import, but arising from the same regard for human dignity and self-determination, is the unwritten constitutional right of privacy found in the penumbra of specific guaranties of the Bill of Rights. *Griswold v Connecticut*, 381

U.S. 479, 484, 85 S. Ct. 328, 13 L. Ed. 2d 339 (1965). As this constitutional guarantee reaches out to protect the freedom of women to terminate pregnancy under certain conditions, *Roe v Wade* 410 U.S. 113, 153, 93 S. Ct. 705, 35 L. Ed. 2nd 147 (1973), so it encompasses the right of a patient to preserve his or her right of privacy against unwanted infringements of bodily integrity in appropriate circumstances. *In re Quinlan,* supra 70 N.J. at 38-39, 355 A. 2d 647. (Saikewicz, 1977)

With the fetal rights cases, therefore, we are confronted with a situation in which a case popularly regarded and even widely cited by the courts in other contexts as standing for the individual's right to control his or her own body is used as authority for drastically curtailing the autonomy of and invading the bodily integrity of pregnant women.

In fact, Justice Blackmun's majority opinion in *Roe* had gone out of its way to disavow the feminist analysis that would have grounded the abortion right in "the sacred right of every individual to the possession and control of her own person" (*Abramowicz v. Lefkowitz,* 1979; complaint cited in Rubin, 1982, p. 49).

It is not clear to us that the claim asserted by some *amici* that one has an unlimited right to do with one's body as one pleases bears a close relationship to the right of privacy previously articulated in the court's decisions. The court has refused to recognize an unlimited right of this kind in the past. (*Roe v. Wade,* 1973)

Instead, Blackmun had cited medical advances that had made early abortion safer than childbirth, conducted a somewhat mechanical balancing of maternal health factors and fetal development, and arrived at a trimester formulation of the right.[7] The final opinion, clearly a compromise, had a bland, stitched together quality. Even those who support the decision have found fault with the Court's failure to articulate a more coherent and compelling constitutional basis (Glen, 1978; Law, 1984; Regan, 1979; Tribe, 1973).

Interestingly enough, public perception—whether hostile or supportive—of the decision has tended to assume a definition of the abortion right that is closer to the feminist argument than to the rationale actually adopted by the Court. Commentators have pointed out that *Roe* (1973) is almost invariably denounced by abortion opponents as standing for "abortion on demand" and hailed by pro-choice activists as a women's rights victory (Harrison, 1983, p. 236; Petchesky, 1984, p. 290). And as we have seen, the lower courts acting in nonabortion contexts such as *Quinlan* (1976) and *Saikewicz* (1977) have relied upon an interpretation of *Roe* (1973) much more akin to the original feminist claim to woman's "possession and control of her own person" than to Blackmun's compromise. The Court's cautious balancing of interests and formulation of a segmented right simply never commanded popular or judicial imagination. *Roe,* perhaps the most quoted, debated, and reprinted of cases, is subject to virtually universal misinterpretation.[8]

But if the *Roe* Court's formulation of the basis of a woman's right to choose abortion lacked clarity, there was no such ambiguity in its analysis of the legal status of the fetus. Justice Blackmun reviewed the Constitution's use of the term "person" and found it applied only postnatally. He noted that the fetus had not been treated as a person by the abortion laws or in other legal contexts. "In short," Blackmun reported, "the unborn have never been recognized in the law as persons in the whole sense" (*Roe v. Wade,* 1973).

Imposing legal restraints and liabilities on women on behalf of fetuses represents a sharp departure from even the pre-*Roe v. Wade* legal and ethical views of the fetus. The notion that the fetus itself has rights breaks sharply with traditional attitudes. Rosalind Petchesky (1984) notes that even

> in those primitive and ancient societies which have regarded abortion as a crime or a wrong, it is not usually the fetus that is considered the wronged party. On the contrary, sanctions against abortion are invoked more often on behalf of the family, the tribe, the state or the husband or maternal uncle (depending on the prevailing basis of patriarchal authority) .... Ancient patriarchal law valued the fetus as the father's property rather than its own right.

As Beverly Wildung Harrison (1983) reports, early Christian condemnations of abortion focused not on the value of the fetus but on the offense of "covering up" the sin of sex or on "rhetorical denunciations of all nonprocreative sex as murder."

> Nearly all extant early Christian objections to abortion, when any moral reasons were enunciated, either directly condemn wanton women (those who seek to avoid pregnancy) or denounce the triad of adulterous, pleasure-oriented sex, contraception, and abortion. These were undifferentiated elements in a disparaging attitude to nonprocreative functional sexuality and a negativity to "promiscuous" women, grounded in what was, within Christianity, the antisensual spirituality of its most ascetic, frequently celibate theologians. The essentially virtuous and morally responsible woman was also to be celibate and could thereby become "manly." But if married, any woman who refused childbearing was thereby a murderer.
>
> . . . Concern about abortion constitutes a minor, episodic matter in Christian discussion until the late nineteenth century. Furthermore, I find no evidence until the modern period that compassion for the presumed "child" in the womb was a

generating source of Christian moral opposition to abortion. Rather, the intertwining of sexual mores and abortion teaching was so complete that there was always a definite correlation between extreme denunciations of abortion and a theologian's objections to sexual intercourse except within marriage for the purpose of procreation.

The traditional pre-*Roe* definition of the fetus in Anglo-American law provides no basis for the current claims of "fetal rights." Before the Civil War, the idea of the fetus as a human person prior to "quickening" and abortion as "murder" was practically unheard of in this country. Later, even the harshest antiabortion laws allowed exceptions for cases in which the life of the woman was threatened, and the penalties for criminal abortion were always considerably less than those provided for homicide.[9] The general common law rule adopted in the United States was that the criminally caused death of a fetus was not homicide unless there had been a live birth—an existence, however momentary, independent of the mother (see, e.g., *Keeler v. Superior Court of Amador County,* 1970; *State v. Larsen,* 1978; *Hollis v. Commonwealth,* 1983).

As the court noted in *Roe,* American law has never treated the unborn as legal persons in the whole sense. The legal status of the fetus varies from jurisdiction to jurisdiction and according to the issues involved. Thus, while the inheritance rights of fetuses are protected, fetuses have no mandatory constitutional claim to benefits under Aid to Families with Dependent Children, are not counted under the census, or regarded as children for income tax exemption purposes (*Burns v. Akala,* 1975; *Roe v. Wade,* 1973).

The states are divided on allowing for recovery for the wrongful death of a fetus. Many of the states permitting such suits require that there have been a live birth or that the fetus have been "viable" at the time of injury. Furthermore, the considerations favoring recovery in such cases are more related to compensating the parents for their loss than to any attribution of personhood to the fetus.[10]

Abortion opponents have attempted to exploit recent legal cases allowing children to sue for injuries caused by prenatal events such as exposure to toxic chemicals, claiming that it is inconsistent to acknowledge a right to sue but not a "right to live." But those cases do not rely on any claim of fetal rights of personhood. The compensation is paid to a person, born alive, who suffers from injuries traceable to prebirth causes. Some suits, like one charging that a negligent blood transfusion given to a young woman caused RH factor problems to the child she later bore, can even involve preconception injuries (*Rensiow v. Mennonite Hospital,* 1976). The essential point, though, is that birth is a precondition for the right to bring such a lawsuit (Gallagher, 1982).

Even in contexts such as inheritance and trust matters where legal protection is accorded to the fetus, it is important to note that the rationale for such treatment is respect for the testator's intent, not a view of the fetus as a separate legal personality (Shaw & Damme, 1976, p.4). The current claim of "fetal rights" then, fly in the face not merely of *Roe* but of the Anglo-American legal tradition as a whole.

Many of the current, allegedly secular arguments for fetal personhood invoke the new scientific knowledge about fetal development or recent medical advances permitting actual *in utero* therapies (Nathanson, 1984). In fact, though, such technological developments seem to have provided a contemporary scientific gloss for an enduring set of essentially patriarchal attitudes. The explosion of technologies that make the fetus seem more accessible to the world at large—visually, medically, emotionally—has spurred a resurgence of powerful and largely unacknowledged social attitudes in which pregnant women are viewed and treated as vessels.

Mary O'Brien (1983), citing Aristotle's belief that "women contribute nothing to the child but this arrested menstrual flow," observes that "This idea that men contribute spirit or soul or some other human 'essence' must have struck chords in the masculine imagination, for it lingered for centuries."

A 1977 study of Catholic attitudes toward sexuality notes the shaping influence of that view of the male seed as "the active principle" and women as "receptacles for the seed—gardens, as it were, for human reproduction" (Kosnicki et al., 1979). As Beverly Wildung Harrison (1983) notes, that "sire-centered view of embryology" has a deep ideological correlation with "the assumption that children are really the fruit, even the possession of men" and with male attempts to control women's reproductive power. St. Thomas Aquinas followed the Aristotelian lead: "He saw man as the vital source of life and women solely as the incubator, the blood transfusion unit. The highest soul was infused by God, forty days after conception in the case of a boy, eighty in the case of a girl" (Warner, 1976).

There are dramatic echoes of these patriarchal views in the rhetoric of the nineteenth-century antiabortion crusade by American doctors who denounced women's destruction of

> the children nestling within them—children fully alive from the moment of conception that have already been fully detached from all organic connection with their parent and only re-attached to her for the purpose of nutriment and growth. (Milbauer, 1983)

Contemporary preoccupation with the fetus, though usually couched in terms of new scientific knowledge or power, reflects many of the same images. Protestant historian

George H. Williams, for example, describes fetuses as "the unwitting and diminutive denizens of that universal and mysterious realm of maternal darkness from whence we all emerge" (Harrison, 1983). Now, writes antiabortion spokesperson Bernard Nathanson (1984):

> We have unimaginably sophisticated methods of communication with the very young infant in utero; an array of instrumentation to diagnose its ills and disorders, even at very early stages of pregnancy; a newly defined stage of our lives, known as prenatality; a new surgical specialty, surgery on the unborn and fetal medicine, that branch of fetology in which we diagnose and treat the unborn child with medications and blood transfusions; and the unborn child asserting its right as a patient requiring a separate physician and a separate legal advocate for its rights in the law.

Recognition and fear of the continuing vitality of that view of women as "burrows" or "gardens" make some feminists flinch at the recent California case in which a pregnant, legally brain-dead woman's body was kept on life-support systems for nine weeks so that her fetus could go to term and be delivered by cesarean section. In that situation, the woman's husband and sister-in-law consulted with doctors and it was decided that the woman herself would have chosen such a course (*Newsweek*, 1983).

Still, there seems no guarantee, given the persistence of patriarchal attitudes toward pregnant women, that the California case won't be imitated in situations in which the woman might not have made that choice. In fact, Right to Life forces around the country are battling to specifically exclude pregnant women from "Natural Death" statutes that allow the terminally ill to refuse artificial or intrusive means of prolonging life (*Right to Life News*, February 24, 1983).

Attempts to enlist court involvement on behalf of a fetal patient or client are usually based on a claim that the fetus is a person covered by the local child abuse or neglect law (Bross & Meredyth, 1979; Doudera, 1982). Much of the legal and philosophical dispute over abortion and "fetal rights" has centered on whether or not the fetus is a person.[11] But when dealing with questions of court-ordered cesareans or other forced medical procedures, the real inquiry should be whether doctors can use or invade a nonconsenting woman's body for the sake of another patient, fetal or born.

Our legal tradition has consistently refused to impose physical burdens and risks on one person for the sake of another. Parents, for example, are not legally required to risk themselves to rescue their born children from danger or to donate blood or organs to them (Regan, 1979). The law draws a sharp distinction between duties normally imposed by ethical or emotional responses to a situation and duties imposed by legal government dictate. The American legal system simply does not recognize the right of *anyone*—born or not—to appropriate the body of another for his or her own use (Regan, 1979; Honneger, 1980).

Some years ago, for example, a Pittsburgh judge had to rule in a case involving a young man dying of a form of cancer that might have been arrested by bone marrow transplants from a compatible donor. His cousin, the only compatible located, would not submit to the transplants. The judge refused to order the procedure. "Morally," he wrote, "this decision rests with the defendant and, in the view of the Court, the refusal of the defendant is morally indefensible." But, the judge insisted, "to *compel* the Defendant to submit to an intrusion of his body would change every concept and principle upon which our society is founded. To do so would defeat the sanctity of the individual and would impose a rule which would know no limits and one could not imagine where the line would be drawn" (*McFall v. Schimp,* 1978).

Indeed, stopping points are hard to find. If the government can force a woman to undergo a cesarean section for the sake of a fetus, why not fetal surgery if that becomes "standard medical procedure" under certain circumstances? Scholarly articles arguing just that position are now appearing in the legal journals. In one such article, John Robertson (1982) proposes the following:

> If she refused the surgery, and the fetus did not survive, she could be prosecuted under state feticide or abortion laws. If the fetus was born but then died later as a result of the failure to use in utero therapy, she could be prosecuted for homicide or child abuse/neglect.

Court intervention can mean drastic invasion, not only of women's bodies but of their liberty. Are judges to become arbiters of women's conduct, ordering them to attempt to conform to the latest prescription for fetal health? Michigan's highest court has held that a father can sue a mother on behalf of their son because he claims that the child's teeth are discolored due to her "prenatal negligence" in taking a drug during pregnancy (*Grodin v. Grodin*, 1980). One legal commentator has suggested that women could be held liable for "negligent fetal abuse" for various prenatal harms including, in cases of some genetic disorders, "exposure to the mother's defective intrauterine environment" (Shaw, 1980). If pregnant women can be legally forced to undergo major surgery, then why not legal restrictions on prenatal diet, work, sex, sports? After all, such restrictions are certainly less "invasive" or "burdensome" than major surgery. Indeed, why not just lock pregnant women up?

In 1981, a Los Angeles juvenile court, acting at the request of the local welfare department, worried about one woman's ability to care for herself, confined her to a hospital for the last two months of her pregnancy by "taking jurisdiction" over her fetus. The woman had, in fact, been examined by psychiatrists who had found no basis for committing her under California's mental health law, and a higher court later overturned the juvenile court ruling. By then, however, the pregnancy—and detention—was over (*In re Steven S.,* 1981). The new prescriptions for fetal health should themselves be treated with a healthy degree of skepticism. Not only do they draw upon and reinforce punitive and controlling attitudes toward women, they all too frequently serve the economic or professional advantage of their proponents. Research has shown, for example, that many of the workplace substances harmful to fetuses are also dangerous to the reproductive health of male workers. And, as Jeanne M. Stellman and Mary Sue Henifin report in *Biological Women: The Convenient Myth* (1982), "There may also be a possibility that toxic agents present in seminal fluid can contaminate the uterine environment." Yet the "fetal protection" policies adopted by many corporations are remarkably gender-specific. Instead of eliminating or lowering exposure to a level safe for all workers, many companies have moved to bar all fertile women—pregnant or not, planning a pregnancy or not.[12]

And even these sex discriminatory policies are applied selectively. Stellman and Henifin (1982) point out that

> many of the jobs from which women are now being excluded are the higher-paying jobs that have traditionally been male territory. There has not been an attempt to exclude fertile women from lower-paying, *traditional* "women's" jobs where they are exposed to known reproductive hazards. For example, nurses, X-ray technologists, and nurses' aides continue to be exposed to radiation; and ceramic jewelry workers to lead.

When it is economically convenient, therefore, the new ideology of "fetal rights" gets combined with and reinforces a one-dimensional definition of women—no matter what their individual choices—as childbearers.

The fetal rights language not only threatens women's access to nontraditional jobs, it undercuts our attempts to exert greater control over the conditions of childbirth. The slogan of "fetal rights" has become a replacement for "Doctor knows best" in the battle for control over decision making in the birthplace. The insistence that the fetus is a patient with full rights of its own provides an effective counterweight to the demand for a less medically defined experience of birth. The growing popularity of midwives and home births, for example, has been met with a wave of prosecutions for "child abuse," or even "murder" or "negligent homicide" (Evenson, 1982). State legislatures or regulatory agencies are pressed to adopt regulations designed to curtail the use of midwives in all but a narrow category of circumstances. Doctors who "back-up" midwives or nurse-midwives find themselves subjected to the loss of hospital privileges, threats to their malpractice insurance, and professional ostracism (Evenson, 1982).

And those women who choose a hospital birth may now find themselves pressured to defer to doctors' choices on behalf of their other, fetal "patient." George Annas, Professor of Law and Medicine at the Boston University Medical Center, worries that the court-ordered cesarean section cases may be used by the obstetrician as a "weapon to bully women he views as irrational into submission" (Annas, 1982).

Court-ordered cesarean sections are a dubious solution to disputes between birthing women and their doctors. Besides being violations of women's rights of bodily integrity and self-determination, they're also very likely to prove unnecessary. The 1981 Georgia case, now pointed to as precedent by lawyers favoring court intervention, actually ended with the woman triumphantly defying the doctors' dire prediction and delivering a healthy child without a section (or as the Journal of the Georgia Medical Society headlined the story: "Georgia Supreme Court orders Cesarean Section— Mother Nature Reverses on Appeal").

In a 1982 Michigan case doctors, claiming that a woman's birth canal was blocked by the placenta, sought a court-authorized cesarean. The patient belonged to a church, the members of which preferred to "trust themselves to God," and she had refused surgery. A juvenile court judge declared the fetus a temporary ward of the court and ordered that, if the woman did not present herself "for medical procedures deemed necessary by the attending physicians" by a specified date and time, the local police were to pick her up and deliver her to the hospital. The woman went into hiding and, two weeks after the court order, gave uncomplicated vaginal birth to a healthy 9 pound, 2 ounce baby boy (*Detroit Free Press,* June 29, 1982).

Ironically, the reports of the forced cesarean cases have coincided with a growing concern and criticism about the number of cesarean deliveries in the United States (up from 5 percent to 18 percent between 1969 and 1980). A 1980 study commissioned by the National Institute of Child Health and Human Development reported that the risk of maternal death rate in cesarean deliveries was two to four times that in vaginal births and urged that reliance on cesarean be reduced.

But the threat posed by the cesarean section cases and the new arguments that nonconsenting women could be forced to undergo fetal surgery is not really measurable in terms of the risk of death or complications, real and dramatic as those might be. The core issue is whether pregnant women are to be accorded the legal autonomy over decision-making that our tradition regards as basic to human dignity.

The cesarean section and other prenatal intervention cases reflect, in a drastically heightened way, the same social/political attitude underlying opposition to legal abortion: a view of pregnant women as somehow less than independent legal beings capable of making moral judgments about whether and how to bear a child. The real question posed by the "fetal rights" phenomenon has much less to do with the status of the fetus than with the status of women. It boils down to a question of control: control over abortion, pregnancy, birth—control over women's bodies and lives.

The insistence that the fetus is entitled to a legal status that would allow the government to compel a woman's "good" prenatal behavior or would justify forced surgery is often linked to an antiabortion stance. Not all "fetal rights" advocates, though, are necessarily antichoice on the issue of abortion. Most of the interventions sought involved late-term, wanted pregnancies. Medical personnel and social workers involved in these incidents have been confronted by situations in which all of their immediate professional, ethical, and emotional instincts are to intervene on behalf of an unborn child. And they have found themselves stymied by some seemingly abstract notion of patients' rights. No doubt many of the women seemed to be behaving in a selfish or irrational manner. The impulse to call in the courts and use whatever legal theory necessary is understandable. But even in those rare instances in which court intervention is appropriate, it's usually possible to find a legal mechanism that doesn't rely on claims of fetal personhood or rights. When closely examined, the fetal rights claims almost invariably prove unnecessary to reaching the "right" result. And given both the continuing passions over abortion and the traditional treatment of pregnant women, legal decisions involving fetuses should be couched in terms less subject to manipulation and distortion.

A headline 1982 case in which a federal judge in Connecticut declared that a fetus could sue for violations of its civil rights exemplifies the sort of sensationalism to be avoided. The court ruling really involved a child—already born—suing for injuries allegedly suffered when his pregnant mother was the victim of police brutality. The judge's choice of legal labels transformed what should have been treated as a standard prenatal injury case into what newspapers described as "an unprecedented federal ruling that a [Right to Life] legal expert said yesterday could be a victory for anti-abortion forces if it sets a trend" (*New York Post*, July 8, 1982).

Such confusion is unnecessary. There are now well-established legal remedies for fetal death or injury that neither undercut abortion rights nor disregard pregnant women's liberty and bodily integrity.[13] *Roe*—now viewed by judges and public alike as a guarantor of human dignity and self-determination—simply cannot be twisted into an authorization for subjecting pregnant women to state-imposed restrictions or, worse, coerced medical treatment or surgery.

The language of "fetal rights" is dangerous. It draws upon and reinforces deeply misogynist attitudes. Ultimately, fetal well-being is not well served by an ideological insistence on framing pregnancy health issues as conflicts between two separate, antagonistic entities. Policymakers and health care providers would do better to encourage an attitude toward pregnancy that emphasizes a woman's respect and care for the fetus, not as a subordination to the unborn, but as affirmation of herself and of her choice to become a mother.

NOTES

1. Four states—New York, Washington, Alaska, and Hawaii—had already adopted reform legislation within the *Roe* guidelines.

2. For a detailed account of the Roman Catholic Church's mobilization, see the opinion in *McRae v. Califano* (1980). Judge Dooling's decision that the congressional cut-off of Medicaid funding was unconstitutional was later reversed by a 5 to 4 Supreme Court vote in *Harris v. McRae* (1980). Nevertheless, the factual detail of Dooling's opinion makes it a rich resource.

3. The Medicaid ban was upheld in *Harris v. McRae (1980)*. The Supreme court has upheld laws requiring parental consent or notification for minors' abortions as long as there is a mechanism whereby "mature minors" can seek authorization from a judge as an alternative to telling their parents. See, for example, *Planned Parenthood v. Ashcroft* (1983). Although ongoing suits challenging the constitutionality of such laws "as applied" may force Court reconsideration.

4. The doctors argued that the fetus was viable and, since *Roe* indicated that the state could assert an "interest" in viable fetuses by banning nontherapeutic abortions, the state could here assert its interest in potential life by ordering surgery.

5. The Georgia case has already been cited as precedential authority for compelling pregnant women to undergo fetal surgery against their will in several law review articles. See, for example, Robertson (1982).

6. See, for example, *In re Osborne* (1972). A Jehovah's Witness injured in an accident refused blood transfusions. His decision was based on religious beliefs. The court refused to order treatment.

Blood transfusion refusals by Jehovah's Witnesses are not always upheld by the courts. See, for example, *In re President of Georgetown College, Inc.* (1964). Judges in such cases seem intent on preserving the patient's religious scruples by taking judicial responsibility for the procedure. The key transfusion cases involving pregnant women (see, for example, *Raleigh-Fitkin Memorial Hospital v. Anderson*, (1964) predate both *Roe* and many of the major right to refuse treatment cases and are thus of dubious precedential value.

7. See paragraph 4 of this chapter for explanation of trimester formulation.

8. This may be a good thing. I would argue that the widespread misperception of *Roe* suggests, better than any law review argument, a need to reground the legal rights in terms more responsive to the emotional and ethical demands of the abortion issue. And that reformulation of the right can now draw upon the many federal and state cases in which *Roe* has served as authority for the recognition of individual rights of personal decision making and bodily integrity. Our understanding of *Roe*'s implicit premise—the terms, in fact, in which it has been popularly perceived—can be enriched by a review of its application in nonabortion contexts. To fail to do so leaves us with what is logically and legally an untenable, scandalously discriminatory situation in which courts recognize a "derelict's" right to refuse leg amputation (*New York Times*, January 11, 1977, p. 37) and bar the forced medication of mental patients and prisoners (*Saikewicz, Rogers*), but countenance unconsented-to, major surgery on pregnant women.

Several alternative formulations of the abortion right have been suggested. See, for example, Tribe (1973), Regan (1979), Karst (1980), Law, (1984), and Brief Amicus Curiae (1982).

9. Mohr (1978) gives an excellent account of the nineteeth century legislation and court decisions.

10. See Janet Gallagher's comments in note 62 in Hubbard (1982). For a recent and sensible approach to the wrongful death issue, see *Dunn v. Roseway Inc.* (1983).

11. Ruth Macklin (1983) analyzes the personhood argument and concludes that scholars either choose a definition of personhood that agrees with their own position in the abortion debate or else claim that personhood is irrelevant to setting moral and legal issues involving the fetus.

12. For an excellent treatment of the workplace hazard issue, see Williams (1981).

13. See, for example, Note (1977), Preconception torts: Foreseeing the unconceived. U. of Colorado Law Review, 48, 621; the wrongful death ruling in Iowa's *Dunn v. Roseway* (1983); and the 1985 New Mexico criminal statute designed to protect women's choice to carry a pregnancy to term (*New York Times*, April 23, 1985).

CASES

Abramowicz v. Lefkowitz, 305 F. Supp. 1030 (S.D.N.Y. 1976).

Burns v. Alcala, 420 U.S. 575 (1975).

City of Akron v. Akron Center for Reproductive Health, Inc. 103 S. Ct. 2481 (1983).

Douglas v. Town of Hartford, 542 F. Supp. 1267 (1982).

Dunn v. Roseway, Inc. 333 N.W. 2d 830 (Iowa, 1983).

Grodin v. Grodin, 102 Mich. App. 396, 301 N.W. 2d 869 (1980).

Harris v. McRae, 448 U.S. 297 (1980).

Hollis v. Commonwealth of Kentucky, 652 S.W. 2d 61 (1983).

In re Osborne, 294 A. 2d 372 (D.C. Ct. of Appeals, 1972).

In re President of Georgetown College, Inc., 331 F. 2d 1000 (D.C. CIR., 1964).

In re Quinlan, 70 N. J. 10, 355 A. 2d 647 (1976).

In re Stevens, 126 Cal. App. 3d 23, 178 Cal. Rptr. 525 (Ct. App. 1981).

Jefferson v. Griffin Spaulding Country Hospital Authority, 247 Ga. 86, 274 S.E. 2d 457 (1981).

Keeler v. Superior Court of Amador County, 2 Cal. 3d 619, 470 P. 2d 617, 87 Cal. Rptr. 481 (1970).

McFall v. Schimp, unpublished, Ct. of Comm. Pleas, Alleghany County, Penn, Civil Division, July 26, 1978.

McRae v. Califano, 491 F. Supp. 630 at 702-727 (E.D.N.Y. 1980).

Planned Parenthood v. Ashcroft, 103 S. Ct. 2517 (1983).

Raleigh-Fitkin Memorial Hospital v. Anderson, 42 N.J. 421, 201 A. 2d 537, cert. denied, 377 U.S. 985 (1964).

Renslow v. Mennonite Hospital, 40 Ill. App. 3d 234, 351 N.W. 2d 870 (1976).

Roe v. Wade, 410 U.S. 113 (1973).

State v. Larsen, 578 P. 2d 1280 (Utah, 1978).

Rogers v. Commissioner of the Department of Mental Health, 390 Mass. 489 (1983).

Superintendent of Belchertown State School v. Saikewicz, 373 Mass. 728, 730 N.E. 2d 417 (1977).

RESOURCES

Annas, G. (1982). Forced cesareans: The most unkindliest cut of all. *12 Hastings Center Report,* 16, 45.

Annas, G., Glants, & Katz (1981). *The rights of doctors, nurses, and allied health professionals: An ACLU handbook.* New York: Avon.

Berg. (1981). Georgia Supreme Court orders cesarean section—Mother nature reserves on appeal. *Georgia Medical Association Journal, 70,* 451.

Bowes & Selegstad. (1981). Fetal versus maternal rights: Medical and l spectives. *Obstetrics and Gynecology, 58,* 209.

Brief Amicus Curiae, Right to Choose v. Byrne. (1982). *Women's Rights Law Reporter, 7,* 285.

Bross, & Meredyth. (1979). Neglect of the unborn child. 3 *Child Abuse and Neglect.*

Cantor, N. (1973). A patient's decision to decline life-saving medical treatment: Bodily integrity versus the preservation of life. *Rutgers Law Review, 26,* 228-264.

Cesarean Birth Task Force, National Institutes of Health Consensus Development Statement on Cesarean Childbirth. (1981). *Obstetrics and Gynecology, 57,* 537.

Clarke. (1980). The choice to refuse or withhold medical treatment: The emerging technology and medical-ethical consensus. 795 *Creighton Law Review, 795.*

Copelon, R. (1981). Danger: A "human life" amendment is on the way. *Ms., 46* (February), 72-74.

Doudera. (1982). Fetal rights? It depends. *Trial* (April), 39.

Ely. (1973). The wages of crying wolf: A comment on Roe v. Wade. *Yale Law Journal, 82,* 920.

Evenson, D. (1982). Midwives: Survival of an ancient profession. *Women's Rights Law Reporter, 7,* 313.

Flanigan, B. (1982). Fleeing the Law: A Matter of Faith. Detroit Free Press, June 29, p. 3, col. 3.

Gallagher, J. (1982). Legal analysis accompanying Hubbard, Ruth, prenatal diagnosis and fetal therapy: Legal and policy implications. *Women's Rights Law Reporter, 7,* 143.

Glen, K. B. (1978). Abortion in the courts: A laywoman's historical guide to the new disaster area. *Feminist Studies, 4* (February): 1-26.

Guillemin, J. (1981). Babies by cesarean: Who chooses, who controls? *11 Hastings Center Report, 15* (June).

Harrison, B. (1983). *Our right to choose: Toward a new ethic of abortion.* Boston: Beacon.

Honneger, B. (1980). Unpublished manuscript in the possession of the author.

Hubbard, R. (1982). Prenatal diagnosis and fetal therapy: Legal and policy implications. *Women's Rights Law Reporter, 7,* 143.

Karst. (1980). Freedom of intimate association. *Yale Law Journal, 89,* 624.

Kosnicki et al. (Eds.). (1979). *Human sexuality: New directions in Catholic thought.* Garden City, NY: Doubleday.

Macklin. (1983). Personhood and the abortion debate. *Milbank Memoriel Quarterly, 61.*

Law. (1984). Rethinking sex and the constitution. *University of Pennsylvania Law Review, 132,* 955.

Milbauer, B. (1983). *The law giveth: Legal aspects of the abortion controversy.* New York: Atheneum.

Mohr, J. (1978). *Abortion in America.* New York: Oxford University Press.

Nathanson, B. (1984). *The abortion papers.* New York: Fall.

Newsweek (1983). *Out of death, a new life comes.* April 11, p. 65.

Newman, S. A. (1983). *Saying no to medical treatment.* New York (October 17), 74.

O'Brien, M. (1983). *The politics of reproduction.* Boston: Routledge & Kegan Paul.

Petchesky, R. (1984). *Abortion and women's choice.* New York: Longman.

Pilpel, H. (1976). The collateral legal consequences of adopting a constitutional amendment on abortion. *5 Family Planning/Population Rep. 44.*

Prosser. (1971). *Law of torts.* St. Paul: West.

Regan, D. (1979). Rewriting Roe v. Wade. *Michigan Law Review, 77,* 1569.

Robertson, J. (1982). The right to procreate and in utero therapy. *Journal of Legal Medicine, 3,* 333.

Rubin, E. R. (1982). *Abortion politics and the courts.* Westport, CN: Greenwood.

Shannon, T., & Manfra, J. (1982). *Law and bio-ethics.* New York: Paulist Press.

Shaw, M. (1980). The potential plaintiff: Preconception and prenatal torts. In Milunsky & G. Annas (Eds.), *Genetics and the law III.* New York: Plenum.

Shaw, M. & Damme. (1976). Legal status of the fetus. In Milunsky & G. Annad (Eds.), *Genetics and the law II.* New York: Plenum.

Stellman, J. M., & Henifin, M. S. (1982). No fertile women need apply: Employment discrimination and reproductive hazards in the workplace. In Hubbard, Henifin, & Fried (Eds.), *Biological woman: The convenient myth.* Cambridge, MA: Schenkman.

Tribe. (1973). The Supreme Court: Foreword. *Harvard Law Review, 87,* 1.

Warner, M. (1976). *Alone of all her sex: The myth and cult of the Virgin Mary.* New York: Alfred K. Knopf.

Williams, W. (1981). Firing the woman to protect the fetus. *Georgetown Law Journal, 69,* 641.

5

CHILDBIRTH MANAGEMENT AND MEDICAL MONOPOLY

Barbara Katz Rothman

The word "professional" is used in a variety of ways. Sometimes we use it to mean a task expertly, even slickly done. Sometimes we say "professional" when we mean well-behaved or appropriately presented. In that sense, a sloppy job or person is criticized as being "unprofessional." Often we use the word to refer to work done for pay, rather than "amateur." Dictionary definitions of "professional" emphasize the knowlege and training that go into making a particular category of worker "professional." Professionals, in the dictionary's use, are those who have studied long and well—though just how long or just how well is never clear.

Sociological definitions of "professional" have a different focus: These definitions, the ones on which I will draw, emphasize power. A profession is an occupation that has social power, social control. In this sense, what makes people "professional" is not their individual worthiness, neatness, expertise, or even knowledge; rather it is their membership in an occupation that has such power. This power plays a significant role in the medical field.

Eliot Freidson (1970), considering the nature of professions, said, "What is critical for the status of medicine or any other profession is ultimate control over its own work." In health care, members of the medical profession have such control: The profession of medicine is dominant and, according to Freidson, it follows that "the status of other occupations participating in a medical division of labor can only be subordinate ... however much their faces may be smoothed by such cosmetics as a code of ethics, a long period of schooling that includes instruction in a body of theory, and a claim to serve humanity (Freidson, 1970). In this one sweeping statement, Freidson dismisses the knowledge, ethics, and service orientation of professions as cosmetic, as so much window-dressing. The bottom line, the critical factor, is control, power, autonomy. What makes an occupation a profession is its place in the organized division of labor: When it comes to its work, a profession is subordinate to no other occupation. Other occupations may coexist, occupations with a long period of training, a body of knowledge and theory, with a code of ethics, and a commitment to the service of humanity. But when it comes down to decision making and the control of work, they must defer to the profession in charge. Freidson calls such subordinate occupations "paraprofessional."

Defining professional work in this way emphasizes its political nature. An occupation becomes a profession not because of the good work of its individual members, but because the occupation as a whole wins a state or social mandate to practice and to monitor itself. Being ethical, being dedicated, even being knowledgeable, may not have a lot to do with it. Leaving issues of ethics and dedication aside, it is certainly clear that medicine developed its professional dominance long before it developed its body of knowledge. Medicine was a profession when medical school took three to six months, no high school diploma needed. Using this definition of profession also takes something of the "name-calling" quality away from discussions of which occupations are, and which are not, professions. The emphasis in the sociological definition is so clearly not on the personal characteristics, the "professionalism," or even the competence of the members. Rather, sociologists consider only the structural position of the occupation in the division of labor. Professionalism in this sense is simply not something that can be achieved by individual hard work and study. Professional status comes from political action.

Just as I am distinguishing here between personal "professionalism" and the social status of the occupation, so too let me distinguish personal power from professional power, personal from professional autonomy. No individual, member of a recognized profession or not, has complete personal autonomy in work. A physician cannot do any particular thing he or she pleases in the management of a labor or birth simply because of membership in the profession. But the standards of what a physician, as a physician, may or may not do, are set by physicians. By physicians, for physicians, the profession determines its own standards of practice.

Contrast professional autonomy with the experience of personal autonomy: Often a midwife will say to me that she has autonomy, that she can pratice her profession as she thinks best, that she can make her own decisions. As we talk about it, she assures me that she has a very good relationship with her back-up doctor or with the head of obstetrics at her hospital who is "very supportive." That is not the kind of autonomy of which I speak. It is not the autonomy or freedom of an individual to practice at the grace of another that is the hallmark of a profession, but the autonomy of the group to set its own standards of practice for its own members.

When we apply this sociological definition to midwifery and to medicine, the situation is clear: Midwives do not tell physicians what they may do, what procedures they may use, to which tools and instruments they may have access. No other occupation makes those decisions for the occupation of medicine. But medicine, as a profession, does indeed control midwifery is just those ways. Midwifery is not, according to the sociological perspective, a profession.

One can readily understand why midwives themselves want midwifery to have full professional recognition: Why shouldn't they want the freedom to make their own decisions, to control their own work? And with professional status comes higher social status, probably also ultimately higher rewards of a more tangible nature as well. Control over needed services, the basic monopoly such as medicine exercises, pays handsomely. Why shouldn't midwives want to "better" themselves, to grow, advance, carve out the best possible place for themselves in the social system?

A better question is, why do I care? Why do I and others—childbirth activists, feminists, mothers—why do we care whether or not midwifery achieves professional status? The struggle between midwifery and medicine goes back for hundreds of years, with no end in sight. Why should the "consumers," the clientele, the birthing women, get involved in this long, maybe endless battle?

Most discussions of midwifery's appeal for "consumers" emphasize the amorphous quality of "attitudes" and the "warmth" of midwives—and the fact that midwives are women, and women often like women birth attendants. That is not a satisfactory argument. I know some very nice, humane, friendly and warm women doctors. I even know some midwives who are not so warm and nice. But even if we were to agree that, on the whole, midwives are the better choice of birth attendant, that is still not sufficient reason to engage the services of others in the struggle for midwifery autonomy. Midwives, especially nurse-midwives, are available as birth attendants. Does it matter to the birthing woman if the midwife taking her blood pressure, if the midwife listening to her fetal heart tones, if the midwife catching her baby, is or is not a member of a state-recognized profession? Yes, I think it really does matter.

Just what is it that a profession "controls" when it controls its work? For medicine, it is the state-supported right, manifested in the licensing of physicians, to what is defined as medical practice. With their license, physicians can legally do what no one else can, including cutting into the human body and prescribing drugs (Conrad & Kern, 1981, p. 151). Where other occupations are allowed to perform these tasks it is with the clear and expressed permission of medicine. Control over an area of practice extends, as I have indicated, to control over other workers. As members of the dominant health care occupation, physicians determine which practices are "medical" and which can be delegated to lower-level practitioners. Physicians further oversee the work of individual lower-level practitioners, and have the right to determine whether their work falls within the prescribed limits. For midwives, this is experienced as the control of the back-up physicians (or physician-directed hospital service) to determine standards of practice.

But control over an area of practice also allows for control over the clientele. If only physicians can do certain tasks, then those who want those tasks done depend on, are under the power of, physicians. Much research, thought, and writing has been produced on the relations between doctors and their patients. In virtually all such work themes of power and control, and their converse, dependency and submission (often dubbed "compliance") emerge.[1] From the point of view of the birthing women, the professionalization, the full coming into its own, of midwifery would mean shifting control from medicine to midwifery. It would not mean a return to power to birthing women, at least not directly—although midwives and their clients tend to identify with each other far more than do physicians and their clients, the two are separate groups with potentially divergent interests.

So, again, why do I, as someone who is not a midwife, feel that it is important that midwifery achieve professional autonomy? It is because there is a third direction, in addition to co-workers and clients, over which professions extend their control. A profession also controls a body of knowledge.

In part, this means that a profession controls access to knowledge. The profession of medicine controls access to medical schools and influences the curriculum content of health-related programs. But even more fundamental is the control over the development of knowledge. In regard to birth, the profession of medicine determines not only who may attend a birth, or what birth attendants may do, but controls also what we know of birth itself.

In its control over practice, the profession of medicine maintains control over research—research in its broadest sense. Data are collected, both formally and informally, to support and to develop the medical body of knowledge. But the data are themselves generated by the medical practices. The methods of observation in medicine have been criticized as not "scientific" enough, but the more fundamental flaw is in not recognizing the social processes involved in the generation of the data, of that which is there to be observed. So it develops that in our society the obstetrical perspective on pregnancy and birth is not considered just one way of looking at it, but rather to be the truth, the facts, science; others may have beliefs about pregnancy, but we believe medicine has the facts. However, obstetrical knowledge, like all knowledge, comes from somewhere: It has a social, historical and political context. Medicine does not exist as something "pure," free of culture or free of ideology. The context in which medical knowledge develops and is used shapes that knowledge. In particular, the setting of practice generates the data on which the knowledge is based.

To begin to make this point clear, I am going to draw examples from two very different worlds, different "settings of practice." I am going to contrast medical obstetrical knowledge with the knowledge of a lay midwife practicing outside of medical settings. The same physiological event, the birth of a baby, can occur in many places—women labor and babies are born in a variety of settings. But the social definitions, our ideas about what is happening, are vastly different in different settings, and these differences create new social realities. In turn, these new realities, or definitions of the situation, create new physiological reality, as the birth process itself is shaped by the settings in which it occurs. Let us begin with a simple, everyday event.

SITUATION ONE

A woman comes to the maternity floor of a large hospital. She is upset, almost crying, holding her huge belly and leaning against her husband, who seems nearly as upset as she is. "My wife's in labor," he states, and hands over a scrap of paper with times marked off—the seven- to twelve-minutes intervals they have timed between contractions. The woman is ushered into a cubicle and examined. The examination might be repeated an hour later. "No," the doctor tells her, "You're not in labor yet. You have not begun to dilate. This is just a false alarm, a false labor. You can go home and come back when you really are in labor."

Here we have a physiological event—the painful contractions of the uterus—defined two different ways, as labor and as not-labor. The woman and her husband are basing their definitions on her feelings, the sensations she is experiencing as she has been taught to measure them—in minutes, for example. The doctor is basing his or her definition on what he or she feels as an examiner, the degree of dilation—how much the cervix has dilated. Each definition of the situation carries with it a way of acting, a set of behavioral expectations, for the actors involved. As not-labor, the doctor is finished with the woman and can turn his or her attention elsewhere. The woman is to go home and stay simply pregnant a while longer. Defined as labor, however, the situation is very different. The woman changes from her status of pregnant woman to the new status of laboring woman. She will put on the appropriate costume (change from "maternity clothes" to a "hospital gown") and become a patient. The doctor will be expected to provide examination and treatment, to begin managing her condition. Only in labor will she become the doctor's responsibility.

SITUATION TWO

Cara (an empirical midwife): I got a call that Roberta was having heavy rushes but wasn't dilating and was having a hard time. I wanted to go see her and help. When I got there, Roberta was writhing with each rush and shaking. She just didn't have any ideas how to handle the energy. Joel was sitting beside her looking worried. The whole scene was a bit grim for a baby-having. I got them kissing, hugging, and had Roberta really grab on to Joel and squeeze him. Joel is a big strong, heavy-duty man. He and I rubbed Roberta continuously and steered in the direction of relaxed. I let her know that she was having good, strong rushes, and that if she'd relax and experience it and let it happen, her rushes would accomplish a lot and open her up, she gradually accepted the fact that there was no getting out of this, except to let it happen and quit fighting it. (Gaskin, 1975, p. 126)

Here we have the same physiological event, a woman experiencing the same sensations and the same lack of dilation, defined along yet other lines. First note the difference in the language being used. The empirical midwife describing this situation is not talking about "contractions," the medical word for what the uterine muscle is doing, but "rushes." This midwife lives and works on The Farm, the Tennessee commune that published *Spiritual Midwifery*. The midwives explain their language:

> On the farm we've come to call these contractions of the uterine muscle "rushes" because the main sensation that happens when these muscles contract is exactly the same as the sensations of rushing while coming on to a heavy psychedelic, which feels like a whole lot of energy flowing up your back and into your head. It leaves you feeling expansive and stoned if you don't fight it. (Gaskin, 1975, p. 346)

This language relies on internal or subjective cues, sensations the woman herself experiences. The medical language, in contrast, relies on external or "objective" cues, information available to the examiner—how much the woman has dilated. Thus when the subjective and objective cues are at variance, in the medical situation the subjective cues are discounted. The woman's sensations of labor are "false" and the doctor's definition is "true." In the midwifery situation, the woman's experienced reality of the rushes is acknowledged. The "problem," the variance between subjective and objective measures, is here defined as the woman's inability to cope effectively, to "let it happen." This definition, of course, also carries with it consequences for the people involved: The midwife and the husband are expected to help her cope, relax, let it happen. For the woman, one of the negative consequences of this definition of the situation is that it tells her that it is in some way her own fault that she is having a hard time. In that way the midwives are doing the same thing as the doctors: imposing their definition of the situation on the laboring woman. The doctor's responsibility is very narrowly defined: only to manage "real" labor. Midwives' responsibility, in contrast, is defined more broadly, to include "helping" or "managing," controlling the emotional as well as the physical situation.

Thus each of these alternate definitions carries with it quite different consequences, consequences that will shape the experience of all those involved, but most dramatically of the pregnant woman. It is one thing to be a pregnant woman, and quite another to be "in labor." And it is one thing to be told that the labor that you are experiencing is "false" and yet again another to be told that the rushes are real and you have to learn how to relax and stop fighting them. The meaning given the particular uterine contractions of any particular woman becomes the basis for the way the event, and thus the woman, is treated.

These scenarios, and their implications, explain why it matters, even to those of us who are not midwives, that midwives come to have professional autonomy. With professional autonomy comes the power to control the setting of birth, and ultimately to control the birthing woman. As someone who is not a midwife, I prefer midwifery control to obstetrical control because obstetrical control, the "objective" medical reality if you will, diminishes the birthing woman. It makes her an object upon whom the art and science of obstetrics is practiced. The underlying ideology of medicine is that the body is a machine. This depersonalizes the birthing woman, making her less than a person, a suitable candidate for being hooked up to yet other machines.

The organization of the hospital maternity floor influences this mechanistic vision of the woman. Labor rooms look more like regular nursing-care rooms; delivery rooms more like operating rooms. As the woman is transferred from one to another, there is basis for more and more narrowly defining the relevant parts of her, as she first loses full personhood to become a patient, and then in the delivery room where all the doctor sees of the woman is the exposed perineum centered in draped linen, becomes simply a pelvis from which a fetus is removed. The alternative birth settings—homes, "birthing rooms," and the like—provide a contrasting image, in which the mother is not lying flat, and is surrounded by friends and family, tied to a full social world. Such a setting may very well encourage the awareness of the social and emotional factors in the birth. Thus, "contractions" may be the salient feature when palpating the abdomen of a semiconscious woman, but "rush" may seem more appropriate when talking to a woman who is experiencing one.

Is the woman I described "really" in labor when she experiences contractions with "no progress?" Who defines? Who sets the policy about whether such a woman could or should be admitted to a particular hospital? If nurse-midwife and physician disagree, upon whose judgment will the insurance companies' decision to pay for the day of hospitalization rely? And so how will we learn which definition of the situation results in better outcome for mother and baby? Unless and until midwifery achieves professional status, it controls neither the birthing woman nor the development of an alternative body of knowledge.

In sum, for midwifery, nurse-midwifery, or midwifery in general, to develop an alternative body of knowledge, to reach new understandings about what is happening in birth, requires midwifery control over the setting of birth. I have come to see that it is not that birth is "managed" the way it is because of what we know about birth. Rather, what we know about birth has been determined by the way it is managed.

And the way childbirth has been managed has been based on
the underlying assumptions, beliefs, and ideology of medicine
as a profession.

What are the implications of this for nurse-midwifery?
Nurse-midwifery is learned in medical settings, in situations
controlled by the profession of medicine. Medical control
thus inevitably limits the development of a unique body of
midwifery knowledge by nurse-midwives. Childbirth must be
managed within the guidelines established in accordance with
"obstetrical facts," but those facts themselves have grown
out of the setting of practice established by medicine. The circle is tight and usually closed. When it is broken, startling
things happen.

I have made a study of the breaking of that circle of
knowledge (Rothman, 1982). I have studied nurse-midwives,
trained within medical settings, who began doing home
births. I am not claiming here that homes are the only, or
even the best, setting for nurse-midwifery practice—that is
a question that I have addressed elsewhere (Rothman, 1983).
But I do claim that home births break the circle.

For a nurse-midwife with standard hospital-based training,
doing home births is a radicalizing experience. It makes her
think hard about her work and its meaning. In this new setting she has to question many of the taken-for-granted
assumptions of the medical setting and medical model. And
she finds herself constructing a new model, a new way of explaining what she sees. This is the process of reconceptualiza-
tion, taking something you've confronted maybe a hundred
times, and suddenly seeing it as something else entirely.

There is a simple experiment that shows this process at
work.[2] People were asked to identify a set of playing cards
flashed on a screen. Most were standard playing cards, but
some were made anomalous, for example, a red six of spades,
a black four of hearts. The subjects were able to identify "normal" cards correctly. However, they not only failed to iden-

tify the anomalous cards correctly, but without any apparent hesitation or puzzlement "normalized" them. For example, a black heart would be identified as a regular red heart, or seen as a spade. When they were allowed to look at the cards longer, however, the subjects began to hesitate. They displayed more and more hesitation until they switched over and began to perceive the cards correctly, identifying a black heart as a black heart, a red spade as a red spade.

For the nurse-midwife making the transition from the hospital to home births, many anomalies will present themselves. The nausea that she was taught was part of her labor may not be there. She may begin to see that in the hospital this discomfort was caused by not letting the woman eat or drink anything during labor. The amount of time something takes, such as expelling the placenta, may begin to look, in this new setting, very different from the way it did in the hospital delivery room. At first she will try to apply the medical model in the new setting, attempting to utilize the knowledge gained in the hospital to what she is seeing in the home. That won't always work for her. When she is faced with an anomaly in the medical model that she cannot ignore or "normalize," she has a radicalizing experience: She rejects at least part of the medical model. She may share that experience with other nurse-midwives, and many such stories are told. Hearing the resolutions achieved by others supports and furthers her own radicalization. What were perceived as facts come to be seen as artifacts: obstetrical constructions, artifacts of the medical setting.

Let me review a small sample of these questioned "facts":

(1) Vomiting and nausea are a common part of labor.

Working outside of medical control, midwives who have not denied food and drink to laboring women have observed that nausea is uncommon. The question: Is the nausea caused by labor, or by the lack of food?

(2) Infection is likely to occur if much time passes after the rupture of the membranes and before the birth.

Careful and frequent vaginal examinations were standard practice in the hospital to assess progress once the membranes , ruptured. Midwives working outside of medically controlled settings, faced with a natural rupture of membranes at term before labor began, have on occasion avoided the examinations, fearing that they may be a source of infection. The question: How likely is infection, and at what interval after the membranes have ruptured, if hospitalization and vaginal examinations do not take place?

(3) Milk does not come in for three days after birth.

Working against what had been standard practice, women (inside hospitals as well as outside) demanded their babies earlier and more often. The new knowledge, now no longer even a question, is that milk comes in more commonly within 24-48 hours after birth when mother and baby have unrestricted access to each other. A corollary of this is that the time required for the infant to regain birthweight has been adjusted downward.

(4) Once full dilation is reached, second stage begins. If it does not, the condition, called second stage arrest, is a sign of pathology.

Working outside of medically controlled settings, midwives sometimes observed a woman who, on reaching full dilation, rolled over, exhausted, and fell asleep. That is not something one would often see on a delivery table. After a nap, the labor resumed, with a healthy baby and mother. The question: What is pathological second stage arrest, and what is a naturally occurring rest period?

The examples abound. Some of the most interesting, like most of these examples, have to do with medical timetables, with how long the various stages of pregnancy, labor, and the postpartum period are claimed to take. Other questions have arisen about the distinctions between vountary and involuntary action—just how much of the birth process can and does the mother control?

Where does midwifery stand amidst these questions? Can we turn to lay midwives or to nurse-midwives to learn answers? The answer: only to the extent that midwives can control the settings of their practice; only to the extent that midwifery emerges as a full profession.

The implications of allowing medicine the monopoly on childbirth management thus go beyond the relatively simple question of the infringement of other occupations' right to practice. What I am arguing is that our usual assumptions need to be turned on their head. As a society we claim that medicine has the monopoly because childbirth is more than anything else a medical event. The truth might more nearly be stated that childbirth is a medical event because medicine holds the monopoly on management.

If birth were moved out of the hands of medicine, if birth were defined in other than medical terms, the implications would be far reaching indeed. Some of the "facts" about the birth, as I have shown, would be seen to be "artifacts" of medical management. But it is not just that a new, more lenient, and more individually varied set of timetables would be developed to replace the obstetrical timetables. As important as this would be, the effects of demedicalizing childbirth would go beyond even this reevaluation. Demedicalizing childbirth would allow us to perceive the experience of childbirth in new ways.

Such demedicalization would open up the possibility of new outcome measurements for birth. As a medical/surgical event, birth outcome is measured in standard medical terms: mortality and morbidity rates. The incidence of postpartum infection, for example, is perceived as a relevant outcome measure, useful for comparing alternative childbirth management strategies. This perfectly parallels the measurement of postsurgical infection rates in comparing, for example, vaginal with abdominal hysterectomy, or alternative treatments of various tumors.

If birth were defined in other than medical terms, other outcome measures would be perceived as equally appropriate. As things stand now, if two approaches to childbirth result in equal mortality and morbidity rates, the two approaches are perceived as being roughly equivalent. Thus home birth is demonstrated to be at least as safe as hospital birth because mortality rates are equal and morbidity rates are lower.

But birth is also an event in the lives of families, and if perceived as such, outcome measures based on familial experience would also be considered appropriate, along with infection rates or other measures of physiological morbidity. To take extremes, childbirth management that routinely leaves older siblings with nightmares and separation anxiety as the mother is removed from the household to return days later engulfed in the care of the new infant, is not the same as a birth that leaves older siblings strongly attached to the newcomer, unshaken in their own secure position within the family—even if the rate of morbidity are the same. A birth management that leaves wives angry at husbands, and husbands feeling that they have failed their wives is not the same as a birth that draws the two closer together. A birth experience that leaves the woman unsure of her mothering abilities and unable to comfort a crying new baby is not the same as a birth experience that leaves the woman feeling confident and competent.

Childbirth is also a learning experience for women. Perceived in those terms, birth outcome can also be measured in terms of the woman's knowledge about her body, her baby, and her birth. With demedicalization, teaching skills, long valued in midwifery and largely ignored in medicine, would be considered important. A pregnancy and childbirth experience, again looking at the extremes, that leaves the woman fearful of her bodily functions, unsure of just what was cut "down there" or why, is not the same as a birth that leaves the woman feeling strong and positive about herself, more rather than less comfortable with her body.

In sum, the medical monopoly on chilbirth management has meant defining birth in medical terms, and so narrowing our scope of perception. A birth management that routinely leaves psychological and social trauma in its wake for the members of families, using this narrow definition, is measured as perfectly successful, unless the trauma is severe enough to be measured in appropriately "medical" terms—that is infant weight gain, or some such crude measure.

Because I challenge the usefulness and the validity of such measures, I thus challenge the medical monopoly on childbirth. The policy implications that follow from this challenge are admittedly radical. If childbirth is redefined in other than strictly medical terms, medicine as a profession loses its long-standing monopoly on childbirth management in the United States. The demand by midwives to practice their profession is to be seen by those in a position to make policy not as an attempt by a less qualified group to engage in the practice of medicine, as it has most often seen, but rather, as the claim of a more qualified group to practice midwifery. The state, as granter of professional licensing, remains in a position to license—or refuse to license—individual midwives or classes of midwives. But redefining birth in nonmedical terms means that it will be midwives and not physicians who determine appropriate midwifery qualifications, who set the standards for midwifery practice, and who advise the state on the licensure of midwives.

The break in the medical monopoly that I seek is much more than simply allowing others access to performing medical functions; it is not simply the granting of hospital privileges to nurse-midwives. Rather, it is the rethinking of the meaning of childbirth. If childbirth is not merely a medical event, then physicians are simply one profession with relevent expertise. The implications of a change in policy that would grant professional status to midwives go far beyond changing the work situation for midwives. This fundamental reorganization has the potential to change the birth experience and the ways that experience is defined.

NOTES

1. For a discussion and criticism of research on compliance, see Mumford (1983, chap. 13).
2. The experiment by Bruner and Postman is discussed in Kuhn (1970).

RESOURCES

Conrad, P. & Kern R. (1981). *The sociology of health and sickness.* New York: St. Martin's Press.
Friedson, E. (1970). *Professional dominance.* Chicago: Aldine.

Gaskin, I. M. (1975). *Spiritual midwifery.* Summertown TN: The book Publishing Co.

Kuhn, T. S. (1970). *The structure of scientific revolutions.* Chicago: University of Chicago Press.

Mumford, E. (1983). *Medical sociology: Patients, providers and policies.* New York: Random House.

Rothman, B. K. (1982). *In labor: Women and power in the birthplace.* New York: W. W. Norton (Reprinted in 1983 as *Giving birth: Alternatives in childbirth.* New York: Penguin).

Rothman, B. K. (1983). Anatomy of a compromise: Nurse-midwifery and the rise of the free-standing birth center. *Journal of Nurse-Midwifery* (Summer).

6

OCCUPATIONAL SAFETY AND HEALTH
AS A WOMEN'S POLICY ISSUE

Graham K. Wilson
Virginia Sapiro

Although comprehensive federal involvement in workplace safety and health is comparatively new, dating back only to the creation of the Occupational Safety and Health Administration (OSHA) in 1970, policy debate over protection of the health and safety of American workers goes back to the beginning of this century and before; safety and health policies at the state and local levels have an even longer history. These policies and policy debates have caused particular difficulties for women's policy analysts. On the one hand, there is general agreement that regulation of workplace practices is essential to the protection of the health and safety of the working population. On the other hand, past experience shows that protective labor legislation, as it applies specifically to women, can be used as a way of securing gender-based job segregation, limiting women's economic opportunities in discriminatory ways, and maintaining gender stereotypes.

Protection of the safety and health of workers in general and of female workers more specifically continues to raise important questions about the nature of public policy as it af-

137

fects women, and about the special problems of women in the workforce. This chapter takes up and examines some of these questions, beginning with an exploration of how the design and purposes of occupational safety and health policies affect women and men differently. Because discrimination in policy effects is not always direct, intentional, or even recognized (Sapiro, 1984), we will first look at some of the ways in which an apparently "gender neutral" policy design discriminates in practice, and will then turn to the more specific role of gender ideology in occupational safety and health policies.[1] From policy design we move onto some aspects of alternative strategies of enforcement. Finally, we will look at the impact of the Reagan era on occupational safety and health policy and at the problems that need to be addressed in the future.

SAFETY VS. HEALTH:
WHAT DIFFERENCE DOES IT MAKE?

Until very recently, discussion among politicians of occupational safety and health was likely to focus more or less exclusively on safety rather than health. That is to say, congressional debates on the hazards of work were concerned almost entirely with the prevention of accidents that can befall workers, and were little concerned with the diseases or illnesses that can be caused by occupational factors. The differences between emphasizing occupational health and safety offer important insights into both this area of policy in general and the ways it specially concerns women.

Industrial accidents are certainly nasty and important enough. They cause more deaths than road accidents among the working population, and inflict dreadful damage on their victims. The number of occupational accidents may actually be underestimated in official figures; because many workers' compensation schemes are parsimonious, less drastic accidents may go unreported as the victims do not take time off from work. But nearly all major accidents are reported, particularly if deaths result. In 1980 there were 13 deaths on the job for every 100,000 workers. About 2 million workers suffered death or disabling injuries on the job. Considering all injuries at work raises the figure higher, and includes about 8 million incidents involving men and 3 million involving women.

In contrast, occupational causes of ill health are much more difficult to identify and count. Many diseases caused by occupational factors have long latency periods; for example, some of the lung cancers caused by asbestos appear thirty years after exposure. In the absence of adequate epidemiological data, scientists are driven back to data derived from experiments on animals, first, to establish that a substance is a hazard, and second, to calculate what exposure limits, if any, are safe. The implications for humans of the results of such experiments are highly uncertain and subject to a number of criticisms about their validity, such as the tendency for experimenters to administer large doses of suspect substances because of the time factors involved in experimenting with more realistic low doses.

The costs of meeting health regulations are generally much higher than the costs of meeting safety regulations. The advocate of health regulations has to overcome the opposition of firms upon which a great cost is to be imposed while armed with data that are much less precise and reliable than data on accidents. Conflicts of interest arise between companies asked to incur major costs to meet regulations designed to protect the health of workers from diseases that may be latent until long after they have left the company. In contrast, safety issues seem to raise more questions of shared interest between employer and employee. The most callous employer could at least understand that stopping an assembly line to remove the victim of an accident and training a replacement would add to costs. Safety, in brief, is a more obvious, certain, and cooperative area for government action. It is little wonder that there are more safety than health regulations and inspections in the United States.

Unfortunately, serious though accidents are, many more people—probably ten times as many—are victims of occupational ill health than occupational accidents. No one is sure how many people die from occupationally caused illnesses. The long latency period of the illnesses and the fact that most doctors are not used to looking for occupational factors in diagnosing illness or death make statistics inaccurate. Identifying the cause of particular illnesses in specific cases is a complex problem that can often stretch scientific diagnostic skill to its limits. Both exposure to asbestos and cigarette smoke are causes of cancer, but cigarette smoking multiplies the dangers of asbestos by at least four and possibly fifty times. Estimates of occupationally related illness is rough at best, but some scientists believe that 40 percent of all cancers are attributable to occupational factors.

Whether protective policies emphasize health or safety makes a vast difference in their impact and in what kinds of workers are likely to benefit from them. The most dangerous industries as measured by the accident rates are not necessarily the most unhealthy. The uses of asbestos apart, the construction industry can be considered highly dangerous in terms of number of accidents, yet probably relatively safe in terms of occupational health. Similarly, meatcutting is a very accident-prone industry, yet it is otherwise a healthy industry. Deepcast coal mining is unusual in combining a high accident and health risk. Otherwise one can say that there is a poor correlation between the risks of occupational accident and ill health.

The balance between health and safety concerns in protective policies has a hidden but profound gender relevance that becomes clear if we focus on the degree of occupational segregation by gender. The proportion of American workers who hold integrated jobs, meaning those in which the gender imbalance is no more than 40 percent to 60 percent, is very small; in 1980 only 11 percent of men and 15 percent of women held such jobs (Rytina & Bianchi, 1984). Most Americans hold jobs that are done primarily by people of their own sex. Job segregation is based on a number of norms defining what is a "masculine" and what is a "feminine" job. One of the characteristics that defines a job as masculine is the degree of danger involved: the likelihood that one might suffer death or injury. Using the examples of accident prone jobs mentioned above, 2 percent of construction workers are women, as are 2 percent of meatcutters and 8 percent of miners regardless of type of mining. The trade and service sectors of the ecomomy, where the bulk of female workers are found, are the safest industries as measured by death and injury from accident.

Women are more likely to be found in industries where health risks appear to be more important problems than accidents. The textile industry, in which women constitute a majority of the operatives, is a case in point. The accident rate is below the average for manufacturing industries, yet the health hazards are manifold. Noise may cause a loss of hearing, and dust threatens the lungs of textile workers with diseases such as byssinosis. In manufacturing women have traditionally been channeled into light industry and, especially, those jobs requiring fast, agile detail work because of the belief that women are particularly good at that kind of work. Workers in these jobs do not suffer heroic deaths and disable-

142 WOMEN, BIOLOGY, AND PUBLIC POLICY

ment, but such long-term health risks as eye strain are problems.

Secretarial work, the largest single employer of women, has long been attractive to women in part because it appears to be a safe and clean alternative to most available types of blue collar work. Few people would believe there are dangers lurking in such an apparently comfortable sit-down job. And yet, typing over the long term is associated with muscular problems in the back and upper arms, long hours in front of visual display units creates eye strain, and many medical authorities are suspicious of the effects of copying machines. Experts suspect that these problems are not temporary and minor complaints but, rather, have lasting effects. People in more female dominated medical jobs—nurses and technicians—are more exposed to the sources of disease than are doctors. Among the occupational classifications most at risk of skin diseases are many predominately female jobs, including medical workers, florists, launderers, food workers—and homemakers (Stellman, 1977). Homemaking, the most female dominant job, is a particularly risky job as far as both safety and health are concerned. These risks go nearly unrecognized, in part because homemaking is not regarded by most people as an occupation. The only legal protections given to homemakers in their workplace are very indirect, including, for example, the regulations of the Consumer Product Safety Commission and the Federal Trade Commission.

For a variety of reasons, many of them not explicitly tied to gender discrimination, most of women's work is not central to protective policies. "Gender neutral" policies are not necessarily gender neutral in effect. The connection is indirect but strong. Women are defined as unsuitable for dangerous occupations as defined by relatively dramatic (masculine?) accident risks. Protective policies are designed primarily to cover these types of jobs, thus leaving women out.

HEALTH AND SAFETY
REGULATION AND WOMEN:
EXTRA CARE OR DISCRIMINATION?

In spite of the fact that current occupational safety and
health policies seem to leave women out, there is a long
history of treating women as a "special case" in matters of
protecting workers. Indeed, for historical reasons, the phrase
"protective labor legislation" generally implies policies aimed
at women. Most members of the public probably assume that
women do receive many special protections and, further, that
this extra protection is justified because women are more at
risk than men due to their lesser physical strength or other
biological characteristics. Phyllis Schlafly and other opponents
of the Equal Rights Amendment consistently argued that the
ERA would hurt women by removing their labor protections
from them.

The history of protective labor legislation is well known to
historians of women's economic lives. At the turn of the century a coalition of feminists, progressives, and trade union
leaders worked together to push for special protective labor
legislation for women and especially legislation that would
limit the hours they worked and certain job conditions such
as weight lifting. Support for special protections for women
workers drew together not just a coalition of different groups
but a coalition of different interests. Some groups, of course,
wanted to protect women from the horrors of exploitation so
common at the time. Most male labor leaders, on the other
hand, had little interest in improving women's economic lives
or job conditions per se; Samuel Gompers, for example, who
strongly supported protective legislation for women, wanted
women kept out of the labor force as much as possible and
even hoped to see additional legislation that would bar
women from government employment. Rather, many of the

labor leaders supported protection for three reasons. They thought that protective labor legislation would keep women from competing in men's jobs, that by eliminating women as cheap competition it would help raise male wages, and, finally, that protective legislation for women would serve as the "thin end of the wedge" to transform a laissez-faire economic system into one that would offer protections for workers in general and in which unions could gain strength.

Although different states experimented with such legislation the Supreme Court remained hostile to any interference with the rights of workers and employers to enter into contracts freely, which is what they defined protective legislation as doing in a 1905 case, *Lochner v. New York*. In 1908 the Court changed its mind by accepting a maximum hours law for women in *Muller v. Oregon*. The case is familiar, but it is worth quoting the key part of the Court's rationale as it concerns the question of health and safety:

> That women's physical structure and the performance of material functions place her at a disadvantage in the struggle for subsistence is obvious. This is especially true when the burdens of motherhood are upon her. Even when they are not, by abundant testimony of the medical fraternity continuance for a long time on her feet at work, repeating this from day to day, tends to injurious effects upon the body, and as healthy mothers are essential to vigorous offspring, the physical well-being of women becomes an object of public interest and care in order to preserve the strength and vigor of the race.

The Court emphasized that these protections "are not imposed solely for her benefit, but also largely for the benefit of all."

Women's health and safety had to be protected for one very specific reason: the "proper discharge of her maternal functions," as the Court said in *Muller.* Women workers were to be regarded as mothers or as potential mothers, and were to be protected as such. From then on most protections ever offered to women in the workforce have generally been justified in terms of reproductive functions, and the most significant effect of protective labor legislation has been to inhibit women's entrance into jobs that are defined as in conflict with the interests of reproduction. The decision over what job conditions are in conflict with reproduction has always been a very subjective one, and one that has been based on prejudices and stereotypes regarding women's and men's "natural" and "biological" roles. As many observers have pointed out, women have been more likely to be "protected" from male-dominated jobs than even similar conditions in traditionally female jobs. For a classic example, women have sometimes been restricted from jobs requiring the worker to lift weights equivalent to the weight of a small child or a load of groceries or laundry. As noted earlier, protective legislation does not apply to homemaking. The ideological base of these policies has led to another consequence: Because reproduction is regarded as a female function, protective policies have been relatively unconcerned with the effects of work hazards on men's reproductive capacities.

The bulk of traditional protective legislation has fallen by the wayside over the years, in part because protection against occupational hazards tends to apply to workers within given occupations regardless of sex and in part because of the effects of equalization policies set in place since the 1960's such as the Equal Pay Act of 1963, Title VII of the 1964 Civil Rights Act and its amendments, and state equal rights amendments. Beginning in 1971 with the Supreme Court case *Phillips v. Martin Marietta* the Court, Congress, and the executive branch began to chip away at practices they saw as discriminating against women as mothers, pregnant people, or potentially pregnant people. The 1978 Pregnancy Discrimination Act, which wrote pregnancy into Title VII of the 1964 Civil Rights Act as an explicit category of women against whom discrimination is prohibited, is particularly important in this regard.

The problems and questions have not ended here. Research is revealing much more clear and reliable information on occupational hazards that are particularly risky to reproductive capacities and to the fetus. Women who are pregnant or who will one day become pregnant are at special risk in certain jobs. Humanitarian motivations aside, if employers know that they may be held responsible for injuries or disabilities caused by their workplaces, especially if there is a known risk involved, shouldn't they be in a position to keep those at risk away from the hazards? Risk to reproduction is not the only type of situation in which employers have attempted to protect themselves; asbestos companies such as Johns Manville have argued that they should be allowed to refuse employment to cigarette smokers because of the fact that cigarette smoking multiplies the risks from asbestos.

Employers who attempt to exclude pregnant or "potentially pregnant" people from certain jobs come into conflict with equal employment policies; most choose a method that excludes women from the places where hazards are located and therefore excludes them from certain jobs. The Occupational Safety and Health Administration debated the possibility of a nondiscrimination guideline in its own regulations in 1980, but dropped the idea. Feminists are justifiably wary of protective legislation that could serve once again to deny women employment opportunities, but many of these hazards are real. Many women may argue that they would prefer to have a choice as informed and consenting adults, but as Vibiana Andrade (1981, p. 78) says, such choices may be paid with women's own flesh.

ENFORCEMENT

The enforcement of safety and health regulations is extremely difficult. The fact that there are only 1,500 inspectors employed by the federal agency responsible, OSHA, adds to these difficulties. Federal inspectors can visit only 2 percent of workplaces in the United States each year, and obviously any imaginable increase in the number of inspectors would leave the vast majority of workplace uninspected each year. Moreover, many safety hazards such as a wet floor or spilled oil have a transitory character. Conditions likely to cause an accident may not be in evidence by the time an inspector calls.

OSHA has been under great pressure since its formation in 1970 to produce a "targeting plan" for inspectors that will maximize the impact of its very few inspectors. Unfortunately, several factors are likely to target inspections to the disadvantage of the female workers.

First, all inspection plans are based on injury rates, not health risk. For reasons explained earlier, it is almost impossible to collect adequate and appropriate statistics on occupational illness, and any targeting policy must necessarily be based on "hard figures." The agency's numerous critics in Congress and the heavy emphasis on "due process" in the American political culture preclude the agency simply convincing courts and employers that it would use its best judgment. All inspection targeting has been done on the basis of injury rates compiled either by type of industry or by the record of the firm. OSHA's targeting programs have therefore reinforced the safety rather than health bias, as the agency has admitted.

OSHA has also been under great pressure to concentrate its inspections on large companies. This is partly because there are economies of scale in inspection. An inspector can check the safety and health regulations for a factory employing

1,000 workers in little more time than checking on the safety and health of workers in a factory employing half that number. There has also been great pressure on OSHA from Congress to treat small-scale employers leniently. Thus appropriations riders have been carried forbidding the imposition of penalities on employers of ten or less people for nearly all first instance breaches of OSHA regulations. As the largest factories tend to be in the male-dominated industries such as steel and automobile assembly, women workers are disadvantaged by this policy.

Inspections are not just triggered by agency decision. Under the OSH Act, workers have the right to request an inspection by OSHA if they believe "that a violation of a health or safety standard exists that threatens physical harm or that an imminent danger exists." Until the Reagan administration, OSHA responded to all requests for inspections— whether written or telephoned—by dispatching an inspector. In practice, requests for inspections came overwhelmingly from union officials. Union officials know the provisions of the OSH Act and where its offices are; most ordinary workers do not. It is in fact suspected that union officials have used the threat of an OSHA inspection as a general bargaining tactic, for example in pay negotiations. How commonly OSHA inspections are requested for the wrong reasons is hotly debated, of course, but even the agency's friends admit that the automatic response of OSHA, sending out an inspector after every such request, has biased its inspection program toward unionized workers. As female workers are much less unionized than are male workers, this bias in OSHA inspections has again biased its program against them.

The contrast between male and female workers should not be overdrawn, however. OSHA has been a beleaguered agency since its inception. OSHA has faced continual attacks in Congress; regulations and decisions have been challenged incessantly in the courts. With an almost ridiculously small number of inspectors and great difficulties, both political and legal, the agency has made very limited progress in protecting any workers, whatever their sex. Even in the field of occupational safety the agency has been argued to have had no appreciable effect on the number of industrial injuries. Such assessment is probably unfair, but few would claim that the agency has fulfilled its sponsors' expectations.

OSHA UNDER REAGAN

OSHA suffered the same fate under the Reagan administration that other social welfare and regulating agencies experienced. Thorne Auchter, the first head of OSHA appointed by President Reagan, set out to change fundamentally the direction that the agency had taken previously. Auchter claims that his goals have been to make the agency less objectionable to industry, weakening the attacks upon it. He argues that OSHA had adopted an adversarial approach to enforcement, and spent too long defending itself from attack and too little securing the voluntary compliance of industry. Auchter's critics—including the vast majority of unions—have argued that Auchter was implementing a general administration policy of reducing the strength of agencies that industry sees as antagonistic. Certainly every change in agency policy made by Auchter has been welcomed by industry. Work has dropped on the creation of new health regulations and staff were diverted to revising existing regulations to make them more acceptable to industry. The number of inspectors employed by OSHA was reduced even further and the inspectors were ordered to adopt a more conciliatory approach to employers. It is possible to view the Auchter regime, which lasted from 1981 to 1984, as marking the demise of a serious federal commitment to improve workplace safety and health. Auchter's Reagan-appointed successor continued this process.

Two aspects of Auchter's regime require particular attention. First, the advent of Auchter brought to an end the quickening pace of creating occupational health regulations that had been the work of his predecessor, Dr. Eula Bingham. Dr. Bingham had made switching the emphasis of the agency's work from safety to health one of her primary objectives. Major drives had been started to develop regulations on carcinogens and textile dust. Auchter brought this drive for health regulations to an end and specifically tried to revise the textile dust regulations to make them more congenial for employers; that is, less protective of the workers. The only major health regulation promoted by Auchter—providing for the labeling of chemical hazards—was intended to prevent more stringent action by the states.

A second and related aspect of Auchter's reign was his attempt to split union opposition to his policies, gaining the support of the construction unions. Construction unions are generally conservative, and are among the unions most supportive of the Republican Party. Auchter sought to exploit the potential gap between the construction and industrial unions by placing greater emphasis on safety and less on health. Inspectors were instructed to pay greater attention to the construction industry as part of a decreased attention to health and increased attention to safety. This change in policy was open to the criticism that many more people die from occupationally caused ill health than occupational accidents, a long-known fact. The switch to safety inspections also had the effect of concentrating attention on the most male-dominated industries. Meanwhile the administration dropped the idea of drawing up regulations to be sure that OSHA policies were enforced in such a way as to avoid sex discrimination.

CONCLUSIONS

Occupational safety and health policies have had special gender-specific effects in two ways. First, apparently gender neutral policies affect women and men differently because women and men do not occupy the same kinds of jobs. The emphasis on safety rather than health in OSHA policies and implementation mean that while few people could argue that American workers in general are well protected against being hurt by their jobs, the types of risks that are covered by public policy are more likely to affect men than women. Implementation that depends, in practice, on union participation also involves hidden forms of inequity as long as unions remain so male dominated, and women's occupations remain less unionized.

Safety and health policies have also had different effects on women and men for reasons related more directly to gender ideology and discrimination. When policymakers have focused specifically on women's economic lives, they have tended to view women through the lens of traditional general ideology: as reproducers first and producers and workers second. The result has been that protective policies first, have tended to reinforce gender segregation in the workforce and, especially, to keep women out of the generally higher paid male-dominated jobs and second, they have tended to reinforce the idea that when we are concerned about reproduction and protection of reproductive functions and capabilities we are concerned exclusively with women.

As we have suggested throughout, few people who want our work lives to be safe and healthy as possible can be pleased with the current state of affairs for women or for men, but protective policies have been more likely to work to the disadvantage of women, or at least to the relative advantage of men. We will conclude, therefore, with a brief and probably incomplete list of the issues that must be raised and the problems that must be solved if protective policies are to help women more in the future.

The first problem, as always, is a question of knowledge and further research. Protective policies have emphasized safety over health because it is easier to know how many people fall off scaffolding or lose limbs in factory machinery than it is to know how many people contract diseases with long latency periods or suffer other health problems that are not immediately apparent. Protective policies that focus on women pay attention almost exclusively to reproduction (and certain limited aspects of it) because everyone "knows" that is what is special about women. In both cases the policies are taking a path of least resistance determined by a paucity of knowledge and inadequate funds channeled into research and development. These funds were cut even further during the Reagan years.

The first problem cannot be solved in isolation from attacking a second, and that is the male bias in research and development. We will never have policies that cover women adequately if the knowledge and assumptions on which they are based continue to operate through a prism of conventional wisdom and traditional gender ideology on women's lives. Research that is not woman-centered, for example, remains ignorant of the dangers that "fit work for women" holds for women. It will be unaware of the way factors other than direct and intentional discrimination against women work to create inequality. It will not take into account research of the type that shows that both sex discrimination and sexual harassment at the workplace are threats to women's health, particularly as they provoke stress and stress-related health problems, and that they therefore not only affect the quality of the lives of women themselves, but the quality of the work they can offer. The male bias in research is related to a larger bias in the dominant ideology of work life: It is more important to save male jobs and male workers than female jobs and female workers. Men are, after all, "the" breadwinners.

A third problem is one that plagues most policy questions modern government handle: policy fragmentation. For all the Weberian theory stating that bureaucracy could rationalize and make efficient any workings of modern, complex government—a bureaucratic office for every problem and every problem in its own office—neither social problems nor bureaucratic offices can be arranged as neatly and coherently as we might wish. Each important problem overlaps with too many others and has too many possible interpretations and ramifications. In general, when government administrations become particularly frustrated at the dispersion of a problem across different offices and agencies, they solve the problem by creating a new office to coordinate the different efforts, thus solving the problem of "big government" by making it bigger.

Fragmentation has been particulary likely to afflict women's policy, and it has created special roadblocks to improvement in occupational safety and health policies as they affect women. The health and safety of woman at work in and outside the home is the responsibility of, inter alia, the OSHA, the Federal Trade Commission, the Environmental Protection Agency, and the Consumer Product Safety Commission. "Women's" questions are generally regarded as a special interest or parochial problem, and certainly not one of important relevance to more general interest "human" questions such as occupational safety and health policy. OSHA, for example, might see special attention to women's employment as irrelevant to them or even as wastefully redundant because of the existence of the Women's Bureau in the Labor Department, for decades the most important location of interest in and research on women's issues in the government, the Equal Employment Opportunities Commission (EEOC), created by the 1964 Civil Rights Act to administer antidiscrimination policy, or the various women's offices of the White House, which have often been mere public relations offices, much to the chargin of some of their more activist occupants such as Bella Abzug or Midge Constanza. Hard-pressed agencies are most unlikely to spread their precious resources to questions they see not only as of secondary interest but as handled elsewhere, even if the president or the Office of Management and the Budget were to allow them to do so.

The most obvious result of fragmentation in our area of concern has been the difficulty of resolving the conflict of interest between protection and equality. There are many ways in which the 1970 Occupational Safety and Health Act can come into conflict with Title VII of the 1964 Civil Rights Act, particularly because the latter now not only bars discrimination against pregnant women, but also bars treatment of workers that has the effect of providing unequal opportunities unless a bona fide occupational qualification is involved. In other words, employers and government agencies are barred not only from directly discriminating on the basis of sex, but also from doing things that are not in and of themselves designed to be sex discriminatory, but have that effect. A further wedge is drawn between the goals of equality and protection because of the nature of the enforcement and implementation processes. The EEOC has no authority to enforce the OSH Act and OSHA has no authority to enforce Title VII. Any conflicts between these goals, therefore, must be thrown to lengthy court battles.

The conflict between protection and equality is a problem that needs serious attention within the women's movement itself. It has long been a source of controversy, back to the time when Alice Paul and Carrie Chapman Catt solidified the split between the National Women's Party and the League of Women Voters over the question of protective labor legislation, which Paul defined as antifeminist, and the Equal Rights Amendment, which Catt abhorred because it would seem to overrule protective legislation. It is not enough to say that we need nondiscriminatory protections for workers that cover women and men equally, because women and men face different problems and different working conditions. The solution lies somewhere between protecting women into an economically disadvantageous situation and giving women and men equal opportunity to be worked to death literally in an uncaring and unprotective system.

NOTE

1. For works that look particularly at protective legislation that is not even, on the face of it, gender neutral, see Andrade (1981) and Chavkin (1984). For a more general view of occupational safety and health policy making and implementation, see Wilson (in press).

RESOURCES

Andrade, V. M. (1981). The toxic workplace: Title VII protection for the potentially pregnant person. *Harvard Women's Law Journal 4* (Spring), 71-104.

Chavkin, W. (Ed). (1984). *Double exposure: Woman's health hazards on the job and at home*. New york: Monthly Review Press.

Rytina, N. F. & Bianchi, S. M. (1984). Occupational reclassification and distribution by gender. *Monthly Labor Review 107* (March), 11-17.

Sapiro, V. (1984). Women, citizenship, and nationally: Immigration and naturalization policies in the United States. *Politics and Society 13*, 1-26.

Stellman, J. N. (1977). *Woman's work, woman's health: Myths and realities.* New York: Pantheon.

Wilson, Graham K. (in press). *The politics of safety and health.* Oxford: Oxford University Press.

7

OLDER WOMEN: LONGEVITY, DEPENDENCY, AND PUBLIC POLICY

Laura Katz Olson

Feminist literature has focused increasingly on the nature, causes, and consequences of the sexual division of labor among younger adults, both in the workplace and in the home. Despite vast increases in women's labor force participation since World War II, and the rapid growth of single female heads of households, women's work continues to be viewed economically and socially as secondary to their "real" roles as mothers and housewives. Job segregation by gender, which assures lower wages, benefits, and status for women, simultaneously perpetuates women's dependency on men and penalizes women living independently. The feminization of poverty is directly linked to the rising number of women with low—or no—wages who are forced (or choose) to support themselves and their families alone.

The economic problems faced by women tend to be exacerbated during old age. Distribution of income among the elderly has a greater variance than that of any other age group. While economic resources are concentrated among a small segment of the aged, older people are disproportionately represented at the lower end of the income distribution scale in American society. In particular, older single women (and blacks) tend to suffer more substantial economic deprivation than either older white males or couples. The latter groups are relatively more likely to receive higher and multiple sources of retirement compensation. Consequently, older married women tend to be just one husband away from poverty or near-poverty conditions.

In this chapter I will argue that the sizable and growing impoverished 65-and-older female population, and the multifaceted problems associated with its lack of an adequate income, are inextricably tied to the sexual division of labor among younger adults and the assumed economic dependency of women on men that is built into old age retirement programs. The economic inequality found among the aged, and the significant percentage of older women living in situations of serious economic deprivation, are functions of market, property, and power relationships set prior to old age.

The availability and level of benefits for retired workers in the United States are based on type of employment, length of labor force participation, and previous wage levels, factors that limit the ability of women workers to earn adequate annuities in their own right. Consequently, the vast majority of women tend to be dependent on their husband's benefits. Under current pension arrangements, these benefits are reduced drastically, and in many cases terminated, at the death of or divorce from the primary worker.

I also will argue that because economic inequality between males and females is intensified by age, a large percentage of older single women are dependent on supportive social programs in order to meet their basic needs. Recent reductions in such programs as Medicare, Medicaid, food stamps, subsidized housing, energy assistance, and the like, disproportionately affect older women and limit their ability to live independently.

LONGEVITY AND INDEPENDENCE

Life expectancy at birth has been increasing steadily over the past several decades, with a growing gap between males and females. In 1900, the average life expectancy was 46.3 years for men and 48.8 years for women. By the early 1980s these numbers grew to 70 and 78, respectively, with a gender difference of eight years (U.S. House of Representatives, 1982b, p. 75).

Men age 65 and older outnumbered women in 1900, when there were 98 older women for every 100 older men. However, by 1983 there were 148 women per 100 men. Gender differences increase dramatically in the older age categories. At ages 65 to 74 there were 131 women, at ages 75 and over there were 180 women, and for the 85 and over population there were 229 women per 100 men (U.S. House of Representatives, 1982a, p. 25).

In 1980, there were 15.2 million women and 10.3 million men age 65 and over, representing over 11 percent of the U.S. population. Between 1970 and 1980 alone, the 65-and-over group grew by 30 percent as compared to less than 10 percent for the under-65 population. Projections by the Bureau of the Census indicate that by the beginning of the twenty-first century there will be approximately 18.6 million older women, representing 7 percent of the population, and that such women will outnumber men by 154 to 100 (Williams, 1980, p.5). In fact, older women are the fastest growing segment of our population. Clearly, the policy implications of women's greater longevity relative to men, and the growing number of older women, particularly in the 75-and-over age category, merit examination.

The socially created dependency of females, encouraged through various aspects of the socialization process, the

educational system, and labor markets, and perpetuated by
old age social programs, is strikingly at odds with older
women's actual experiences and conditions. Women's greater
longevity, along with their tendency to marry men who are
older than they, increasing divorce rates among middle-aged
couples, and the decreasing availability of men for remarriage
at older ages, all foster independent living arrangements for
large numbers of older women. In 1981, over 6 million
women age 65 and over lived alone as compared with less
than 1.5 million men age 65 and over (U.S. Department of
Commerce, 1982, p. 44). According to a 1982 report by the
U.S. House Select Committee on Aging, only 18 percent of
men age 65 to 74 and 31 percent of men age 75 and over were
single as compared to 50 percent and 77 percent, respectively, of women (U.S. House of Representatives, 1982a, p.
2). Nearly 85 percent of all women will end their lives alone,
primarily as widows (U.S. House of Representatives, 1982b,
p. 43).

DEPENDENCY AND INCOME STATUS

The onset of old age does not occur at a biologically
prescribed age but, rather, is socially defined. Chronological
age is not a reliable predictor of an individual's capacity to
work, social behavior, political values, or even physical condition. Old age is a socially constructed category that ar-
bitrarily restricts labor force participation and defines
eligibility for specific public programs and benefits, regardless of ability to work or economic need.

Nor is older people's dependency on pension programs for
income support inherent to the aging process. As I have
noted elsewhere (Olson, 1982, p. 28),

Before the advent of factories and mechanized farming, economic superannuation was unknown. Few people attained old age, but those who did experienced economic insecurity, along with the rest of the household, primarily through crop failures, pestilence, and other natural disasters, rather than as a result of forced retirement or loss of wages. On the farm, or in trade and business, only physical incapacity determined whether an individual would withdraw from full-time productive labor.

Most older women and men who were no longer able to work were cared for and supported by their children and relatives, with the older members of the family generally retaining ownership (and in many cases control) of the farm or business until they died.

Since the mid-nineteenth century, industrialization, mechanization, structural unemployment, mandatory and informal retirement policies, and other government and corporate practices have generated the social dependency of older people. The transition from an agrarian society to an advanced capitalist economy brought loss of control over an individual's own productive means, growing dependency on employers for subsistence wages, and the removal of older workers from the labor force without sufficient pension income to meet their needs.

Employment of male workers age 65 and over fell steadily from 63.1 percent in 1900, 45.8 percent in 1950, and 33.1 percent in 1960, to 26.8 percent by 1970. At the end of 1982, only 19 percent of the 65-and-over male population was employed. Despite the dramatic entry of women into the labor force during the twentieth century, reaching nearly 60 percent by 1983, the employment rate of older women has hovered between 8 and 10 percent from 1900 to 1983. Older women who want to work continue to face even greater employment barriers than their male counterparts.

The growing number of "retired" workers became increasingly dependent on public and private support systems, with whatever pension benefits they were eligible for derived from their labor and wage histories. Most women became dependent not only on employers for wages, or their husband's employers for wages, but also, in older years, on secondary pension rights derived from their husband's labor and wage histories. And these secondary pension rights have been even less adequate than those available to the primary, and usually male wage earner. For most men and women, retirement is accompanied by severely reduced and often inadequate income. However, under current pension arrangements, women tend to suffer even further income loss as widows or divorcees. The income problems experienced by older single females today are related to the inadequacies and inequities of our pension systems overall, and to the sexual division of labor upon which these pension plans are based. Retirement programs reinforce a woman's economic dependency on the male wage earner, and penalize her when she is thrust into an independent social status, relegating a large percentage to poverty or near-poverty conditions.

In 1980, the 6.3 million older women living alone had a median income of $4,957, nearly one-third were living at or below the poverty level (income below $3,941), and 50 percent lived in near-poverty conditions (U.S. House of Representatives, 1982c, p. 13). Older minority women are the most vulnerable, having a median annual income of $3,558. Two-thirds were classified as officially poor and 82 percent experienced near-poverty conditions (U.S. House of Representatives, 1982c, p. 12). These income figures can be contrasted with the $12,881 median income earned by older families, and the $22,548 earned by younger households (U.S. House of Representatives, 1982a, p. 8).

THE SOCIAL SECURITY SYSTEM

The social security system assumes and encourages dependency among women in a number of ways. As Burk-hauser and Holden (1980, p. 8) note,

> The OASI system of 1939 was tailored to provide old-age income to the typical family of that day: a family headed by a male who worked full time in the labor force and a wife who worked full time caring for children and maintaining the home.

Although the original intent of spouse and survivor benefits was to protect homemakers,[1] these women are relegated to secondary roles rather than viewed as equal partners in a marriage.[2]

Even in dual earner couples,[3] the woman's social security pension is likely to be dependent on her husband's wage record, despite the fact that she may have paid into the social security system during her entire working career.[4] Social security benefits are based on both the level of wages and the number of years in the paid labor market, and women tend to have significantly lower earnings and more interruptions in their work histories than their husbands. Consequently, the spouse or survivor benefit often is greater than that which the woman would receive in her own right. In fact, married couples with, or survivors of, two-earner couples generally receive less in benefits than one-earner couples with the same total lifetime earnings. Thus preference is given to the non-working, dependent spouse over the working wife; low-earner couples are affected most adversely. A woman who never marries must rely solely on her own employment and wage record; this benefit may be considerably less than that available to the dependent or working wife of a high-income earner.

Despite the dependency role of married women on male wage earners assumed under the social security program, most women will require income or receive benefits as either widows or divorcees at some point in their lives. Yet surviving widows under 60 are entitled to benefits only in their role as mothers; no pension is available to these homemakers if their children are over age 16. At age 60, the benefits of surviving widows (which are wage-indexed only to the year of the spouse's death) are reduced by 28.5 percent. Such women have difficulty obtaining employment; the unemployment rate for women between the ages of 55 and 64 are double that of men. Despite their economic need, these "displaced homemakers" are not eligible for Medicare, Supplementary Security Income (SSI), social services under the Older Americans Act, or other major benefits until they meet the chronological age requirements of the various programs. Nor are they eligible for welfare if their children are over eighteen years of age.

The single and female beneficiary also suffers serious loss of income if her husband dies after retirement age. While the couple is entitled to 150 percent of the worker's primary insurance amount (PIA),[5] surviving spouses receive only the PIA, which represents two-thirds of their previous benefit. Moreover, the primary pension itself is likely to have been actuarially reduced by up to 20 percent if the wage earner had obtained initial benefits prior to age 65. Approximately 60 percent of all retired workers receive reduced benefits due to such factors as job mobility, mandatory and informal retirement pressures, poor health, and unemployment. In July of 1981, the average benefit for a worker with a dependent allowance was $576.71 per month or $6920.52 on an annual basis, as compared to $344.66, or $4135.92 per year for widows and widowers (U.S. House of Representatives, 1982a, p. 6).

Many divorced older women have been full-time homemakers during much or all of their husband's working years. According to Deckard (1979, p. 421), "The work the full-time homemaker does has been estimated at being worth from $10,000 to $20,000 per year." Despite such contributions to the household, the divorced older woman receives only one-third of the couple's previous pension (a benefit that had been designed originally as a supplement for a dependent wife), while the primary worker receives two-thirds of the total. Divorced women must have been married for a least ten years and be at least 60 years old to be eligible for any benefits at all. Importantly, widowers and divorced men are likely to remarry, at which time they may become eligible for full couple benefits again.

The social security system has been credited with the sharp decline in officially defined poverty among the aged overall, a rate that decreased from 35 percent in 1959 to 16 percent in 1980. However, it is clearly less effective in reducing the incidence of poverty among single women. During that period, the poverty rate of older women living alone decreased from 63 percent to only 32 percent. Critically, for 60 percent of all single women over 65, social security is the primary source of income. Nearly 2 million unmarried women rely on the program for their entire income support. The recent elimination of the minimum social security benefit, and increase in the age of entitlement for full benefits from age 65 to 67, will reduce pensions for most older people. Widows and divorced women will suffer even more serious hardship as a result of the legislation.

PRIVATE PENSION SYSTEMS

Most single older women are forced to rely on social security (and Supplementary Security Income—SSI) for most of their support because private and other pension systems do not protect them adequately. Only about 20 percent of retirement age women receive a state, local, or private pension on their own or their husband's employment record (U.S. House of Representatives, 1982c, p. 14). Approximately 10 percent of women over age 65 receive money from a private pension plan, as compared to 25 percent of men. Due to limited coverage, stringent vesting rules, low benefit levels, integration with social security, and the failure to provide cost-of-living adjustments, most workers in the private sector do not receive any benefits, and when they do, the pension amounts tend to be small. Adequate pensions accrue only to long-term, highly paid employees.

Surviving spouses of those retired workers eligible for a benefit receive only 50 percent of an actuarially reduced amount, and only if the primary worker had elected the joint-and-survivor option, a decision that rests exclusively with the primary worker. In addition, most plans do not provide preretirement survivor benefits, and when they are offered, annuities are only fractionally related to the original pension. Moreover, because few plans provide regular cost-of-living adjustments, inflation can erode the purchasing power of benefits considerably, a problem experienced most severely by those in the oldest age groups.

Divorced women have no rights to an ex-husband's annuity under current private pension plan regulations; the treatment of pension assets at divorce is subject to state by state approaches. Where community-property rules prevail (8 states), the former spouse has the right to petition the court for that portion of the benefit accrued during the period of the marriage. However, her share can be claimed only when the ex-husband actually retires.

In most other states, the courts are empowered to distribute spousal property but "the precise definition of property and whether it is inclusive of pension expectancies or deferred benefits may differ somewhat in different jurisdictions" (King, 1980, p. 217). Most divorced women either receive no benefits or insignificant amounts based on their husband's work record. Although state case law on spousal rights when a marriage dissolves is still evolving, it is unlikely that such women will be protected adequately in the future.

Working women are considerably less likely than men to receive a private pension in their own right because they tend to be concentrated in low-wage, uncovered job categories. Approximately 40 percent of female as compared to 55 percent of male full-time employees in the private sector participate in these plans. Job mobility and intermittent work histories limit women's vesting possibilities, and their predominantly low-wage work is translated into even lower annuities, relative to men, at retirement. Thus most working women, although subject to mandatory and informal retirement policies, are not protected economically by the private sector during their older years.

SUPPORTIVE SERVICES:
THE IMPACT OF REAGANOMICS

Growing old in the United States can be accompanied by a host of social problems, most of which stem from having an inadequate income. As suggested earlier, women are particularly vulnerable because they tend to live longer and have fewer financial resources than men. Clearly, our retirement systems have failed to serve the economic needs of older women, many of whom also have to cope with increasing chronic ailments that limit their mobility. Lack of an adequate income contributes substantially to their inability to care for themselves, to provide adequate health care, transportation, housing, heating, and nutrition, or to meet other basic needs. Single and often impoverished older women who are attempting to maintain independent living arrangements are forced to rely on supportive benefits and services available to them in the community. The oldest groups, those women age 75 and older, are most dependent on public programs. As noted by Storey (1983, p. 29),

> The very old depend more on public transportation and social services; they need more health care; ... and they may have less opportunity to receive family support since their children are often in old age themselves.

Despite the growing federal budget devoted to older people, representing $173 billion in fiscal 1981 or 26.4 percent of the total, the social problems faced by older women living alone have not improved markedly, and since 1981 actually have worsened for the very low-income population. Most of the federal outlays fund Medicare ($35.8 billion) and social security ($97.1 billion), with only $11.8 billion representing cash and noncash benefits exclusively for the needy, and $6 billion for other services benefiting the elderly (Storey, 1983, p. 20). Supplementary Security Income (SSI), of which 73 percent of the participants are older women (U.S. House of Representatives, 1982c, p. 4), totalled $2.6 billion. Medicaid ($6 billion), food stamps ($.9 billion), and housing assistance

($2.3 billion) accounted for a mere $9.2 billion (Storey, 1983, p. 28).

Recent cuts in federally subsidized housing, food stamps, energy assistance, and public transportation, have threatened the ability of growing numbers of older women, particularly those age 75 and over, to maintain their independence. According to a recent analysis by Storey (1983, p. 28),

> Older Americans with low income have suffered a net loss overall as a result of the policy changes under the Reagan administration. Among the low-income elderly, the oldest members of the group have been affected the most by budget cuts.

The low-income group, defined by Storey as those with household money income of less than $5,000, includes approximately 50 percent of all single older women.

Only 23 percent of older households living below the poverty threshold actually received food stamps in 1980 (U.S. House of Representatives, 1982a, p. 6). Cuts in eligibility and benefits under the program, which serves 2 million older people, have amounted to 23 percent since 1981 (Storey, 1983, p. 29). About 70 percent of the participants in this program are women.

Federally subsidized housing covers less than 12 percent of all older households living below the poverty threshold (U.S. House of Representatives, 1982a, p. 6). In 1980, the programs served only one million low-income older households, of which 75 percent were elderly women living alone (U.S. House of Representatives, 1982c, p. 14). Moreover, legislation enacted in 1981 increased rents for participants over a five-year period from 25 to 30 percent of income. For most of these women, this increase will reduce even further their ability to provide for essential needs.

In real dollars, there also has been a one-third reduction in state grants for low-income energy assistance since 1981 despite escalating heating and utility costs. Energy costs amount to nearly 50 percent of the budgets of the elderly poor in some regions. Mass transit subsidies also have been cut by one-third, cuts that will limit substantially the mobility of people in the oldest age groups, many of whom do not own automobiles (Storey, 1983, p. 29).

HEALTH CARE: THE IMPACT OF REAGANOMICS

Health care expenditures have become increasingly burdensome for older people not eligible for Medicaid. Rapidly growing premiums, deductibles, and co-insurance under Medicare, along with rampant inflation in health care costs (averaging about 16 percent annually), and the decreasing number of physicians willing to take assignment, have forced the elderly to contribute a high and increasing percentage of their income for medical needs. In 1981 alone, deductibles for hospital and physician services were raised by 12 percent and 25 percent, respectively (Storey, 1983, p. 35). Medicare also does not cover many essential services such as optical and dental examinations, dentures, eyeglasses, prescription drugs, and hearing aids.

Health care outlays for older people are, on average, 3.4 times greater than those for people under age 65. Yet despite Medicare, out-of-pocket expenses for the elderly amount to about 43 percent of their total health bill. For the very old low-income population, the need for (and costs of) health care are even greater, causing growing numbers to forego services entirely. Moreover, low-income urban and rural communities have only limited medical facilities and physicians. For older women with substantial mobility limitations and inadequate public transportation, medical care has become increasingly inaccessible.

In 1982, new hospital reimbursement procedures utilizing Diagnostic Related Groups (DRGs) were enacted for Medicare recipients. Under DRGs, Medicare will reimburse hospitals a set amount for a particular type of illness or medical procedure, regardless of the actual cost to the hospital or individual need of the patient. If the hospital provides the services at less cost, it keeps the difference; if the service is more expensive, the hospital absorbs the loss. DRGs are likely to reduce the quality of medical care for older people, increase costs for private-pay patients, and remove some elderly from hospitals before they recover sufficiently from an illness or operation. This will be particularly burdensome for those people living alone.

The Medicaid program, which serves as a supplement to Medicare, covered only 35.9 percent of older households living below the poverty level in 1980 (U.S. House of Representatives, 1982a, p. 6), or about 14 percent of the low-income elderly population overall. Growing medical costs have led to consistent retrenchment in the program. States have steadily reduced benefits, types of services available, and eligibility. Many states also have begun to impose cost-sharing expenses on recipients. In 1981, the federal government cut its matching funds to the states, engendering even more stringent eligibility standards, fewer services, and more cost-sharing provisions in the state programs. Further, because reimbursement rates to providers have not grown commensurate with their charges, increasing numbers of physicians refuse to serve Medicaid recipients. Storey (1983, p. 29) argues that the cuts in social programs since 1981

will have a particularly severe effect on those low-income elderly who depend on multiple public benefits. For example, a Food Stamp recipient who lives in subsidized housing may experience all of the following reductions in benefits and services over a span of one or two years: a rent increase, a reduced Foot Stamp allotment, a decline in public transportation, fewer social services and reduced access to free medical care.

Already inadequate funds for supportive community services and benefits, along with recent program reductions, foster (and will foster even further) the unnecessary institutionalization of older women.

Over 75 percent of our nursing home population is female, with about 80 percent age 75 and over. The vast majority of these older women are single (83 percent) and impoverished. In American society, poverty, loneliness, isolation, abandonment, unemployment, and homelessness often are treated with nursing home placement (U.S. House of Representatives, 1982b, p. 81).

The bias of public funding for nursing homes when community benefits and services may be more appropriate also contributes to unnecessary institutionalization. In 1980, fully 40 percent of federal and state Medicaid outlays flowed into the coffers of old age institutions (OAIs).

As I have argued in detail elsewhere, Medicaid and Medicare funding practices, and other public policies related to nursing homes, have prompted rising public spending for and enrichment of the nursing home industry, without commensurate gains for the elderly. The care of institutionalized older people for profit, coupled with cost-plus reimbursement formulas to fund the indigent, have encouraged pervasive and acknowledged exploitive practices by nursing home operators, ranging from financial to patient abuses. Further, spiraling costs for OAI care and changing eligibility requirements under Medicaid have contributed substantially to the impoverishment and dependency of the institutionalized population. Private pay residents, who make up 50 percent of those people entering OAIs, must exhaust their limited savings before they arc eligible for any public assistance (Olson, 1982, pp. 139-145).

CONCLUSION

Women have entered the labor market steadily over the last several decades, accounting for nearly 60 percent of those of working age by 1984. However, the vast majority remain segregated in low-wage jobs that are not covered under private pension systems. Thus the percentage of women earning a meaningful social security or private pension in their own right probably will not increase significantly.

Under current structural arrangements, social security and private pension systems provide for women primarily as dependents of male wage earners. However, the social reality is that most women will live alone at some point during their older years, whether due to divorce or widowhood. Their newly independent status has been and will continue to be accompanied by severe pension reductions. In the case of private pension systems, the surviving spouse or ex-wife may lose the entire annuity. Recent revisions in the social security system, such as the future increase in the age of entitlement for full benefits, will affect most adversely those people at the lower ends of the benefit scale who rely on the program as their sole or primary means of support.

At the same time, the percentage of younger female heads of households has doubled since 1970, representing 14 percent of all households by 1984. These women, who generally have poverty-level incomes, will be even poorer during their old age under current pension policies.

Although the Medicare program was aimed at removing some financial barriers to health services for the aged, older people have been burdened by increasing out-of-pocket costs, rendering medical care steadily less affordable. The uniform, and regressive cost-sharing provisions, which have grown rapidly in response to inflation in health care costs, serve as major and increasingly greater deterrents for the low-income and oldest age groups who often have the highest health care needs.

Consequently, most single older women have difficulty in meeting their basic needs or maintaining their independence. Even the limited funding for supportive social programs, such as food stamps, energy assistance, federally subsidized housing, and Medicaid, has been reduced drastically since 1981. Yet the percentage of single older women, particularly those over the age of 75, is projected to rise rapidly over the next twenty years. If current trends continue, there will be growing numbers of impoverished older women who will be confronting fewer available community services. Many of these women, particularly those with limited mobility, could find themselves forced into institutionalized care.

NOTES

1. Currently less than 1 percent of men receive spouse benefits. See Fierst (1982).

2. Homemaker credits, and particularly earnings sharing, would address some of the problems of homemakers. As Fierst points out, earnings sharing would avoid placing homemakers in a dependency role. See Fierst (1982, pp. 66-72). For a full discussion of alternative options for women under social security, see U.S. Department of Health, Education and Welfare (1979) and Sommers (1978).

3. By 1983, nearly two-thirds of couples were made up of two earners.

4. Women workers, because of their concentration in low-wage jobs, are disproportionately affected by the regressivity of social security's payroll tax.

5. The Primary Insurance Amount (PIA) is the basic monthly benefit that would accrue to a retired worker, based on his or her average monthly earnings (AME), and since 1977 on his or her average indexed monthly earnings (AIME), if the worker received the initial social security benefit at age 65. It is also used as the base for computing other benefits payable on the basis of the worker's earnings record, such as the dependency allowance.

RESOURCES

Burkhauser, R. V., & Holden, K. C. (1982). Introduction. In R. V. Burkhauser & K.C. Holden (Eds.), *A Challenge to social security: The changing roles of men and women in American society*. New York: Academic.

Deckard, B. S. (1979). *The women's movement: Political, socio-economic and psychological issues*. New York: Harper & Row.

Fierst, E. A. (1982). Discussion. In R. B. Burkhauser & K. C. Holden (Eds.), *A challenge to social security: The changing roles of men and women in American society*. New York: Academic.

King, F. P. (1980). Occupational pension plans and spouse benefits. In R. V. Burkhauser & K. C. Holden (Eds.), *A challenge to social security: The changing roles of men and women in American society*. New York: Academic.

Olson, L. K. (1982). *The political economy of aging: The state, private power, and social welfare*. New York: Columbia University Press.

Sommers, T. (1978). *Commentary on report of HEW task force on the treatment of women under social security*. Unpub. mimeo.

Storey, J. R. (1983). *Older Americans in the Reagan era: Impacts of federal policy changes*. Washington, DC: The Urban Institute.

U.S. Department of Commerce. (1982). *Statistical abstract of the United States*. Washington, DC: Government Printing Office.

U.S. Department of Health, Education and Welfare (1979). *Social security and the changing roles of men and women*. Washington: DC: Government Printing Office.

U.S. House of Representatives, Select Committee on Aging. (1982a). *Every ninth American*. 97th Congress, 2nd session, July.

U.S. House of Representatives, Select Committee on Aging. (1982b). *Problems of aging women*. 97th Congress, 2nd session, September.

U.S. House of Representatives, Select Committee on Aging, Hearings before the Subcommittee on Retirement and Employment. (1982c). *The impact of Reagan economics and aging women*. 97th Congress, 2nd session, September.

Williams, B. (1980). Profile of the elderly women. In M. Marshall Fuller & C. A. Martin (Eds.), *The older woman*. Springfield, IL: Charles C Thomas.

III

DOMESTIC TRANQUILITY AND THE COMMON DEFENSE

8

AN ANALYSIS OF BIOSOCIAL THEORIES OF CRIME

Susette M. Talarico

In the late 1970s the presidents of two influential professional associations, John C. Wahlke of the American Political Science Association and C. Ray Jeffrey of the American Society of Criminology, argued for biological approaches to the study of social and political phenomena. In a 1979 article, Wahlke argued that the behavioral revolution in political science did not live up to its name and that political research could benefit from the biobehavioral sciences. He illustrated his point by demonstrating how ethological knowledge could provide a theoretical perspective for identifying political problems worth studying and by describing how neurophysiological knowledge could correct erroneous conceptions of the relationship between attitudes, words, and actions in politics (Wahlke, 1979, p. 9).

In the journal *Criminology,* Jeffrey called for a behavioral scientific approach to the study of crime. Jeffrey argued that criminology was shaped by nineteenth century psychosocial conceptions of man, while criminal justice was directed by eighteenth century assumptions of political man. He emphasized that these assumptions must be challenged and that criminology must move from a social to a biosocial model of learning (Jeffrey, 1978, p. 151).

Not surprisingly, both of these articles and the conference addresses that preceded them prompted considerable discussion and debate. Whereas political scientists had not taken biobehavioral approaches to the study of political behavior seriously in the past, criminologists had considered and then roundly dropped biological theories of criminal conduct. In the words of Donald Cressey (1978, p. 182), "The biological determinism theory of criminal conduct went down the tube long ago." Responding to Wahlke's call, political scientists questioned the competence of social scientists in the biological sciences, the state of contemporary biobehavioral knowledge, and the resulting policy implications. Criminologists, on the other hand, directed many of their criticisms to earlier and rejected theories of crime and questioned the appropriateness of a return to earlier, reductionist conceptions of criminal behavior.

Wahlke and Jeffrey's emphasis on biobehavioral research in the social sciences was grounded in the broader approach to the study of animal behavior, including human, referred to as sociobiology. This emerging discipline was highlighted in Edward O. Wilson's (1975) *Sociobiology: The New Synthesis.* While the bulk of Wilson's treatise focused on organisms and lower animals, the last chapter applied sociobiological theories to human behavior.

Wilson's work was roundly criticized (e.g., Gould, 1978). The philosopher Charles Frankel (1979, pp. 39-40) observed that "it was immediately attacked as a thinly disguised revival of Spencerian rugged individualism, as a prescription for technocratic social engineering, as a defense of inequality and male chauvinism, as a restatement of racist doctrine, and as a contemporary version of the ideas which led to the gas chambers of Nazi Germany." More dispassionate though no less sharply concerned critics like biologist Richard Lewontin (1979) focused on the problems of arbitrary agglomeration, reification, conflation, and confusion of levels (1979).

The debate on sociobiology raged in the late 1970s. Socio-biologists such as Robert Trivers (*Time,* 1977) boldly predicted that "sooner or later, political science, law, economics, psychology, psychiatry, and anthropology will all be branches of sociobiology." These exaggerated claims prompted critics to denounce sociobiology as "pseudo-science" and to call for the abolition of biobehavioral research in the social sciences. While the conflicts associated with the introduction of sociobiology and its applications in political science and criminology have abated, fundamental problems and substantive policy issues remain.

In this chapter I look at the development of biological theories of criminal behavior and analyze the resulting problems and policy implications. The chapter is divided into three parts: (1) an examination of pertinent criminological theories; (2) an analysis of the problems related to the biosocial model of criminality; and (3) a consideration of the policy implications of such perspectives. Underlying this review are four basic points. First, there is a tendency in both the social sciences and contemporary politics to search for overarching theories of crime and criminal justice. Biosocial criminology is one such overarching theory. Second, this reductionist tendency in both science and politics reinforces the search for simple solutions to complex problems and typically results in an overemphasis on criminal law. Third, when criminal law reforms are grounded in reductionist theories of behavior, women, minorities, and juveniles are likely to be singled out for special and possibly discriminatory treatment. Fourth, biosocial conceptions of criminal behavior do offer questions and hypotheses for research. Such study, however, must proceed in rigorous scientific fashion with serious consideration of the ethical and legal implications of both the research strategy and the applicability of results.

This analysis is particularly appropriate for an anthology on biology and women's policy. Like many other issues of public policy that actually and potentially condition the status of women in society, the development of biosocial criminology presents both a unique and a typical challenge. The development of biosocial criminology and the resulting policy issues pertinent to women are unique in that the general study of sociobiology is fraught with limitations and hazards particular to that intellectual effort. In this sense, biosocial criminology and its policy implications for women suffer from the broader limitations of sociobiology. However, the development of biosocial criminology and the application of related theories to the treatment of women in criminal law also illustrate how sexism affects policy formulation and implementation. As this chapter demonstrates, women, minorities, and juveniles have been and are likely to be singled out for discriminatory treatment when criminal law is directed by reductionist conceptions of criminal behavior. While there are several reasons for this, the historical and contemporary fact of sexism in law, politics, and society cannot be dismissed as a contributing factor. In this sense, the study of biosocial criminology and the resulting policy implications for women suffer from more typical limitations.

BIOSOCIAL CONCEPTIONS
OF CRIMINAL BEHAVIOR

There have been and are a variety of competing schools of thought regarding the cause and functions of crime in society. In her widely adopted text, *Crime and Criminology,* Sue Titus Reid (1979, pp. 123-172) classifies theories of crime as

(1) individualistic, (2) social-structural, and (3) social-process. Individualistic theories of crime are the oldest and feature the historically dominant classical and positivistic approaches. Social-structural theories focus on the purpose crime serves in society and on the artifical character of the lawmaking process. Included in this category are the consensus interpretations of Durkheim and his followers, and the conflict theories grounded in Marxist or other critical analyses (e.g., Quinney, 1977). The third category focuses on crime from the social process perspective. The labeling theory advanced by Howard Becker (1963) is a leading example.

Only the individualistic theories of crime are pertinent to this discussion of biosocial criminological theories. By their very nature the structural and process theories do not look at individual variation as the cause of criminal behavior. Consequently, we turn to the two dominant individualistic theories of crime, the classical and positivist schools (see Radzinowicz, 1966).

As Reid (1979) and Jeffrey (1978), among others, have pointed out, the classical and positivistic approaches differed sharply along the lines of assumption, emphasis, and implication. Classical criminologists put considerable stock in the free will of people and argued that criminals simply weighed the costs of crime against the perceived benefits. They emphasized the importance of deterrence in criminal law, and argued for fixed and definite penalites for criminal transgressions. Focusing on the legal process, classical criminologists were convinced that crime could be prevented if the punishment outweighed the benefit. Additionally, they were convinced that the criminal justice system did not need to intervene prior to the actual administration of the law. Contemporary advocates of this utilitarian-like calculus, James Q. Wilson (1975) and Norval Morris (1984), do not put the same stock in the deterrent calculus as the original classical criminologists, but they do define issues in cost-benefit terms.[1]

In contrast and reaction to classical criminology, positivistic thinkers argued that crime was determined by a variety of factors, none of which approached the rational calculus of the classical school. "Arguing that it was physical, psychic, social or economic," the positivist school emphasized the deterministic character of crime (Reid, 1979, p. 146). While positivistic criminologists considered the environmental factor that would later feature in competing paradigms, most of thoses now associated with this school focused on physical and psychic causes.

According to positivistic criminologists, it was inevitable that some people would commit crimes. Responding to these crimes, law served primarily a treatment and not a deterrent function. With substantial confidence in science and medicine, positivistic criminologists argued for indeterminacy in punishment and individualized treatment. Unconcerned with the legal or ethical dimensions of the treatment model, they were also not disturbed by the absence of a basic theory of human behavior in either psychology or sociology (Jeffrey, 1978, p. 152). Like the classical school, however, positivistic criminology did not put any emphasis on intervention prior to the time the criminal came in contact with the system.

Obviously, the school of criminology most influenced by biological assumptions of human behavior was the positivist. Clearly, there was little room for physical causes of any kind in the rational model of classical criminology. Some of the early and primitive positivists argued that crime was biologically determined and that criminals were "born, not made." These included the now disregarded Lombroso, Garofalo, and Ferri of the so-called Italian School. All three of these early criminologists focused on the idea of the born criminal, albeit in varying degrees. Ferri (1913) introduced the term, Lombroso (1911) classified criminals as such, and Garofalo (1914) stressed the concept of abnormality. Arguing that the relationship between abnormality and physiological causes was unsettled, Garofalo was more cautious than Lambroso in his analysis of criminality. Particularly, he acknowledged that environmental factors might play a part. For his part, Ferri distinguished born criminals from the insane, habitual, and occasional varieties (Reid, 1979, p. 145). All, however, placed at least some emphasis on the biological factors in explaining crime. In spite of their empirical claims,[2] the methods of the Italian School were basically grounded in analogy and anecdote (Reid, 1979, p. 138).

Not surprisingly, the positivistic conceptions of the Italian School have been roundly criticized and generally disregarded. The criticisms ranged from the extreme to the moderate. Sutherland and Cressey (1978), for example, argued that Lombroso delayed the progress of criminology and made no substantive contribution to our understanding of crime, while Sellin (1937) accepted that Lombroso's ideas were challenging. Most of Lombroso's extreme critics were particularly bothered by his failure to acknowledge the social dimension of crime and by his rugged determinism.

The general disrepute with which the Italian School was held did not diminish the impact of positivistic criminology generally. Other criminologists and reformers drew attention to a range of physical and psychological causes. Convinced that modern medicine and psychology, as well as penology, held the cure to social problems such as crime, these reformers succeeded in passing a considerable number of rehabilitatively oriented laws. These included the indeterminate and indefinite sentences, parole, probation, juvenile courts, and the modern penitentiary (see Gresens, 1972; Wheeler, 1978; Rothman, 1971).

In spite of the criticisms levied at Lombroso and others who argued for biological conceptions of criminality, several twentieth century criminologists have picked up on themes reminiscent of the early determinists. In his 1950 treaties on female criminality, Otto Pollack argued that, as assumed, women did not commit fewer crimes than men. He emphasized that the criminal justice system was not able to detect the crimes commited by women because they were inherently more cunning and devious than men. Additionally, he stressed that female criminality was determined by women's biological nature. Pollak's thesis was not as bold as Lambroso's. In a study of female criminality, Lombroso and Ferrero argued that women were biologically more primitive than men, and that when they did commit crimes they displayed biological abnormalities distinct from their basic and primitive nature (Bowker, 1978, p. 29). Pollak's work, however, is important to note because it testifies to the lingering emphasis on biological causes of crime and because it illustrates the fact that gender was frequently seized on as a distinguishing biological variable in the explanation of criminal behavior.

Contemporary criminology includes at least three kinds of theorizing about biology and crime. First, there is the "born criminal" thesis of Yochelson and Samenow (1976). Second, there are those, like Jeffrey (1978), who advocate a biosocial model for criminology. Third, there are scholars who stress that criminality cannot be understood without extensive testing of biological, phychological, and social factors.

Samuel Yochelson, a psychiatrist, and Stanton Samenow, a psychologist, studied inmates confined in St. Elizabeth's Hospital in the District of Columbia. Specifically, they focused on patients confined because of insanity defense acquittals. Conducting long interviews with over 240 patients, the two researchers came to the conclusion that criminals were

born and not made. Arguing that none of the inmates commited crimes because of mental illness, Yochelson and
Samenow claimed that hardcore criminals displayed approximately 52 erroneous thinking patterns that accounted for
their behavior. These thinking patterns were not environmen-
tally affected. Though Yochelson died in 1976, his colleague
Samenow continued this project and has traveled the country
preaching this particular gospel. Yochelson and Samenow's
work has come under particular scrutiny for the authors'
reliance on an extremely unrepresentative sample and for
their failure to follow standard scientific research methods.

Fascinating as a piece of phenomenological investigation,
Yochelson and Samenow's (1976) work did not focus sustained attention to the deterministic effect of gender. Rather,
they emphasized thought patterns critical to criminal deviance in general. Samples of these thought patterns include
the following: balking at acquiring skills and experiences
(1976, p. 370); constantly building oneself up (1976, p. 351);
refusing to endure pain (1976, p. 401); and refusing to
acknowledge the possibility of conviction (1976, p. 226). The
simplistic and scientifically unreliable approach of Yochelson
and Samenow hearken back to an earlier era in criminology
and to the born criminal thesis of a Lambroso.

More thought provoking and more seriously considered is
the work of C. Ray Jeffrey (1978). As a former president of
the American Society of Criminology, his interest in the
biological causes of crime has lent a certain legitimacy to this
particular enterprise. As previously explained, Jeffrey (1978)
argues that contemporary criminology rests on nineteenth-
century views of the psychosocial nature of man, while
criminal justice administration is largely conditioned by
eighteenth-century conceptions of politics. Both of these
orientations contribute to inadequate criminology and ineffective criminal justice, according to Jeffrey.

Arguing that criminology must move from "deterrence, punishment, and treatment to prevention," from a "social to a physical environment," and from "a social to a biosocial model of learning" (1978, p. 158), Jeffrey emphasizes that behavior is the result of two kinds of variables: physical environment and physical organism. As this stands, it is difficult to take considerable issue with Jeffrey's argument. What has generated particular controversy, however, is Jeffrey's prescriptions for criminal justice. Emphasizing the preventive character of law, Jeffrey advocates private clinics where problematic and disturbed people could be brought for diagnosis and treatment. Supported by state funds, these clinics would take the place of the formal criminal justice system and would not be restrained by either traditional criminal law processes (e.g., arrest, adjudication) or constitutional safeguards (e.g., privilege against self-incrimination).

Jeffrey's work to date is largely polemical in character. There is, however, a growing body of research directed to the scientific testing of hypotheses drawn from both the social and biological sciences. These studies examine the relationship between a variety of physical and physiological factors regarding criminal behavior in particular and aggression in general. The now reorganized and considerably scaled down LEAA published a comprehensive bibliography of such research reports (Brantley & Kravitz, 1979), though it must be emphasized that initial results do not yield the claims to support either Yochelson and Samenow's (1976) born criminal thesis or Jeffrey's (1978) proposal for preventive, private criminal justice.

Much of this recent research has focused on delinquency (e.g., Hippchen, 1978). In particular, researchers have examined learning disabilities and drugs (Cott, 1978), biochemical correlates (Bonnet & Pfeiffer, 1978), and information processing defects (Slavin, 1978). More pertinent to this chapter is research directed to biological correlates of crime (see Brantley & Kravitz, 1979, for a comprehensive list). A difficulty here, however, centers on the fact that women do not commit much crime. As Nagel and Hagan (1983) emphasize in their review of gender and crime, women commit certain kinds of visible crimes (prostitution, infanticide, shoplifting, and fraud), whereas men dominate the more serious offenses against person and property.[3] Obviously, research is limited by this sheer dearth of numbers. Additionally, research is limited, as Peterson (1978, p. 1000) reminds us in his analysis of premenstrual cycles and politics, by the absence of direct and valid measures of the physiology of sex.

METHODOLOGICAL AND POLITICAL PROBLEMS

To be sure, serious students of crime cannot ignore potential biological and physiological correlates of crime. Similarly, environmental factors such as socialization, labeling, and politics must also be considered. There are, however, problems with this general enterprise. While these problems do not imply that efforts to develop scientifically reliable and valid studies of the interaction of nature and nurture in crime will be fruitless, they do caution against premature generalization (see Gould, 1978). More important, they caution against the premature application of research results in public policy.

The problems facing serious students of crime are methodological and political in character. Primary methodological problems include (1) the absence of adjacent disciplines, (2) reliability and validity concerns, (3) the limitations of reasoning by analogy, and (4) the limited applicability of experimental research strategies.

In his work on sociobiology, E. O. Wilson (1975) puts considerable emphasis on adjacent disciplines. Specifically, he argues that it is possible to move from the biological to the social sciences, especially if one accepts the premise that there is something of a linear relationship between the acceptance of new, untried methods of research and the distance between disciplines. Given the lack of congruence in basic concepts, not to mention contrasting research methods and strategies, it is obvious that the biological and social sciences are not adjacent. Furthermore, it is not clear that simple reliance on the same research methods would change the character of that relationship.

Reliability and validity are, of course, the canons of the scientific enterprise. Reliability refers to the stability and consistency of measurements; validity focuses on substantive integrity. Both reliability and validity problems surface in the general criminological enterprise and undoubtedly will continue to do so (Gertz & Talarico, 1977). While there are many problems with criminological research that touch on reliability and validity, a central character of criminal law relates to both and conditions the potential of the biosocial study of criminal behavior.

Crimes are defined by a variety of governmental authorities and can be found in an equal variety of places. State legislators define the prohibitions included in state codes, local lawmakers the ordinances that deal with less serious offenses, and regulatory agencies a range of social welfare prohibitions. Historically, even judges were involved in the definition of common law offenses. Whether one argues with a consensus theorist that these definitions are the product of norms and customs shared by a majority of society or whether one agrees with a conflict theorist that these prohibitions are imposed on the politically impotent by those in power, it is obvious that they are, in large part, artificial. This characterization is illustrated in the fact that criminologists and criminal law scholars typically distinguish between offenses that are wrong in themselves (*mala in se*) and those that are wrong simply because they are prohibited (*mala prohibita*). It is important to note that the second category encompasses the majority of contemporary criminal prohibitions.

Definitions of crime change. The use of narcotics, for example, was only regulated in criminal law in the twentieth century. Likewise, the criminal prohibition of abortion has not been consistently included in Anglo-American criminal codes. This political fact of life, so to speak, obviously affects the reliability and validity of research efforts. How constant are crime measures over time? How can one be sure he or she is studying what he or she wants to study? The artificial character of the definition of crime makes the scientific study of crime hazardous as research is likely to focus on crimes that are restricted to particular social and economic classes (e.g., the visible crimes of person and property[4]) and to ignore those offenses committed by the politically advantaged (e.g., white-collar offenses). Here, it is important to note that women, minorities, and juveniles typically commit the visible crimes, whereas adult, white males more typically violate white-collar and regulatory prohibitions.

Many of the more popular works in the broad area of sociobiology (e.g., Ardrey's 1961 *The Territorial Imperative* and Morris's 1967 *The Naked Ape*) are grounded in basic analogy.[5] The authors generalize from one species to another because there is no correspondence between biological and social science concepts. As Lewontin (1979) has emphasized, this is a serious obstacle to the general scrutiny of biological causes of human behavior.

Many of the limitations of reasoning by analogy are evident in sociobiological analyses of aggression. A political scientist who advocates the study of the biology of human behavior, Glendon Schubert (1973) argues that Ardrey, Tiger, and others have adopted a suspect variant of the scientific method. Specifically, Schubert (1973, p. 249) emphasizes that these general sociobiological advocates assert a hypothesis, look for evidence to establish the proposition, and then conclude that the hypothesis has been proven or verified. Schubert contends that this reliance on analogy sharply contrasts with standard scientific procedure where testable hypotheses are developed, measurements are outlined and collected, and the resulting evidence analyzed with no preordained outcome.

Lewontin (1979) makes a similar point in his cogent and incisive critique of sociobiology as an adaptationist program. In particular he focuses on the problem of conflation where categories originally derived from the study of human social relations are applied to animals and then to humans as though they were derived in reverse order, specifically, from animals to humans. Lewontin is also critical of the popular work on aggression where reasoning by analogy substitutes for rigorous testing of scientifically derived hypotheses. Lewontin (1979, p. 8) states that "political aggression derives from political and economic causes, not from gut feelings of territoriality, xenophobia, and aggression."

The limitations of reasoning by analogy point to a related methodological problem—the character of research. In order to determine the effect of biological and physiological factors on human behavior such as crime, one has to be able to identify the manifestations of particular types of alleged causes, control for other factors potentially related to the phenomenon in question, and measure the impact of the factor under scrutiny. This experimental method is more suited to the sciences that do not concentrate on human behavior, though it is not always easy to apply that method in those arenas either.

Researchers studying human behavior in "nature and nurture" fashion have recourse to two strategies: twin methods and studies of adopted families. In the former, investigators compare the behavior of individuals who share the same genetic heritage. As David Rosenthal emphasizes, this strategy assumes that because "both members of each pair are reared in the same home environment... differences in concordance rates between the monozygotic (MZ) or identical and the dizygotic (DZ) or fraternal twins reflect the genetic contribution to the trait under scrutiny" (Rice, 1973, p. 16). The second strategy involves the study of children raised by adoptive parents. Such research tries to determine, for example, if a child with a criminal, genetic parent is likely to commit crime even if raised in a stable and supportive family.

These two strategies are fraught with tenuous assumptions. For example, in twin studies one assumes that the parents of identical and fraternal twins do, in fact, rear and relate to them in identical fashion. There is nothing that supports such an empirical assumption. In fact, everyday experience suggests that parents do not relate to children in identical fashion, even when explicitly trying to be fair. Interestingly, data derived from twin studies served as some of Jensen's (1969) evidence in his controversial *Harvard Educational Review* article in which he concluded that the intelligence test differences observed for black and white children were attributable to genetic causes.

Obviously, it is very difficult to apply rigorous experimental methods in the study of biological and environmental causes of any behavior, crime included. Even if a wide range of methods were not only available but perfected, the use of experimental strategies raises serious political problems and issues. These include (1) the failure of sociobiologists in general and biosocial criminologists in particular to set a reasonable research agenda, (2) ethical and constitutional considerations, and (3) the general tensions associated with any paradigmatic change.

One of the political problems associated with the general enterprise of sociobiology and the particular study of biosocial criminology is the failure of leading proponents to set out reasonable research agendas. While questions related to biological variation and human behavior are undoubtedly legitimate, those who would pursue such scientific study need to set out feasible research programs. C. Ray Jeffrey's (1978) premature outline of a private criminal justice system built on biosocial criminological tenets, for example, appears to ignore the fact that proximate and fundamental questions have not been extensively pursued in the sociobiological study of criminal behavior. This is especially interesting as Jeffrey (1978) puts considerable emphasis on basic research in his *Criminology* article.

Proximate questions focus on the more particular and less dramatic aspects of the relationship between biological and social variables. For example, how do biological attributes associate with behavior patterns and responses? Proponents of a biosocial study of criminal behavior are more likely to receive research support if they initially focus on the more proximate questions. Fundamental questions related (1) to the degree to which variation in human behavior can be attributed to and/or constrained by genetic composition and (2) to the relationship between cultural evolution and genetic development await developments in both the biological and the social sciences. It is obvious, for example, that cultural change proceeds rather rapidly, at least in the twentieth century. Genetic change does not move at the same speed, and competing paradigms within the biological sciences themselves make it difficult to explore the more fundamental questions of the interaction of nature and nurture.

This does not imply that we should not ask basic questions. It simply means that those who would study general human behavior and criminal behavior from a sociobiological perspective need to set a research agenda that recognizes the current limitations of both the biological and the social science and that sets out questions that can be addressed with existent science. Even if we recognize with Schubert (1973) that some of the objections to the biological study of human behavior are based on erroneous assumptions,[6] it is nonetheless obvious that a reasonable research agenda must be built. This line of research undoubtedly breaks new ground and must proceed on an accurate appreciation of the disciplines related to both nature and nurture. Furthermore, it must proceed, at least initially, with evidence on the more proximate questions.

In order to conduct the research required for adequate theory testing, experimental research on human subjects is required. This method raises a host of ethical issues and problems especially if subjects are to be deceived in the research process or manipulated without their knowledge.

Legally, experimental research methods raise constitutional issues of due process and equal protection. For example. if one were interested in examining the impact of certain kinds of treatment on some offenders, experimental methods would dictate the application of different penalties to equally serious criminals. While such research strategies are not common, they raise obvious issues of equal protection and due process.

An example of an actual experimental study illustrates these problems. *Predictive Sentencing: An Empirical Evaluation* (1976) is a report of a seven-year study of the disposition of juvenile traffic offenders in eight Oklahoma communities. Four authorities, a judge and law professor, a LEAA-project director, a former probation chief, and a research associate at the Oklahoma Center for Continuing Education conducted the experiment and reported the results (Whinery, Nagy, Sather, & Fisher, 1976). The researchers divided juvenile offenders into similar groups, subjected each group to alternate punishments/treatments, measured the effectiveness of the different penalties, and tried to predict the link between offender type and the efficacy of alternate punishments. Concluding that the predictive sentencing of youthful traffic offenders had limited practical utility, Whinery et al. (1976, p. 44) pointed out that "the judge, in sentencing, should concern himself more with reinforcing society's moral condemnation of the conduct in which the offender has engaged than with more complicated preventive sentencing techniques." While the careful and thoughtful conclusion suggests that the researchers were sensitive to some of the implications of their experimental approach to sentencing, the project itself raised serious ethical and constitutional questions. In spite of Norval Morris's comment in the foreword that the work represented "one of the few serious attempts at principled sentencing of any type of criminal." it is obvious that the application of different penalties to groups of offenders convicted of identical offenses raised serious questions regarding the appropriateness of the research itself and the equal protection of the law. Interestingly, the subjects of the scientific experiment were juveniles.

A final political obstacle hinges on the very nature of paradigmatic change. Philosophers of science have observed that the process of science revolves around two seemingly contradictory principles: proliferation and tenacity. If we define proliferation as an expansion of hypotheses and theories, and if we accept the procedural regularity and rigidity that tenacity entails, it is not difficult to appreciate the controversy surrounding the development of a biosocial approach to crime. The use of and reliance on biological theories as potential predictors[7] of criminal behavior certainly suggest new hypotheses and theories to the study of crime. At the same time, the tenacity of the scientific community seems to resist the challenge, albeit for a variety of reasons, many legitimate. The political character of paradigmatic change undoubtedly contributes to the controversy surrounding biosocial criminology.

POLICY IMPLICATIONS

One of the greatest concerns of many criminologists is the practical or policy implication of biosocial criminology. Fueled in part by Jeffrey's (1978) bold policy prescription in his *Criminology* article, these critics center on the way in which criminal justice processes would be structured if criminality were assumed or demonstrated to be biologically determined (e.g., Platt & Takagi, 1979). As summarized earlier, Jeffrey called for a private system of criminal justice in which individuals identified with biological determinants of criminality would be treated prior to any actual criminal behavior or crime, much less official apprehension and adjudication.

Jeffrey's prescription for a preventive, private criminal justice system represents the biosocial perspective carried to its extreme but logical conclusion. Less radical implications, however, are as consequential and controversial. These include the expansion of the state's police power in the interest of prevention, the deemphasis of legal principles such as liability, and the character and function of prisons. If criminal law were grounded on biosocial conceptions of criminal behavior, the state would focus on the prevention of crime and widen the nature and scope of the public authority of police. Law enforcement officials would be able to intervene in citizen lives without even the suspicion of criminal conduct.

This obviously has the potential of affecting a great number of lives, as well as the legal conception of personal responsibility central to criminal law. Liability simply consists of responsibility for action. Although there are signs pointing to increasing emphasis on *actus reus* in criminal law (the erosion of mens rea and the rehabilitative ethic points to an emphasis on strict liability), it is important nonetheless to recognize that biosocial criminology could challenge the very concept of liability. Simply put, punishment could be applied without criminal action. Only the disposition to violate the law would be necessary.

In the third stage of the criminal process, that is, punishment and treatment, it is clear that any expansion of our understanding of the causes of human aggression, criminal actions, and general nonconforming behavior carries substantial consequences. Witness the impact of positivistic theories of criminal behavior and the systemic consequences of a corresponding and earlier emphasis on rehabilitation. As mentioned previously, the positivistic assumptions of behavior underlying the rehabilitative ethic were clearly reflected in a variety of criminal laws and criminal justice institutions. These include the indeterminate and indefinite sentences, and the institutions of parole, probation, and juvenile courts. Though some might argue that organizational pressures (e.g., overcrowded prisons) contributed to the adoption and continuation of some of these institutions, it is obvious that none of them can be justified by nonpositivistic conceptions of criminology.

Defined with virtually no limits, the indeterminate sentence assumed that individuals could be cured of or treated for the causes of criminality. Because no individuals respond to treatment in the same amount of time, no limits were set in sentencing. Theoretically and practically, those convicted were sentenced from zero to life. Release hinged on parole judgments of cure and readiness for limited legal custody. While few states adopted the indeterminate sentence for the majority of crimes, two points are worth noting. First, women and children were usually singled out for such sentences (see Hand & Singer, 1974). Second, the same rationale governed the indefinite sentences and the institutions of parole, probation, and juvenile justice.

CONCLUSION

This review of biosocial conceptions of criminality and the corresponding problems and policy implications leads to four conclusions. First, there is a tendency in both the social sciences and contemporary politics to search for overarching theories of human behavior. Witness the competition between contrasting schools of criminology and the tendency of scholars to proclaim an all-inclusive model of criminal behavior. Studying a limited sample and confining their attention to a very particular class of offenders, for example, Yochelson and Samenow (1976) boldly proclaimed that criminals were born, not made, suggesting that they had discovered a theory of crime. Failure to recognize the potential influence of either environmental or biological factors of crime and failure to appreciate the fact that the social sciences do not advance an all-encompassing theory of human behavior in general will reinforce this tendency.

Second, a reductionist approach to this study of and solution for complex social problems typically results in an overemphasis on criminal law. If we persist in searching for a single explanation for criminal behavior and a single solution to the problem that crime presents to society, we are likely to ask law to compensate for the faliure of other social institutions and for whatever limitations inhere in the human condition. Witness the dependence on law in the wake of emphasis on the rehabilitative ethic and all-encompassing goals ascribed for prisons, juvenile courts, and other treatment-based institutions.

In the event that we continue our insular approach to the study of crime, women, minorities, and children are likely to be singled out for particular treatment and potential discrimination. There are several reasons for this conjecture. First, women, minorities, and juveniles are the most legally vulnerable groups in society. Throughout American history much of the struggle in civil rights has focused not only on the emancipation of blacks, but also on full citizen rights for women and all minorities. Furthermore, the history of criminal procedure illustrates that many due process gains were made in cases involving blacks, women, and juveniles. The continuing debate over the equal rights amendment, the controversy over affirmative action programs, and the inconsistent application of due process guarantees to juveniles indicate that the legal positions of women, minorities, and children are still unresolved.

Second, women, minorities, and juveniles are likely to be singled out if criminal law is directed by reductionist conceptions of criminality because sex, race, and age are obvious and easily measured biological characteristics. Futhermore, these three variables are routinely collected by criminal justice agencies. While the available evidence is not unequivocal, there is evidence that minorities are more likely to be arrested for criminal offenses than whites, that women suffer two contrasting forms of discrimination in the criminal system (excessive paternalism and leniency or punitiveness), and that female delinquents are frequently singled out in the enforcement of status (i.e., noncriminal) delinquent offenses.[8]

Third, as mentioned previously, women, minorities, and juveniles are more likely to commit the visible crimes of person and property than are older white males. Because the criminal justice system is directed to the apprehension and punishment of this category of offenders, it is likely that these three groups will have a greater chance of discriminatory treatment. Additionally, it is likely that women, minorities, and juveniles will be apprehended for victimless offenses more frequently than older, white males. A good example can be found in the administration of laws against prostitution. In her well-received study of the changes in the New York state criminal code, Pamela Roby (1976) pointed out that even when the state penal code had been changed to emphasize both male and female offenders in prostitution, law enforcement authorities continued to direct their efforts to prostitutes and not to clients. Because all victimless offenses are selectively enforced, it is likely that minorities, women, and juveniles will be the focus of a considerable portion of the law's effort.

Finally, it is important to realize that criminologists cannot ignore the possible impact of biological and physiological factors in explaining criminal conduct. Obviously, these factors must be analyzed as they interact with environmental forces. Equally obvious is the fact that research examining this interaction is fraught with difficulties. However, we should not hesitate in raising new questions or advancing new hypotheses. We must, however, hesitate in drawing premature and/or false conclusions and in applying research results that are scientifically suspect or ethically or legally unacceptable.

NOTES

1. Morris (1984) does not seem to be as cost-benefit conscious as J. Q. Wilson (1975), though the social utility argument in his recent book, *Madness and the Criminal Law,* evokes that line of reasoning. See Morris (1984).

2. Lombroso considered himself a "slave to facts" (Reid, 1979, p. 138).

3. Recent research describes the typical female offender as young, black, poorly educated, unemployed or unskilled and unmarried (Wolfe et al., 1984). Obviously, a young, black women faces the greatest possibility of discriminatory treatment if the impact of membership in three vulnerable classes actually compounds the discrimination in each.

4. Abraham Blumberg (1971) distinguished three classes of offenses: upperworld (white-collar); organized (underworld and victimless); and visible (offenses against person and property).

5. For an analogy that appears to attribute moral systems and the possibility of crime among birds and plants see Barash's (1979) discussion of rape among ducks and flowers.

6. Schubert (1973, p. 241) argues that the lack of education in modern biology, the confusion of the twentieth century evolutionary biology with ninteenth century social Darwinsim, and the conviction that the natural and social sciences are absolutely separate contribute, erroneously, to our longstanding disdain for investigating the biological roots of political behavior.

7. Samuel Hines emphasizes that one of the important contributions of sociobiology may be to demonstrate the independence of explanation and prediction.

8. Social science research has not yet yielded conclusive evidence on the impact of either race or sex in criminal justice processes. Though there is evidence on the direct and indirect impact of race, the statistical patterns are not constant across all courts and time periods. The same holds for research on sex, though there is ample evidence on the two patterns summarized. For a summary, see Myers and Talarico (1984).

RESOURCES

Ardrey, R. (1961). *The territorial imperative: A personal inquiry into the animal origins and nature of man.* London: Collins.

Barash, D. (1979). *The whisperings within.* New York: Harper & Row.

Becker, H. (1963). *Outsiders: Studies in the sociology of deviance.* New York: Free Press.

Blumberg, A. S. (1971). Criminal Justice in America. In J. D. Douglas (Ed.), *Crime and justice in American society* (p. 4). Indianapolis: Bobbs-Merrill.

Bonnet, P. L., & Pfeiffer, C. C. (1978). Biochemical diagnosis of delinquent behavior. In L. J. Hippchen (Ed.), *Ecologic-biochemical approaches to treatment of delinquency and criminals.* New York: Van Nostrand.

Bowker, L. H. (1978). *Women, crime, and the criminal justice system.* Lexington, MA: D. C. Heath.

Brantley, J. R., & Kravitz, M. (1979). *The etiology of criminality: Nonbehavioral science perspectives.* Washington, DC: Government Printing Office.

Cott, A. (1978). The etiology of learning disabilities, drug abuse, and juvenile delinquency. In L. J. Hippchen (Ed.), *Ecologic-biochemical approaches to treatment of delinquency and criminals.* New York: Van Nostrand.

Cressey, D. R. (1978). Criminological theory, social science, and the repression of crime. *Criminology, 16*(August), 171-191.

Ferri, E. (1913). *The positive school of criminology.* Chicago: Kerr.

Frankel, C. (1979). Sociobiology and its critics. *Commentary* (July), 39-47.

Garofalo, R. (1914). *Criminology* (R. W. Miller, Trans.), Montclair, NJ: Patterson Smith.

Gertz, M. G., & Talarico, S. M. (1977). Problems of validity and reliability in criminal justice research. *Journal of Criminal Justice, 5* (Fall), 217-224.

Gould, S. J. (1978). Biological potential vs. biological determinism. In A. L. Caplan (Ed.), *The sociobiology debate: Readings in the ethical and scientific issues concerning sociobiology.* New York: Harper & Row.

Gresens, J. W. (1972). The indeterminate sentence: Judicial intervention in the correctional process. *Buffalo Law Review, 21* (Spring), 935-957.

Hand, R. C., & Singer, R. G. (1974). *Sentencing computation laws and practice.* Washington, DC: American Bar Association Commission on Correctional Facilities and Services.

Hippchen, L. J. (Ed.). (1978). *Ecologic-biochemical approaches to treatment of delinquency and criminals.* New York: Van Nostrand.

Jeffrey, C. R. (1978). Criminology as an interdisciplinary behavioral science. *Criminology, 16* (August), 149-169.

Jensen, A. R. (1969). How much can we boost I.Q. and scholastic achievement. *Harvard Educational Review, 38*(Winter).

Lewontin, R. C. (1979). Sociobiology as an adaptationist program. *Behavioral Science, 24* (January), 5-14.

Lombroso, C. (1911). *Crime, its causes and remedies* (H. P. Horton, Trans.). Boston: Little, Brown.

Morris, D. (1967). *The naked ape: A zoologist's study of the human animal.* New York: McGraw-Hill.

Morris, N. (1984). *Madness and the criminal law.* Chicago: University of Chicago Press.

Myers, M. A., & Talarico, S. M. (1984). *Determinants of intrastate sentencing variation.* Report to the National Institute of Justice. (see especially Chapter One).

Nagel, I. H., & Hagan, J. (1983). Gender and crime: Offense and criminal court sanctions. In M. Tonry & N. Morris (Eds.), *Crime and justice: An annual review of research, Vol. 4.* Chicago: University of Chicago Press.

Peterson, S. A. (1978). The menstrual cycle and politics: A preliminary exploration. *Social Science Information, 17,* 993-1000.

Platt, T., & Takagi, P. (1979). Biosocial criminology: A critique (in special issue, Crime and Social Justice). *Criminology, 11* (Spring-Summer), 5-13.

Pollak, O. (1950). *The criminality of women*. New York: A. S. Barnes.

Quinney, R. (1977). *Class, state and crime: On the theory and practice of criminal justice*. New York: David McKay.

Radzinowicz, L. (1966). *Ideology and crime: A study of crime in its social and historical context*. New York: Columbia University Press.

Reid, S. T. (1979). *Crime and criminology*. New York: Holt, Rinehart & Winston.

Rice, D. (1973). Born bad. *Health Services World* (March), 16-18.

Roby, P. A. (1976). Politics and criminal law: Revision of the New York state penal law on prostitution. In G. F. Cole (Ed.), *Criminal justice: Law and politics*. North Scituate, MA: Duxbury.

Rothman, D. J. (1971). *The discovery of the asylum*. Boston: Little, Brown.

Schubert, G. (1973). Biopolitical behavior: The nature of the political animal. *Polity, 6,* 240-275.

Sellin, T. (1937). The Lombrosian myth in criminology. *American Journal of Sociology, 42,* (May), 898-899.

Slavin, S. H. (1978) Information processing defects in delinquents. In L. J. Hippchen (Ed.), *Ecologic-biochemical approaches to treatment of delinquents and criminals*. New York: Van Nostrand.

Sutherland, E. H., & Cressey, D. (1978). *Criminology* (10th ed.). Philadelphia: Lippincott.

Tiger, L., & Fox, R. (1971). *The imperial animal*. New York: Holt, Rinehart & Winston.

Time (1977, August). Why you do what you do, sociobiology: A new theory of behavior, pp. 54-63.

Wahlke, J. C. (1979). Pre-behavioralism in political science. *American Political Science Review, 73* (March), 9-31.

Wheeler, G. R. (1978). *Counterdeterrence: A report on juvenile sentencing and the effects of prisonization*. Chicago: Nelson-Hall.

Whinery, L. H., Nagy, T. J., Sater, G. A., & Fisher, K. D. (1976). *Predictive sentencing: An empirical evaluation*. Lexington, MA: D. C. Heath.

Wilson, E. O. (1975). *Sociobiology: The new synthesis*. Cambridge, MA: Belknap Press of Harvard University Press.

Wilson, J. Q. (1975). *Thinking about crime*. New York: Basic.

Wolfe, N. T., Cullen, F. T., & Cullen, J. B. (1984). Describing the female offender: A note on the demographics of arrests. *Journal of Criminal Justice, 12,* 483-492.

Yochelson, S., & Samenow, S. (1976). *The criminal personality*. New York: Jason Aronson.

9

WOMEN'S BIOLOGY AND THE U.S. MILITARY

Judith Hicks Stiehm

Gen. John W. Vessey, Jr., chairman of the Joint Chiefs of Staff, said early in 1984 that "the greatest change that has come about in the United States forces in the time I've been in the military service has been the extensive use of women. That's even greater than nuclear weapons, I feel, as far as our own forces are concerned" (*Washington Post,* 1984).

When the draft was abolished in 1972, the armed services did, indeed, begin to increase their recruitment of women. However, because laws or military regulations prohibit the use of women in combat, the military argues strenuously that it cannot use even 10 percent women personnel. To many in the military, 9, 8, 7 percent are probably too many. What is it about the biology of these token women that causes more disarray than nuclear physics? Women can't be used in combat, but most military personnel are not used in combat. What are the military's expressed concerns? Biologically, they seem to be three: fitness, physical strength, and pregnancy.

Fitness is a concern both at enlistment and also during service. Establishing physical standards for enlistment has proved relatively easy and noncontroversial; establishing and enforc-

Author's Note: Thanks to M. C. Devilbiss for reading and commenting on an earlier version of this chapter.

ing fitness standards for continuing service has been more problematic.

Physical strength has become an issue as women have (1) moved into jobs that require heavy work, (2) been integrated into units that were previously all-male, and (3) become a significant proportion of the personnel in particular units and specialties.

Pregnancy used to present no problem for the military. Pregnant women were discharged. But in 1975 the Department of Defense directed an end to involuntary discharges for pregnancy and the services had to develop policies concerning both pregnancy and maternity. For the last ten years those policies have been evolving. New policies are proposed with regularity. The truth seems to be that the military has not yet made peace with pregnancy (or maternity, which is, of course, not a strictly biological problem). Let us consider in turn military policies concerning fitness, strength, and pregnancy. Policies are crucial because they tend to have the force of law. Both the Congress and the courts are loath to question military practice.

FITNESS

Lack of fitness has not been a major barrier to women's enlistment as compared to men's enlistment, nor has it been a major reason for women's discharge from service. One should remember, though, that military service is selective. Some 22 percent of youths are automatically excluded on the basis of their Armed Forces Qualification Test (AFQT) scores or because of failure to meet education standards; if another 15 percent are excluded for failure to meet physical standards (the most frequent cause of rejection being overweight), and if still others fail to meet moral standards, the pool for enlistments may be composed of 60 percent of young people. Again, however, lack of fitness, does not seem to reduce women's access to the military more than men's, and more women and men are rejected for lack of mental ability (or stability) than for failure to meet physical standards. It should be noted that both physical standards and mental standards can be reduced in time of emergency. It has been U.S. policy, however, to have a single enlistment standard at any particular time. The expectation is that every service person is available for "worldwide assignment" (Military Manpower Task Force, 1982, p. I-2)

Today women's entrance physicals routinely include gender-specific items such as pelvic examinations. Standards for nongender specific items such as vision are the same for women and men. Neither was always the case. When women were first recruited for the Women's Army Auxiliary Corps (WAAC, which became the Women's Army Corps, WAC, in 1943), men's standards were used and therefore no pelvics were given. Later, a Consultant for Women's Health and Welfare was appointed to establish appropriate health standards for women. In general the Director of the WAC wished to hold women to higher standards than men and also to screen them more thoroughly. Her goal was to reduce greatly disability discharges for gynecological and psychoneurotic reasons—reasons responsible for three-fourths of women's World War II disability discharges (Treadwell, 1954, pp. 176-177). The WAC Director's efforts to build a corps above criticism also included careful monitoring of women already in service. For instance, she requested that all women scheduled to go overseas take a complete physical including a test for pregnancy. The Army refused, saying such a procedure would be too time-consuming, too expensive, and the men were not screened at embarcation (Treadwell, 1954, pp. 580-581). As it turned out the medical evacuation rate for women in the European, Indian, and Chinese theaters was approximately the same as that of noncombat men; it was substantially higher, however, from the Southwest Pacific. The high rate was apparently not so much a matter of physical health as of command policies (Treadwell, 1954, pp. 439-440).

Another World War II inclusion-of-women problem involved the U.S. Army's practice of checking every soldier every month for healthy feet, mouth, and teeth and for the absence of vermin and venereal disease. For women an adequate venereal examination would have included a monthly pelvic and some commanders insisted on this. Other commanders did not. Eventually a regulation was issued stating pelvic exams would be done (1) only as needed, (2) rectally "where indicated," and (3) with a woman officer present. If women's "higher degree of modesty" and, therefore, the need to provide women officer witnesses was experienced as a bother, it should be noted that the military medical setting was mostly male. Whether women would have been "near rebellion" if their physicians had been women, or whether men would have become suddenly modest in a setting composed of women physicians and aides is unknowable (Treadwell, 1954, pp. 608-609).

Maintaining fitness involves physical training and also physical testing. The latter is now conducted on a regular basis; the former is sometimes left to the individual and sometimes conducted as a group activity. Penalties are provided for failure to meet physical standards but few discharges result. Indeed, most fitness failures are due to overweight and the usual remedy is to place the individual in a weight reduction program. In general, physical fitness standards vary by sex, age, and service. Physical training practices vary by service and unit; however, all members of a particular unit are usually expected to participate in the same training.

Physical training is a major component of basic training. While fitness is one goal, in this setting physical training is also used as a tool for the development of unit cohesion and discipline. Programs are not designed solely to build bodies; sometimes they are intended to induce fatigue or to test mental discipline; they may also be intended to develop the habit of obeying commands.

The Marines have always conducted separate and different basic training for enlisted women and men. The Army conducted integrated basic training from 1978 to 1982. Before 1978 women's basic was conducted by the Women's Army Corps (WAC). Then, when the WAC was disbanded and women were integrated into the Army generally, basic training was also integrated. Resegregation occurred four years later. The Army's explanation was that women's presence negatively affected men's performance by not challenging them sufficiently (*Baltimore Sun,* 1982). It should be noted that basic training is just that—basic. It is the shared introductory experience of all enlisted personnel. (In the Air Force, it is so shared all basic training actually occurs at the same location.) Basic is not combat training; even the infantryman goes on to Advanced Infantry Training (AIT) after basic. Basic is the common denominator—except that it is not common for Marine and Army women and men.

Basic is a highly structured activity. Trainees sleep in open-bay dormitories; they are together and their activity is directed around the clock. Organization is both hierarchical and residential. Because dormitories are segregated by sex, the smallest and lowest unit of organization is by definition sex-segregated. Sex integration, then, occurs at a particular level. When an activity is conducted at the lowest organizational level, the squad, it is conducted by dormitory residence and is de facto sex-segregated. This means rugged physical conditioning can be conducted as an integrated or as a segregated activity simply by manipulating the level of organization on which it is conducted. Sex education, too, can be conducted in sex-segregated groups simply by controlling the level at which it is offered. Platoons (which are composed of squads) of women can be combined with other platoons of women to maintain sex segregation at the next level of organization, the company (about 150 people), or they can be combined with men's platoons to integrate the company level of training. In fact, when the Army "resegregated," it did not institute a return to the complete separation and difference of the past. Basic for women and men remained similar; what was new was the fact that it became separate up through the level of the company. Both women and men instructors were retained to train both women and men. It was not a complete reversion to the pre-1978 pattern of training.

Both the Air Force and the Navy describe themselves as conducting integrated training. However, because of residential segregation it is possible for them to conduct some elements of training in sex-segregated units. Nevertheless, if the problem is one of providing equally taxing workouts to a heterogeneous population, one would think ability grouping would be the best answer. This, in fact, was the answer chosen by West Point in the assignment of its cadets to running groups; however, it is an answer at odds with the principle of uniformity (identicalness)—a principle some deem crucial to the development of cohesive units (Stiehm, 1981, ch. 5).

After training is completed, Marine and Army work units are more likely to conduct regular and strenuous physical exercise than Navy and Air Force units. This training is conducted in (integrated) work groups rather than by (often segregated) residential units. Training may involve daily, hour-long workouts. Running is a favored activity but calisthenics are also a normal part of the routine. Thus women may be spared physical training with men in basic only to have to participate with men in their first work assignments!

Training or conditioning sessions typically begin or end a day. Their arduousness depends very much on the commander and the work of the unit. At one Army base in Korea in 1982, early morning runs (in combat boots) were the norm; at a base in West Germany running (in jogging shoes) was a late afternoon but not daily event. At the first base alternate forms of exercise were permitted, but the effect of this policy was blunted by the offering of a unit prize based only on competition in running. This meant women who might have preferred aerobics, dance, or another form of exercise felt pressured to run instead. Unless women had been athletes before coming into service, most of them would not have experienced such a strenuous regime previously. If they were in poor shape, it would not be fun. Still one suspects that the social climate surrounding exercise (whether it rewards efforts and whether it offers positive reinforcement) is as important to women's attitude and performance as is the specific content of "P.T." (physical training).

The Army's "Fit to Win" program includes testing on (1) pushups, (2) situps, and (3) a two-mile run. This testing applies to both active duty and reserve personnel. In addition, the program includes a change in the Army's master menu to reduce both salt and calories—nutrition being considered integral to fitness. Finally, skinfold measures are used to assess percent body fat when there is a question about an individual's being overweight. The minimal required scores for age 17 Army men and women in 1983 were reported to the Defense Advisory Committee on Women in the Service (DACOWITS) in the fall of 1983 as being as follows:

	MINIMAL SCORE		MAXIMUM SCORE	
	M	**F**	**M**	**F**
Pushups	40	16	66	40
Situps	40	27	69	61
Two-Mile Run	17:55	22:14	13:05	13:40

The Navy emphasizes "fitness for life" and building a healthy "life-style." Thus its program includes education about nutrition and exercise but also education about smoking, accidents, substance abuse, high blood pressure, and stress management.

The Air Force has required an annual 1.5 mile run for some time. Personnel under 29 years of age are expected to complete that run in 14:3 minutes if male and in 15:36 minutes if female. Personnel over 50 may use up to 17 minutes if male and 18:15 if female. A new height/weight standard (without age differences) is being phased in. In 1983, 5' tall women had a 130 pound maximum, and 5'4" women had a 139 pound maximum. Men 5'9" could not be over 189 and men 74" were not to exceed 218. If they did, they had to join a rehabilitation program that required women to lose three pounds a month and men five (DACOWITS Briefing, Fall, 1983).

The Marines do not just give tests. They make training mandatory. All its personnel, regardless of age, sex, or rank, do a minimum of three hours of physical training a week during duty hours. In addition, a test consisting of a flexed arm hang, situps, and a mile-and-a-half run are required. Women 5'4" can weigh 102 to 138 pounds or can have under 26 percent body fat. "Food abusers" enter a six-month program to "take care of the problem." (The Army's body fat maximum for women is 28 percent; its West Point women average 22 percent.)

Clearly there is pressure to maintain fitness; that pressure is strongest in the Marine Corps, which includes detailed information on expectations in its public affairs pamphlet "Women Marines in the 1980's." Fitness standards seem reasonable and do not affect women more adversely than men. The increased attention given fitness is in part a 1980s response to a "more military" presidency. Attention to fitness may also be a response to questions about women's capacity to do their share of heavy work in integrated units. Such questions have given rise to a new personnel issue—physical strength testing for job specialities.

PHYSICAL STRENGTH TESTING

Being strong and being fit are not necessarily the same. Weight lifters and football linemen serve as illustration. Indeed, an Air Force football coach was incensed once to learn that one of his star players was not eligible for an officer's commission because he was overweight (Stiehm, 1981, ch. 6); also, the Navy has noted that bulky enlisted personnel can be extremely useful aboard ship even though they are not "fit" (Robertson, 1984).

A 1976 report by the Comptroller General, "Job Opportunities for Women in the Military: Progress and Problems," noted that women in new job specialties were not always doing all the tasks associated with those specialties. The report did not determine the reason for this, but suggested attitudes of supervisors and of women and lack of physical strength might all play a part. The report recommended that attention be given to developing physical tests for job specialties because an increasing number of women were entering fields other than medicine and administration (Comptroller General, 1976, pp. 13-27).

The Air Force had actually already developed such a test and the Marine Corps had plans to do so. The Air Force called its "Physical Work Capacity" score the X factor. New Air Force enlistees were assigned physical strength profiles at Armed Forces Examining and Entrance Stations (AFEES) as early as January, 1976 (Comptroller General, 1976). Subsequent testing showed the AFEEs' subjective testing was underestimating men's and overestimating women's scores. Thus a machine was ordered for this testing in 1978. The X-1 standard was set at lifting 70 pounds to a height of 6 feet. This was held to represent a capacity for "'heavy work over prolonged periods" (Assistant Secretary of Defense, 1981, p. 83). It was required for placement in 85 skills with 123,000 slots or 28 percent of all Air Force enlisted jobs. (Air Force officers are not tested for strength.) These were principally in mechanical or electronic specialties. An X factor score of two qualified an individual for "sustained moderate work over prolonged periods." The test was to lift 40 pounds to elbow height. This score applied to 227 specialties with 190,000 slots or an additional 43 percent of enlisted jobs. Thus 71 percent of Air Force jobs were deemed to require more than mere fitness.

Virtually all men were able to meet X-1 standards, although only 29.4 percent of women could meet that standard. This meant that Air Force strength testing eliminated 70 percent of women from 28 percent of the jobs—jobs open to all men—presumably because equipment had been designed so that men in general could use it. (The X-3 factor, the minimal score, involved lifting 20 pounds to elbow height. Virtually every enlistee could meet this requirement.) (Comptroller General, 1976, p. 19.)

By the end of 1981 the Air Force had raised its standards for X-factor scores (U.S. Air Force, 1983). The new X-1 standard became lifting 100 pounds to 6 feet, X-2 became lifting 70 pounds to 6 feet, X-3 became lifting 40 pounds to elbow height, and X-4 became lifting 20 pounds to waist height. While 80 percent of men can meet the X-1 standard, only .3

percent of women can do so. Thirteen Air Force Specialty Codes (AFSCs) were designated as requiring the X-1 qualification.

Both Air Force test systems were put into place with little notice or justification to the public. The lack of test validation caused no outcry. Perhaps this was because the tests "made sense." Meanwhile, the Air Force, describing these as interim measures, contracted with Texas Institute of Technology in 1982 to develop validated scores for assignment to AFSCs that would include stamina as well as strength as a factor and that would also provide physical tests appropriate for those assigned to flying duties.

The Navy approached physical strength testing more conservatively. While women represented 8 percent of the Navy by 1983, they represented only 2 percent of the personnel in the 26 occupations the Navy had identified as requiring special physical strength. For this reason the Navy decided not to act until its jobs had been analyzed and tests appropriate to job demands had been developed and validated. Much of its work was and is being done at the Navy Personnel Research and Development Center at San Diego. There it was decided that approximately one-fourth of Navy jobs were physically demanding, but that common shipboard demands (such as fire-fighting) might be made of all persons aboard ship regardless of their work assignment. On the other hand, Navy researchers noted that within each specialty there would be certain tasks (alpha tasks) required of everyone, and other tasks (called beta tasks) to which only the strongest crew members need be assigned. These assumptions recognized that work was usually done in a group although testing would be done on individuals rather than on a work team. A further complication was noted—some jobs were literally done by a team, for example, carrying a stretcher or loading bombs (Robertson & Trent, 1983).

The Navy's study is not complete. While it notes the wide separation of score distributions between men and women, it suggests differences can be minimized by (1) applying standards only to the one-fourth of jobs with substantial demands, (2) using only alpha tasks as criteria, (3) allowing a discount procedure to allow for gains in strength and technique, and (4) reviewing tasks to identify ways of redesigning equipment and procedures. For instance, it was found that virtually all women could open a watertight steel hatch with one arm if they kept their arms straight and lifted (with their legs) by climbing up the ladder, instead of climbing the ladder, grasping the handle and then trying to lift the handle by straightening the arm.

The Army has long considered the problem of just how many women it can "utilize." A 1942 study suggested 19 percent and a 1958 study 25 percent (at a time when law proscribed more than 2 percent). Today's estimates (under 10 percent) are much lower although they use the same principal criteria—physical strength and relation to combat (Sternberg, Greenberg, & Fuchs, 1958).

The 1958 study estimated that less than 25 percent of Military Occupational Studies (MOSs) required lifting and carrying 50 pounds as part of their regular duties. It also estimated the number of suitable duty positions within an MOS rather than trying to determine whether or not a whole MOS was or was not suitable.

To measure empirically the physical requirements of all Army MOSs would have been expensive and time consuming. Thus the Army elected to use a rating method for establishing standards (Myers, Gebhardt, & Fleishman, 1980, p. 49). This involved ratings by job incumbents of (1) physical ability, (2) criticality, and (3) team work requirements of particular MOSs. The ratings proved reliable, that is, repeatable. In general the overall rating of an MOS tended to be similar to that of the MOS's most demanding task. Estimates of criticality (learning difficulty, tolerance of delay, and consequences of inadequate performance) were also reliable. However, efforts to assess which tasks were, in fact, performed as a team were not reliable. Moreover, the 1980 work did not establish either the construct or discriminant validity of the ratings (Myers et al., p. 49). The data, then, were not adequate.

The Army began to develop dependable information about women's physical abilities only in the late 1970s. The integration of basic training at the company level that began then did not have data to use in developing its program. Reports from the "major commands," though, did note a "general consensus" that "on the average women have less strength and stamina than male soldiers and a lower level of physical fitness." From Korea it was reported that "the daily three-mile run is almost impossible for most" (The Deputy Chief of Staff for Personnel, 1976, pp. 12-18). Such a "run" represents the kind of demand that may be made of all members of a unit or of all personnel in a particular environment irrespective of MOS. In one sense the run may be irrelevant—it may have no impact whatever on an individual's ability to perform his or her work. In another sense it may be most serious—it may affect unit morale or cohesion to have laggards or nonparticipants in the group.

At this time discussion inside the Army about the utilization of women was vigorous even though Carter administration policy was that women's usefulness was not to be doubted. It is important to understand that strong feelings existed about such things as the effect of women's participation on Russian perceptions of U.S. strength, a possible lessening of unit morale, and civilian support for the military. At least one memo said, "The Army should take no more women." Strong as these views were they would not prevail—directly. What would later (1980) make it possible for the Army to "take no more women," that is, to hold the number of the women in the Army constant, was a combination of restrictions based on the old criteria of (1) physical strength and (2) proximity to combat. The more passionate concerns, for example, pregnancy, would not be confronted directly.

In 1978 the panel for Evaluation of Women in the Army (EWITA) proposed restrictions on enlistment based on the percentage of women estimated as being able to do the work of some 133 MOSs. A rating group assigned a difficulty rating to MOS described by individuals at the schools. That rating was based on the most difficult requirement of the occupation. The ratings were based on lifting weights of 50, 75, 100, and 125 pounds. Two MOSs were estimated to require the ability to lift 125 pounds; 43 to require the ability to lift 100 pounds, 48 to require the ability to lift 75 pounds, 18 to require the ability to lift 50 pounds, and 22 to have no lifting requirement.

After requirements were assigned to a particular MOS, an estimate was made as to what percentage of women and men would be able to meet the total requirements of the MOS. Thus there were 43 jobs that were estimated as requiring being able to lift 100 pounds. Almost all men could lift 100 pounds. However, 100 percent of men were not estimated to be able to do all 43 jobs. In fact, 100 percent of men were estimated to be able to do only 36 of the 43 jobs, and 2 jobs only 50 percent of men were estimated able to do. The estimates as to the percentage of women able to do the 43 jobs with a requirement for lifting 100 pounds were both lower and more varied: 100 percent of women were estimated able to do only one of the jobs; no women were estimated able to do 6. Other estimates were 9 jobs 5 percent; 5 jobs 10 percent, another set of 5 jobs, 25 percent, and 5 other jobs, 50 percent; 4 jobs 35 percent; 3 jobs, 15 percent; 2 jobs 75 percent; and 1 job, 40 percent, 1 job, 80 percent, and 1 job, 90 percent. Overall it was estimated that 95 percent of men could do 121 of the 133 jobs studied; it was estimated that 95 percent of women could do only 32 of the 133—and 22 of these had no strength requirement at all.

Again, physical strength had not been a primary complaint of commanders. Nevertheless, as job analyses emerged based on each person being able to do every element of a job, and with equipment and job definitions designed for a male population, physical strength requirements emerged as a sure and "objective" way of dramatically reducing opportunities for women. It restricted both the number and the variety of jobs available.

Work on appropriate standards continued (Deputy Chief of Staff for Personnel, 1982, ch. 2). The work was extensive. But when physical standards were finally put into place late in 1983, they were used for recruit counseling, not for assignment. Adherence to the standards was described as voluntary on the part of the recruit. A positive interpretation could see this decision as reasonable, even as generous, as leaving the decision to women. A more negative interpretation is that the decision was based upon the Army's failure to validate the tests and thus upon the knowledge that they would not withstand legal scrutiny.

The physical standards the Army finally settled upon did not begin by developing a list of tasks for each MOS and then identifying the physical demands of those tasks. Instead, the Army created job clusters of MOSs based on required upper body strength under combat conditions. This was done even though the Army's policy of not permitting women to serve in combat would have suggested that women might have served in some MOS in noncombat as contrasted to combat assignments. The method used held women to the ability to fill the most vigorous rather than the most regular duty (Deputy Chief of Staff for Personnel, 1982).

Much was made of using long-established Department of Labor (DOL) standards for physical demand testing.

However, it was Army Training and Doctrine personnel who assigned individual MOSs to particular categories. Moreover, the Army did not, finally, use the categories—sedentary, light, medium, heavy, and very heavy—as established by the DOL. According to the DOL, "medium" work consists of lifting 50 pounds maximum and frequently lifting 25 pounds. "Heavy" work consists of lifting 100 pounds maximum and frequently lifting 50 pounds. "Very heavy" involves lifting over 100 pounds. The Army found 100 percent of men and 74 percent of women qualified for "medium" work, 82 percent of men and 8 percent of women qualified for "heavy" work, and 3 percent of women and 80 percent of men qualified for "very heavy" work (Deputy Chief of Staff for Personnel, 1982, pp. 2-14).

The Army separately determined that the 100-pound lift disqualified individuals from 64 MOS that required more than a 50-pound lift but less than the next cutoff, 100 pounds. It argued, "The heavy category neither conforms to the distribution of jobs nor does it optimize the physical capacity of women." Based on this observation, a new category was created. The new category, "moderately heavy," was set at a lift of 80 pounds and frequent lifting of 40 pounds (Deputy Chief of Staff for Personnel, 1982, pp. 2-14).

What was the effect of the new category? It was to create a separate category for 64 MOS (44,000 jobs)—a category with a standard that 26 percent of women could meet. It also represented a standard that 100 percent of men could meet. Thus the cut moved the 18 percent of men who had previously been in a "medium" category with 74 percent of women into a new category they shared with only 26 percent of women. The men's and women's "overlap" was minimized, and no group of men was left as a minority in a group of women. What the new category did was to create a special category not just for the top 26 percent of women, but also for the bottom 18 percent of men. This put 100 percent of men in the top categories. It also created an overlap category with about the same percentage of men and women but with much larger numbers of men. Small men were not left behind.

In applying physical standards, a "predictive physical capacity" factor is planned that will permit enlistees to select MOSs for which they have not successfully tested. Because other studies suggest men gain more than women in the same development program, this may work more to men's advantage than to women's.

The net effect of the new Army standards is that only 8 percent of women are expected to be able to do heavy or very heavy work; 82 percent of men are expected to be able to do this work. These categories include 440,000 of the Army's 572,000 slots; this is 76 percent of all jobs. In 1982 over half of the Army's women were serving in these job categories; though there was a clear understanding that women as a group were not as strong as men as a group, women's lack of strength was not a primary complaint nor was there evidence that women's strength impeded unit performance. Yet the application of the system developed in 1982 (which uses combat criteria and which takes no account of group performance) will sharply reduce recruitment possibilities for women.

The fact is that cutoff scores for mental qualifications are regularly varied; the military wishes to get "enough" draftees/enlistees and does so. The same thing will surely occur with physical standards, but when the categories are large and the tests skip from 50- to 80- to 100-pounds lifts, small adjustments will be more difficult and visible than they are for changes in mental qualifications.

Almost unaddressed are questions about scaling equipment and tasks to women's size. U.S. forces regularly share equipment with men of other nations whose size and strength are significantly different from that of U.S. personnel. No literature has appeared to suggest this creates a difficulty; also, the U.S. population is becoming more ethnically diverse and different groups do have different average heights and weights. Does the Army really want, for instance, to have men of Asian descent concentrated in particular types of jobs because of size and strength measures? Or does the Army (and the country) want all of its male citizens available for any assignment? During World War II Japanese Americans were used as fighting men; Senator Daniel Inouye has described himself at 5'6" as a "big" man in his unit. He noted that some of his men wore size 4 shoes (Good Morning America, Radio-TV Log, 1982, pp. 67-70). In short—in the past and even now—the military seems to have accommodated men of many sizes. Physical strength has not previously been an issue. Individuals were simply used as needed. The real issue, then, seems to be extending the range of size (and strength), with women not extending the range per se.

Further, there seems to have been no analysis made of how less physical strength might be balanced by other desirable qualities, for example, education, an enlistee might offer. It is almost as though physical strength testing is a device being used to reduce opportunities for women in an objective, gender-free way because women are "a problem," not because strength has been a problem. Strength has never been a criterion for men's participation except in certain elite organizations. It is not clear the Army really wants to use it as a criterion for men, because a crucial element of the draft is fairness. By fairness is usually meant inclusiveness—equal risk. It would be very awkard for the Army to have to tell large men that small men do not have to go into combat.

Finally, if the Army really wishes to utilize fully the available pool of personnel, it should reserve the "light," "medium," and "moderately heavy" jobs for persons who cannot meet higher standards. This would mean that about one-fourth of the Army's jobs would be reserved for the 74 percent of women and 0 percent of men not eligible for heavier jobs. Competition would then be more or less balanced, although over one-third of the youth pool would be competing for a quarter of all jobs. More MOSs might become female "traditional" if this were done, but it has not been an obvious disservice to the Army to have, for instance, a Nurse Corps that is mostly women.

One study the Army did not undertake was to see how women who could not pass the proposed physical strength test were actually doing in their jobs. Is strength truly necessary? Have women found other ways to do the work? In its own analysis the Army found five jobs rated "heavy" or "very heavy" that had substantial numbers of women already working in them. In these particular cases the Army redefined ("separated") the MOS to remove the onerous duties from the job description (Deputy Chief of Staff for Personnel, 1982, pp. 2-29). Thus the Army made women more likely to qualify for the jobs they were in. The jobs were the following: wire systems installer operator, ammunition specialist, motor transport operator, medical specialist, and military police.

The Marine Corps has taken a different approach entirely. It considers Basic Training its physical standards test. If one can get through Basic one is fit to be a Marine. The Marines tend to wonder just exactly what other services' "basic" is about if large numbers of women and men can pass it and still not be able to do the services' jobs!

PREGNANCY AND THE MILITARY

Mattie Treadwell has documented the Army's early experience with the pregnancy of military women. During

World War II the medical aspects of pregnancy were secondary because pregnant women were immediately discharged. The primary pregnancy issues were ones of morality, of the women's corps' reputation. Military women were mostly young; in the military setting they were greatly outnumbered by men, many of whom were away from home and family and suffused with the sexual aggressiveness of a military environment (Gray, 1970). The military's anxiety about the safety and virtue of its women is demonstrated by the sometimes elaborate security offered women's housing—in at least one instance women's barracks were surrounded by barbed wire and floodlit—to protect them from their fellow troops (Treadwell, 1954, pp. 420, 437, 449). Nevertheless, there were many rumors about the morality of military women. Indeed, the rumors were so strong that recruitment was affected and the FBI was asked to investigate to determine whether or not the rumors were the result of "Axis influence" (Treadwell, 1954, pp. 195-218). They were not, and, in fact, the 1943 pregnancy rate among unmarried Army women was approximately one-fifth that of civilian women (Treadwell, 1954, p. 193). In the North African theater, enlisted women's rate of pregnancy was less than that of civilian women and about the same as that of nurses in the theater. Some 1944 data suggested a rate less than half that of civilians (Treadwell, 1954, p. 620). Although the data are inexact, it seems clear that pregnancy was not endemic and that the "morality" of military women was at least as good as that of civilian women.

The impulse to fastidiousness that resulted in the use of the word "cyesis" rather than pregnancy in official data and in less than "honorable" discharge of unmarried pregnant nurses was modified during the course of the war and was less punitively managed in services other than the Army (Treadwell, 1954, pp. 501-502). Needless to say, men who fathered children received no punishment and men were regularly provided prophylactics "to prevent disease." Women were not, and even sex education that was "very frank" rather than "moralizing" was "obliged to desist" (Treadwell, 1954, p. 399).

Discharge was required for pregnancy, but during the war even becoming married was grounds for requesting discharge. By the 1960s marriage alone was no longer grounds to request discharge and married women could join the military (Holm, 1982, p. 289). The new issue that would eventually result in a changed pregnancy policy concerned the presence of minor children in a married woman's home. Even if the children were teenagers and the husband's from a previous marriage, military women had to obtain waivers to remain on active duty. Then, in 1970, a seaman, Anna Flores (unwed) miscarried before discharge and asked to remain on active duty. The Navy said no. She (with the assistance of the American Civil Liberties Union) went to court and won. The issue to the court was her nonexistent responsibilities of motherhood rather than the pregnancy or the morality of the pregnancy. The next challenge came from an Air Force woman officer—an attorney named Struck. As a result of her challenge, the Department of Defense decided in 1970 that retention and nonretention could be decided on a case by case basis. Waivers would be granted when deemed appropriate by the separate services. The Army implemented this policy in 1971 for married women; in 1973 it made its policy consistent by making waivers available to unmarried woman as well (Deputy Chief of Staff for Personnel, 1976, pp. 7-12). By 1973 some 60 to 80 percent of waivers were being approved. On average about 6 percent of military women left service each year because they were pregnant (Holm, 1982, p. 300).

In June of 1974 the Department of Defense directed all of the services to make discharge for pregnancy voluntary by May 1975. The Army adopted this policy for officers but requested postponement of the policy for enlisted women. The request was denied. However, the Army has, ever since, periodically requested a return to the old policy of involuntary discharge.

Army discussion has come a long way since discharge of "moral offenders" was routinely accepted by both men and women, since policy required the separation of married couples, since unmarried nurses were discharged "dishonorably" for getting pregnant, since service women were given armed guards (Holm, 1982, pp. 85-87). Now the Army's discussion of pregnancy focuses on "readiness," "mission accomplishment," and "deployability." An intermediate kind of discussion that continues today involves complaints about disrupted or exempted training, the need for special medical treatment, the dangers to women and their fetuses, and the adverse effect of pregnancy on unit morale.

One reason morale is negatively affected is that military policy does not permit temporary replacement of pregnant women. This means existing personnel must make up any work a woman cannot do. In addition, men feel that they get extra and more onerous assignments because of protection granted pregnant women. For example, medical staff women may be removed from X-ray work or from wards with contagious illnesses. The expression of this resentment is interesting. The same persons who resent women doing almost but not quite all the work seem to be quite content to have women at home doing no work at all. It appears convergence creates problems and hostility that do not occur when sex roles are kept wholly separate.

It would seem that if the policy of not replacing a pregnant women creates morale problems or work overload, it would be reasonable at least to discuss changing the policy. Replacement needs for pregnancy and maternity are very predictable. However, the policy seems to be taken as given. Proposals for replacement relief are few. One must conclude that sharing the work is either practicable or that some officials hope that by maintaining an irritating policy, they can obtain a different change in policy, that is, the discharge of pregnant women.

The data on pregnancy suggest that there are significantly different pregnancy rates among the services and within different units. In its 1976 Women in the Army study, the Army reported 3.8 percent of its women as pregnant. It also said the average number of days lost from work by a pregnant women was 105, and that 40 percent of women who delivered babies in service separated from service after using their postnatal leave (Deputy Chief of Staff for Personnel, 1976, pp. 7-17). In its 1978 Evaluation of Women in the Army, The Army said "pregnancy is perceived by the Army in the field as the greatest impediment to the full integration of women." It is also declared that 15 percent of enlisted women became pregnant in 1977 and that 39 percent of them carried to term." The report concluded that "in general, unit leaders do not cope well with the entire pregnancy issue." The report's recommendation was that women should be involuntarily separated when "no longer deployed," or that the women should be put on leave without pay other than medical care and be permitted to return only when fit for service and when fully deployable.

Criticism of the post-1975 policy on pregnancy remains vigorous. The general policy has been as follows: (1) pregnant women could be honorably discharged on request, (2) pregnant women would be discharged if they were participating in training they could not continue because of their condition, (3) pregnant women would be discharged if they were pregnant prior to entry. In addition, pregnant women would not be sent overseas, they would work as long as "feasible," and would be placed on "sick-in-quarters status" approximately four weeks before delivery, and would receive up to six weeks convalescent leave. Originally women were allowed to wear civilian maternity clothes but one by one the services created regulation maternity uniforms. Also, one by one the services began to refuse discharge to some women who requested it. Complaints about letting women be discharged "just because" they are pregnant first arose over women who had received expensive specialized training or enlistment bonuses. Thus the military began to move in two directions at once as it reviewed its policies. Both directions would reduce women's choice. First, the military wishes to retain those women it wishes to retain. Second, it wishes to discharge those it wishes to discharge.

By 1981 women had succeeded in establishing the principle that "lost time" was a general rather than a pregnancy problem. The available data then gave pregnancy rates varying from 7 to 10 percent. The data also suggested, however, that even though women lost more time for medical reasons than men, overall lost time was not very different (Assistant Secretary of Defense, 1981, p. 78).

One reason the 1982 Army study on women was held up for so long was the Army's failure to settle on a new pregnancy policy. What finally happened was that the issue was passed to the (civilian) Department of Defense. A proposed policy that met some favor was that first term soldiers who became pregnant would be discharged if an individual determination was made that this was in the Army's best interest. Another Army proposal was that pregnant women be sent to the Inactive Ready Reserve. The Air Force proposed involuntary discharge during the first three years of service. In all cases the crucial constraint on policy change seems to have been legal. That is, changes have been limited principally by what the services estimate the courts will permit (Department of the Army, 1981).

In one memo gathered for the 1982 Army study, it was noted that pregnant women would be evacuated with other noncombatants and also that it was "not indicated that pregnancy has a significant effect on the deployability of

their [the women's] units." This is not "evidence," but it
does raise the question as to whether or not deployability data
are like mobility data—not as available as would be helpful—
and, also, possibly showing that men and women are not so
different in deployability even if their reasons for non-
deployability differ. More than one commander has noted that
non-English-speaking wives who cannot drive are in some
ways as dependent as the child of a single mother. Also, some
problems are the result of too few rather than too many
women. For instance, when women were more widely diffused
with the abolition of the WAC, facilities such as beauty
parlors, which were heavily used when women were concentrated, became an economic burden. Similarly, having to
fly hundreds of miles for a Pap smear or to drive for a day to see
a gynecologist at first looks like a new expense caused by
women. The visibility of these costs does not make them unnecessary nor does it prove women are more expensive than
men whose expenses have long ago faded into budgets as
routine overhead.

Much of the concern about pregnancy has focused on
women's availability for work and on attrition. Being pregnant is something only women do and it does affect time at
work and attrition. The conventional assumption has been
that restrictions should, therefore, be placed on women's
enlistment. However, policy for all women should not be
based on the behavior of some women. The data show marked variation among groups with regard to completion of
enlistment. In particular, black women's attrition is significantly lower than white women's (Nogami, n.d.). Thus to
restrict women's enlistment generally because of white
women's attrition could be to penalize black women for white
women's behavior.

Wouldn't it be ironic if data were to show that single-parent
women were more likely to stay in service than married?
Wouldn't it be ironic if old policies that especially sought to

discharge single mothers and that were rooted in an endeavor to attain respectability in fact worked in direct opposition to the military's goals of readiness and effectiveness?

CONCLUSION

Fitness is not a special problem for women. Pregnancy is, but women seem to have adapted to being pregnant in uniform far better than military men have adapted to their being pregnant. Pregnancy is the first thing male commanders of women complain about. Many women in uniform do not seem to appreciate how distressed men are by maternity uniforms and swollen stomachs. But physical strength testing is the way commanders will probably relieve their anxiety about women. It may be that instead of confronting pregnancy head on, the services will capitalize on strength differences to restrict the number of women in the military and the jobs women may have far beyond the restrictions imposed by the combat exemption. This can be done through job requirements that assume extreme circumstances, through failure to redefine jobs or redesign equipment, and through failure to assume the use of teams rather than individuals. If there were a genuine desire to use women or to give them maximum access, it might well be that a number of military specialties would become as dominated by women as are the nurse corps today. It might also be that certain geographic areas (like Washington, D.C.) would become dominated by women. However, concepts like rotation base and career progression continue to be used to reserve numerous slots women could fill for men. The argument is that to permit women to dominate in the jobs open to them results in discrimination against men!

Physical strength testing has an aura of objectivity that will be difficult to dispel. Coupled with the difficulty of obtaining the technical materials needed to analyze policy decisions, and slick devices like the making of test results advisory rather than mandatory, makes one pessimistic about women's freedom to choose. As noted above, the Air Force is now conducting a study of strength needed to be a pilot. I am sure that if the study is released it will show a substantial number of women are not strong enough to be pilots. I am equally sure that if women were the purchasers of the planes, manufacturers would design planes 100 percent of women would have the strength to fly. There is little evidence that the services are serious about redesigning equipment for women's use. The most recent struggle involves standards the Navy and Marine Corps wished to apply to future pilots. The length of torso, arms and legs was the issue (*Air Force Times,* 1984a, 1984b). Standards in use up to January 1, 1984, excluded 39 percent of college-age women and 7 percent of men. Standards set in January and in place into May excluded 73 percent of women and 13 percent of men. These were rescinded by the Secretary of Navy as "unintentional" discrimination. Nothing was said about safety, the original justification for the change, the remaining discrimination, or Air Force standards that are "close to" the suspended standards (*Norfolk Virginia Pilot,* 1984a, 1984b).

Increased utilization of women was forced on the military by the end of the draft. When and if a draft is reinstituted, I would expect the services to use without complaint men the same size as women the military says now it cannot use. I would also expect the military to find other reasons for limiting the use of women. It appears that it is women's sex and not their biology that the military finds so hard to incorporate.

RESOURCES

Air Force Times. (1984a). *Navy tightens size requirements for flyers.* June 4.

Air Force Times. (1984b). *Tougher size rules for navy fliers rescinded.* June 11.

Assistant Secretary of Defense. (1981). *Women in the military.* Washington, DC: Department of Defense.

Baltimore Sun. (1982). *Army to end coed companies in basic training.* May 4.

Comptroller General of the United States. (1976). *Job opportunities for women in the military: Progress and problems.* Washington, DC: Government Printing Office.

Department of the Army. (1980). *Comprehensive evaluation of total integration of women in the army.* Washington, DC: Government Printing Office.

Department of the Army, Memorandum: DAJA-AL. (1981 June 19). *Changes in pregnancy separation policy.* Washington, DC.

Deputy Chief of Staff for Personnel. (1976). *Women in the army study.* Washington, DC: Headquarters, Department of the Army.

Deputy Chief of Staff for personnel. (1982). *Women in the army policy review.* Washington, DC: Department of the Army.

Good Morning America Radio-T.V. Log. (1982). Washington, DC., September 13.

Gray, J. G. (1970). *The warriors: Reflections on men in battle.* New York: Harper & Row.

Holm, J. (1982). *Women in the military.* Novato, CA: Presidio Press.

Military Manpower Task Force. (1982). *Executive summary.* Washington, DC: Government Printing Office.

Myers, D. C., Gebhardt, D. L., & Fleishman, E. A. (1980). *Development of physical performance standards for army jobs: The job analysts methodology.* Technical Report 446. Washington, DC: United States Army Research Institute for Behavioral and Social Studies.

Nogami, G. (n.d.). *The impact of MOS traditionality and soldier gender on first term attrition.* Alexandria, VA: Army Research Institute.

Robertson, D. W. (1984). Telephone interview. Navy Personnel and Development Center. San Diego, CA, August.

Robertson, D. W., & Trent T. T. (1983). *Predicting muscularly demanding job performance in navy occupations.* San Diego, CA: Annual Convention of the American Psychological Association.

Sternberg, J. J., Greenberg, F. & Fuchs, E. F. (1958). *Identifying army jobs suitable for WAC assignment.* Research Studies 58-3. Washington DC: Army Personnel Research Office.

Stiehm, J. H. (1981). *Bring me men and women.* Berkeley, CA: University of California Press.

Treadwell, M. E. (1954). *U.S. army in world war II, The women's army corps.* Washington, DC: Office of the Chief of Military History, Department of the Army.

United States Air Force. (1983). *DCS/MP fact book*. Washington, DC: Department of the Air Force.

United States Army Administration Center. (1978). *Evaluation of women in the army. Executive summary* (1-29). Fort Benjamin Harrison, Indiana.

United States Army Research Institute. (1977). *Women content in units force development test (MAX WAC)*. AD A050022.

United States Army Research Institute. (1978). *Women content in the army reforger 77 (REF-WAC 77)*. Special Report S-7. Alexandria, VA: Army Research Institute.

Washington Post. (1984). *General Vessey sees women as biggest military change*. February 3.

10

WOMEN AS "AT RISK" REPRODUCERS: BIOLOGY, SCIENCE, AND POPULATION IN U.S. FOREIGN POLICY

Jane S. Jaquette
Kathleen A. Staudt

This chapter analyzes some of the ways in which the scientific paradigm and the biological models of medicine and demography affect women by their influence over population policy, an important aspect of our foreign policy in the Third World. We will argue both that the scientific paradigm has significantly shaped U.S. population policy and that it has had specifically negative effects on women. We further suggest that the detrimental impact of U.S. population policy on women, inherent in the scientific and technological approach, has been strongly reinforced by bureaucratic decision making, itself a product of scientific influence. The single-mindedness of the policies we criticize did not arise simply from the overzealousness of one individual, however comforting it may be to have a specific target for our frustration, but derived from approaches, habits of thought, and patterns of decision making that are deeply embedded in our society, and that will consequently be difficult to change.

Authors' Note: We would like to thank Irene Diamond, Abraham Lowenthal, and Jane Rubin for their thoughtful comments on this chapter. The errors and obstinacies that remain, of course, are ours.

The scientific approach to population policy has made a key difference in a number of ways. It has determined the definition of the population problem and supported techno-logical rather than structural solutions. It has mandated a medical relationship between population programs and women, with all the attendant asymmetries that have characterized relations between a male-dominated medical establishment and female patients. It has encouraged the treatment of women as objects, to be manipulated by social engineering and experimented on in contraceptive research. Thus bureaucratic decision making and the scientific paradigm have key elements in common, elements that com-bine to produce the greatest distance between bureaucrats and medical experts, on the one hand, and the "target population" of fertile women, on the other.

In the Agency for International Development (AID),[1] women are viewed primarily as "at risk reproducers." This biological definition of women has coincided with their exclu-sion from the highly technical, productivity- and growth-oriented forms of assistance. Despite the 1973 congressional mandates that AID promote "growth with equity" to the "rural poor majority" and "integrate women in develop-ment," it is virtually only through population policy and related maternal/child health programs that AID reaches women. This overwhelming orientation toward women as mothers reinforces a narrow view of women and ultimately prevents any genuine redistribution of aid resources between men and women.[2]

U.S. POPULATION POLICY:
A BRIEF HISTORY

General Draper's report on military aid (Ravenholt, 1969, p. 51) recommended as early as 1959 that the U.S. government provide population assistance to nations that requested it. This did not become official policy until Richard Gardner made a speech containing an offer of such assistance before the U.N. General Assembly in December, 1962, which was confirmed by President Kennedy in April 1963. President Johnson announced a program to "seek new ways to help deal with the explosion of world population and the growing scarcity in world resources" in January 1965, which provided the executive mandate for AID's involvement. The program grew rapidly, from $2.1 million in FY 1965 to $50 million in FY 1969, leveling off at $200 million per annum in the late 1970s. In 1966 the U.S. Congress amended the Foreign Assistance Act of 1969 and included specific provisions in the Food for Peace Act of 1966 "to assist voluntary family planning programs in countries requesting such help (Ravenholt, 1969, p. 53).

Initially, AID—chief U.S. bilateral assistance agency to more than sixty developing countries—was reluctant to become involved in birth control programs. As a relatively unpopular agency dealing with an issue that lacks widespread public support in the United States, AID is heavily dependent upon what has been termed a "four-fold Congressional obstacles course" in authorizing and appropriating assistance. For this, AID must not only maintain good relations with Congress, but also create constituencies that assist it through these hurdles.[3] In the early 1960s, AID feared Catholic opposition in Congress to overt family planning. Indeed, only in 1963 did a birth control advocate replace the birth control opponent who directed AID's health program. Moreover, AID itself had placed contraceptive devices on the prohibited list for commodity assistance since 1948.[4] Such self-limitations are explained by the bureaucratic protectionist strategies AID pursues.

Important changes in AID's political environment prompted greater risk-taking on AID's part. Various congressional committees, above and beyond those monitoring foreign assistance, aired population matters. A bureaucratically aggressive epidemiologist, Dr. Reimert T. ("Ray") Ravenholt, was hired in 1966 and pushed vigorously for removing contraceptives from the prohibited list and for increasing funding, particularly earmarked funding, in defiance of higher level agency executives who jealously guard the autonomy of their internal budget process. Earmarked funding was perceived to have cut into other programs at a time of declining appropriations. The late 1960s and early 1970s were low points in AID's already minimal popularity, given AID's association with an overall foreign policy that included opposition to Allende in Chile, AID's large Vietnam program, and counterinsurgency programs elsewhere. By contrast, the population issue was on the upswing, and new visibility for AID's role here became part of a strategy for agency survival.

Bureaucratic changes reflected the new emphasis. Within AID, the Population Branch of the Health Service became the Population Service. The Bureau of Population and Humanitarian Assistance was created in 1972, in population's "heyday," with dramatic increases in specialized staff in Washington and in the country Missions. The purpose of family planning had been spelled out by Congress in Title X of the Foreign Assistance Act of 1967 as follows:

> Voluntary family planning programs to provide individual couples with the knowledge and medical facilities to plan their family size in accordance with their own moral convictions and the latest medical information can make a substantial contribution to improve health, family stability, greater individual opportunity, economic development, a sufficiency of food, and a higher standard of living. (Ravenholt, 1969, p. 54)

At the first population conference held by the Organization for Economic Cooperation and Development (OECD) in

1968, Ravenholt outlined "fundamental principles" of AID's population policy: (1) to give aid in response to specific requests "to stimulate and supplement a country's own efforts" (Ravenholt, 1969, p. 56), (2) to consider only programs in which individual participation is "wholly voluntary" as eligible for support, and (3) to provide needed assistance on request rather than insist on "any specific population policy" for another country. These self-imposed restrictions are carefully geared to both popular consensus and foreign acceptability.

What emerged from this set of directives was a program of funding, half of which was bilateral and half of which went through intermediaries such as the United Nations Fund for Population Activities and the International Planned Parenthood Federation, to multilateralize U.S. assistance in this area. In addition, funds were given to smaller organizations seeking more innovative programs. Substantial resources were invested in research efforts, both in applied demography (what factors appear to affect birth rates and the likelihood that women will "accept" contraceptives) and medical research for improved contraceptive methods. This commitment to research was dictated in part by the need to understand the various factors relevant to an effective policy, but early funding strategies must be understood primarily in terms of AID's constituency-building efforts, and the fact that the Population Office was unable to spend all of its appropriations.

As might be expected, in an area combining intense personal value conflicts on the one hand, and ambivalence about the U.S. role and power on the other, the population program has been subjected to a variety of criticisms. On one end of the spectrum, as exhibited most dramatically during the World Population Conference in Bucharest in 1974, the United States is accused of doing too much, of mounting a "genocidal" policy directed at the nonwhite peoples of the world.[5] At the other end, critics charge that voluntary family planning programs cannot make a measurable dent in rapid population growth rates that threaten to outrun food supplies and the ecological balance of the planet. These critics have accused AID of doing much too little and have advocated stronger measures, including withholding food aid from countries that do not have effective programs of population control.[6]

Ravenholt's own approach, which could be called a policy of inundation, emphasized maximum availability of contraceptives. Inundation has provoked criticism on grounds that the popular female contraceptives (the pill and the IUD) cannot be provided in the absence of public health support without endangering the health of the women using them (Sullivan, 1978). Others have argued that the Population Office's purchasing policies allowed unethical drug companies to "dump" contraceptives (such as the Dalkon Shield or Depo-Provera) that were not FDA approved, or for which approval had been withdrawn,[7] thus exhibiting a double standard for women in rich and poor countries.

The description of these programs, which were generally popular in the United States, often exhibit a quantitative bias and a mechanical notion of bureacratic output as a measure of success. AID's inundation approach was summarized thus in 1968:

> During the past decade oral contraceptives have far outpaced other forms of contraception in LDC's assisted by AID. Through FY 1976 AID had purchased more than 450 million monthly cycles of oral contraceptives. The price has been kept below 15 cents per monthly cycle by consolidated central purchasing of guaranteed quantities of oral contraceptives. Since the advent of lubricated, colored condoms, the usage rate of this method has increased rapidly—more than 8 million gross have been purchased by AID. IUDs continue to be an impor-

tant element of the program, but have not increased in usage as have pills and condoms. In order to make sure that everyone has contraceptive services consistent with their ethical and religious beliefs, AID also provides diaphragms, spermacides, thermometers, charts, and support for the utilization of the safe period methods. (Boynton, 1978, pp.78-79)

Although a variety of methods were available, the pill and the IUD were more heavily promoted. Abortion was not among those, as it was explicitly barred by the Helms Amendment. Sterilization was encouraged, but injectable progesterones like Depo-Provera, which had not received FDA approval, could not be supplied by AID directly. UNFPA and IPPF, however, were free to do so.

ECOLOGY AND EVOLUTION:
DEFINING THE POPULATION CRISIS
AND CREATING POLITICAL CONSENSUS

Books began to appear in the mid-1950s calling attention to an unprecedented explosion in population growth, warning that population in the near or medium term would outrun the resources to feed and maintain it (e.g., Sax, 1955, 1956). However, it was not until Paul Ehrlich's *The Population Bomb,* published under the auspices of the Sierra Club in 1968, that popular attention was focused on the issue. Aspects of Ehrlich's approach have remained fixed in the public's mind: that we are entering a severe Malthusian crisis, that the solution to that crisis can only be found in population control, that we have the technical means to reduce birth rates significantly, and that we can mount an effective policy if we create the political will to do so.

Ehrlich's (1968, p. xi) prologue set the tone: "The battle to feed all of humanity is over. In the 1970s and 1980s hundreds of millions of people will starve to death in spite of any crash programs embarked upon now." A central feature of Ehrlich's approach is the use of "scenarios," set in the United States, to aid the reader in imagining the effects of population in the future. In one, an average housewife (of a university professor!) is trying to feed her family in 1983, not coincidentally one year shy of Orwell's "deadline" for Western civilization:

> Jane Gilsinger was not worried about anyone's nuclear capacity [the previous paragraph had her husband worried about development of Japanese nuclear capacity and the possibility of war]. Like most American housewives in 1983, she was preoccupied with how to feed her family adequately and safely. George made a good living. ... Still, at a cost of $12 a pound, steak had become a memory for them as for most other Americans. She didn't really understand what the failure of the corn crop had to do with beef prices—but apparently it was a lot. (Ehrlich, 1968, pp. 52-53)

She then asks her husband about the president's plan to introduce food rationing, and husband endeavors to educate her on the full extent of the crisis:

> Even with rationing, a lot of Americans are going to starve to death unless this climate change reverses. We've seen the trends clearly since the early 1970s, but nobody believed it would happen here, even after the 1976 Latin American famine and the Indian Dissolution. Almost a billion human beings starved to death in the last decade, and we managed to keep the lid on by a combination of good luck and brute force. (Ehrlich, 1968, p.53)

The Population Bomb was intended to bring expert opinion to bear on a situation that required crisis planning. It had the effect of mobilizing a constituency in support for population programs in the United States and, more significantly, abroad. Yet the sexism and racism of Ehrlich's appeal have persisted in the public's understanding of the issue. In conditions of scarcity, the wealthy countries can justify the use of "brute force." Men are the scientists who can understand the complex relationships relevant to this issue, but women cannot even see the linkage between the supply of corn and the price of beef. The split between the far-seeing "scientific" rationality of man and the day to day reproductive irrationality of woman is at the heart of the analysis.[8]

To enhance his credibility, Ehrlich appeals to "scientific fact." Statistics are used to show how small differences in population growth rates will sharply reduce the time it takes for a population to double, the demographic significance of the fact that over 50 percent of the world's population is under the age of 15, and the dramatic impact of modernization on reducing death rates even in less developed regions. Ehrlich further argues that potential increases in food production are very limited and that pollution levels are increasing geometrically, creating a statistical image of disaster, similar to that of the Club of Rome's equally influential model of impending global breakdown in *The Limits to Growth* (Meadows et al., 1972). An additional message is sent: Scientists can see these trends, using their specialized expertise, and scientists must have a role in finding a solution to the problems they have identified if the world is to be saved from imminent self-destruction.

If Ehrlich is aware of the traditional uses of Malthusian arguments by the rich to limit the demands of the poor (Harvey, 1974; Segal, 1973), he gives us no sign of this. Despite his implicit extension of his case to the entire globe, he does not recognize the importance of cultural differences, particularly as they affect women's needs and motivations. All women are seen to be like "Jane"—that is, nonproductive, nonthinking women with nothing to do with their spare time but have children. Ironically, his negative assessment of women's limited choices will give the population movement common ground with the feminist movement, critical for its own reasons of the family and of women's reproductive roles.

Ehrlich lumps women together as reproducers of the species. In evolutionary terms we are all equal, and evolutionary science is substituted for an understanding of the cultural context of human fertility:

> A self-reinforcing selective trend developed—a trend toward increased brain size.

> But there was, quite literally, a rub. Babies had bigger and bigger heads. There were limits to how large a pelvis could conveniently become. To make a long story short, the strategy of evolution was not to make a woman bell-shaped and relatively immobile, but to accept the problem of having babies who were helpless for a long period while their brains grew after birth. How could the mother defend and care for her infant during its unusually long period of helplessness? She couldn't, unless Papa hung around. The girls are still working on that problem, but an essential step was to get rid of the short, well-defined breeding season characteristic of most mammals. The year-round sexuality of the human female, the long period of infant dependence on the female, the evolution of the family group, all are at the roots of our present problem....Sex in human beings is necessary for the production of young, but it is also evolved to ensure their successful rearing....Our urge to reproduce is hopelessly entwined with most of our other urges. (Ehrlich, 1968, p. 14)

It is not clear if readers are to conclude from this that women are biologically at fault for the year-round manipulation of male urges and their imposition of marriage, or simply that we should not get bogged down in the variety of cultural determinants of fertility behavior.

For AID, family planning now became the priority, separate from and prior to AID's stated goal of promoting stable economic development. State Department Deputy Assistant Secretary for Environment and Population Affairs Christian Herter testified that "without continued resolve... unchecked population growth will continue to contribute to social malaise, unemployment, internal tensions, and possible conflicts among neighbors (U.S. House of Representatives, 1976, p. 628). Their language tended to be crisis-oriented, militaristic, and designed to eliminate value considerations. Economists' cost/benefit analysis on the "number of births averted" figured from $150 to $1,000 savings in their formulae (Montgomery, 1979, p. 45). Dean Rusk referred to our "losing battle to feed the hungry," and argued that population problems could be "as dangerous as nuclear problems" (U.S. Senate, 1967, p. 790), and Senator Clark equated the Vietnamese refuge camps with "rabbit warrens" (U.S. Senate, 1967, p. 619). Charts were carted to Capitol Hill with figures on excess numbers of births over deaths per year, week, day, and hour; AID's 1971 report on population even calculated this down to the second (Agency for International Development, 1971, p. 5)! "Science" had been mobilized to define the crisis and help solidify to political consensus for a major investment of resources and a new foreign policy thrust.

MEDICINE: FERTILITY
VERSUS TECHNIQUE

Ravenholt's (1969) inundation strategy—the initial and primary strategy of the Population Office—gave doctors the key roles in inventing and promoting particular contraceptive methods and designing and staffing the "delivery systems" by which most female contraceptives—the IUD, the pill, sterilization, and abortion—are provided to women. Barbara Ehrenreich and Dierdre English have already identified some of the effects that the development of "scientific medicine" in the nineteenth century had on women. The victory of "scientific" medicine over other forms of healing made possible the development of a medical profession that restricted entry in general, but from which women (who had been midwives and herbalists in the first half of the century) were virtually proscribed. In addition, the profession relied heavily on the earnings gained from treating middle- and upper-class women, for "invalidism and physical and emotional frailty" were an integral part of the Victorian feminine ideal (Brown, 1979; Delamont & Duffin, 1978). As E. Richard Brown (1979) notes in his study of the *Rockefeller Medicine Men*, the nineteenth century bequeathed to women an image of weakness as a result of their reproductive systems. Women's illnesses were associated with their reproductive organs, which meant that upper- and middle-class women were subjected to unnecessary surgery and excessive medical attention, whereas lower-class women received little or no medical care:

> Gynecological surgeons preyed upon the supposedly delicate nature of the upper-middle-class women and the terrible consequences of having a "tipped" uterus or sexual appetite. Hysterectomies, ovariotomies, and cliteridectomies were prescibed for these and other female maladies. (Brown, 1979, p. 92)

In the United States and overseas, the medical establishment is deeply involved in population programs. In most countries, only licensed doctors can prescribe pills, sterilize patients, or perform abortions (Gray, 1974), although the pressure to expand programs has outrun available manpower and paramedical staffs have been trained to insert IUDs and in China to perform abortions. In contrast to the Victorian United States, medical "profits" are relatively low, and doctors do not treat patients almost exclusively drawn from the middle class. But the hierarchical relationship between doctor and patient, the view that female fertility is a kind of sickness and the primary reason for health services to treat women, and the relative exclusion of women from the medical profession are factors common to both situations.

The influx of funds into population programs has ensured employment for a significant class of medical and paramedical bureaucrats, mostly male, at the national and international level. It has not reduced the gap between women's needs and the objectives—and practices—of population programs. AID's postpartum program, proudly described in annual reports, teaches women about family planning techniques in the obstetrics ward. Such women are definitely part of the "target" group, obviously fertile, and acceptance rates are high. These glowing reports usually begin with the obligatory tribute to Margaret Sanger, emphasizing human rights, women's rights, and choice (Agency for International Development, 1971). But such programs are designed to reach women when most vulnerable to these usually male experts. The language used to describe women often depersonalizes them, labeling them "acceptors" or "targets." In setting goals for contraceptive use, the term is "number of monthly cycles" reached. Although it pays lip service to the need for studies on women's opportunities, family concepts, values, and the like, AID's Population Office does otherwise in actual practice. When members of Congress queried Ravenholt on children as "social security," his response was how he had heard this "ad nauseam.... Ask women in maternity wards. They want help" (U.S. House of Representatives, 1976, p.736).

In the *Rockefeller Medicine Men,* Brown links scientific medicine and capitalism. Medicine is a means of cultural domination: "Medicine can convert and colonize the heathen" (Brown, 1979, p.122). Medical research institutes funded by Rockefeller were the "temples of the new religion," each helping to "spread abroad in the public mind a respect for science and for the scientific method" (Brown, 1979, p.127). Brown concludes that "scientific medicine, as part of the fervent campaign for science, helped spread *industrial culture,* albeit a *capitalist* industrial culture, throughout the land and indeed the world" (Brown, 1979, p. 17).

Part of the explanation he offers for this is the identity between the scientific world-view and industrialism, both of which are alien to traditional cultures. Scientific medicine turns attention away from competing values and ideologies, focusing instead on the research for appropriate technique:

> Members of any society or social class whose existence is intimately tied to industrialism will find scientific medicine's explanations of health and disease more appealing than mystical belief systems. The precise analysis of the human body into its component parts is analogous to the industrial organization of production. From the perspective of an industrialist, scientific method seems to offer the limitless potential for effectiveness that science and technology provide in manufacturing and social organization. Just as industry depends upon science for technically powerful tools, science-based medicine and its mechanistic concepts of the body and disease should yield powerful tools with which to identify, eliminate, and prevent agents of disease and correct malfunctions of the body.

> Rockefeller money did not support medical research that investigated the relationship of social factors to health and disease. ... It ignored the impact of the social, economic and physical environment on disease and health. (Brown, 1979, p. 119)

In the Third World the process is reversed and the successes of scientific medicine pave the way for industrial capitalism. We would argue that, through the population program, women are the front-line recipients of this assault.

The process of advancing capitalism through scientific medicine and advancing medicine through population control has two significant implications for women. "Technique" has translated into the emphasis on contraceptive devices—how to make them effective (if not always safe), and how women might be induced to use them—and not on the broader political, economic, or social context, and not on a primary commitment to women's definition of their own needs.

Second, the convergence of medical and industrial values has had an impact on sexuality in general, and women's sexuality in particular. It is worth asking how science and modernization, or more specifically urbanization and industrialization, combined historically to create a new sexual economy and the moral underpinnings for a new industrial order. We would argue that there are parallels between the population control movement of our generation and the "purity movement" of the nineteenth century:

> The metaphors and symbols of the (purity) reformers expressed external fears of Oedipal conflict and the potentially destructive power of sexuality. But they also provided an ideal sexual and moral regimen for the newly urbanized Northeastern middle class, some of whom listened to their lectures, read their books, and participated in health reform organizations. The purity advocates' belief in a closed energy system and their insistence that work and energy be directed toward socially acceptable goals helped industrialize and bureaucratize a once agricultural people. The purity reformers stressed the values of deferred gratification, hard work, sobriety, seriousness, individualism, and good health.

In the precarious world of antebellum America, these habits
were valuable attributes, for too early a marriage, too many
children, or too dissipated a life could mean financial and
social ruin. (Sokolow, 1983, p. 93; on "control" see Freund,
1982)

Female sexuality is under traditional, often patriarchal
control in most Third World societies. Modernization and
population control apparently share the goal of restraining
male sexuality as well, in the interests of "seriousness,"
"sobriety," and upward social mobility. And, learning to
"control" sexuality—by taking the pill, replacing the IUD
regularly, or going through the kinds of future calculations
that are required to decide on sterilization—is learning to
control "nature," to calculate, to "reckon" costs and time.
If nineteeth century U.S. history is a valid example, control
of male sexuality was an important element of increased
female power (Rosenberg, 1982) and consonant with increased
female autonomy in the family, the key element that, according to historian Carl Degler (1980, p. 189) explains fertility decline in the nineteenth century, a decline that occurred
despite the lack of safe and reliable contraceptives.

A woman's capacity to control her fertility—with or
without male knowledge—has potentially profound implications for the traditional patriarchal patterns of male-female
relations. But when women are taught to see contraceptive
methods as just a technique, they will be less able to conceive
of control over their own fertility as a means to independence
or as a power resource. The close association of family planning and medical science makes U.S. promotion of contraceptive use much more palatable to Third World elites and
reduces any potential danger to the existing distribution of
power between the sexes. And if Degler is right, policies that
do not challenge that power ratio are unlikely to succeed.

BUREAUCRACY AND THE
POLICY OF INUNDATION

The Population Office's declared policy emphasizing supply of contraceptives, labeled by both its supporters and detractors as "inundation," came under attack during the 1970s from a variety of critics. Some saw AID's policy of distributing contraceptives in bulk as dangerous to women's health and as an inappropriate image for U.S. foreign policy (e.g., Ehrenreich, Dowi, & Menken, 1979). Many criticized the Office for failing to take broader developmental issues regarding women into account. Others argued that the program wasted resources in creating and delivering a supply for which it had not created an adequate demand.

Many saw inundation as the personal creation of Dr. "Ray" Ravenholt, arguing that he was too zealous to see the population issue in its broader developmental context or that his attitudes about women were extremely sexist. There is no doubt that Dr. Ravenholt's priorities—or biases—with regard to Population Office strategy ruled the day. We would argue, however, that different leadership might well have settled on the same strategy. Any office given this specific mandate in this area would have moved in the same direction. Inundation is a typical bureaucratic product, not simply a result of the demographic and medical biases of those who made population policy in the 1970s. Specialized offices survive in AID (or any other bureaucracy subject to congressional or budgetary review) because they perform their tasks visibly and efficiently, or can create the image of doing so. Under this hypothesis, any expenditures made by the Office that are not directed toward the maximum dispersion of contraceptive devices (provided that there is also reasonable proof that they are used) are subject to criticism on cost-effectiveness grounds. As early as the 1967 Population Crisis Hearings, the direct approach was praised as being "simplest" (managerial-wise) and cheapest."[9]

But the Population Office had to face the fact that supply did not always create demand, and this dictated that some proportion of its budget would go toward research intended to increase use—including efforts to create more acceptable contraceptive devices, and pilot programs to develop effective delivery systems, attitudinal research, and analysis of the social variables that condition fertility decisions. Also, changes were taking place in the international and domestic political contexts through the central Population Office's ten-year reign. Besides the new mandates of 1973, which gave the egalitarian advocates inside the agency some legitimacy, a variety of United Nations conferences criticized both the U.S. overemphasis on population control and the worldwide neglect of women in the development process. The International Women's Year Conference, expanded into the International Women's Decade, stimulated the expansion of international feminism and mobilized specific women-in-development and feminist domestic constituencies. In addition, there was growth, diversity, and hybridization in the population constituency itself. Over-laying all this was the periodic reorganization within the AID, efforts to "decentralize" to regional Bureaus and Missions during the mid 1970s, and various opportunities for bureaucratic players to vie for the superiority of their definition and control over population policy. This resulted in competition between the "demand-siders," also known as "developmentalists," as they called themselves, and the "supply-siders" epitomized by Ravenholt. Years of careful maneuvering shifted the balance of bureaucratic power.

In the 1976 AID policy paper, "U.S. Population Related Assistance," analysts concluded that the direct supply of contraceptives was not sufficiently effective in reducing world birth rates, but that broader policy reforms were needed to support smaller families, development, and variables that increased demand. AID submitted language to Congress leading to the creation of Section 104. d of the international Development and Food Assistance Act, which called upon AID to administer all AID projects so as to build motivation for lower fertility by modifying conditions that support higher fertility. Internally, 104.d prompted new internal procedures that required that "fertility impacts" of projects be considered (joining the procedural environmental-, economic-, and woman-impact statements). The responsibility for oversight fell to the Policy Bureau rather than the Population Office.

DEMOGRAPHY: BIOLOGY
UNDER SOCIAL CONTROL

The move away from the inundation strategy meant decreasing dependence on medical science and its biological image of women and increasing reliance on the science of demography. Although demography is based on the general assumption that the human desire to reproduce is a primary drive, its sociological approach has provided a means to identify and explore the relationships among the "factors" that are correlated with increases or decreases in birthrates. Demography's major contribution to policy has been its theory of "demographic transition": societies tend to achieve lower birth rates, whether or not modern contraceptives are available, as they become more "developed"—that is, as they become more industrialized, urbanized, and adopt "modern" values.

As development is a complex process—and population policies are not directed toward solving the "development problem" in the Third World—a number of hypotheses have

been developed to identify the key variable that will explain
lowered fertility. Knowledge of and access to contraceptive
techniques do not predict actual use of contraceptives, so the
search has spread to the factors that affect household decision making and to the education, employment, and legal
status of women. Household analysis—the "new home economics"—has looked at the present and future economic
value of children, with the result that the most significant
decline in birth rates, associated with urbanization, industrialization, and a sustained level of economic development, is explained by demographers in a large part by the
changing "cost/benefit" ratio of child rearing: as societies
modernize, the cost of raising children increases, but they are
less essential—and less likely to support parents in their old
age.

The majority of countries, including those with the highest
birth rates, have not achieved sufficient modernization to
have entered this phase, however. In these countries, the
search for the magic variable has proven frustrating (Birdsall, 1976). This makes it difficult for those who want to
argue, within AID and other donor organizations, that improvements in female status, education, and employment will
bring about the much desired reduction in fertility. The effort
continues, however, for the tactic of slipping "women in
development" in under the population issue is made necessary by the sad fact that there is a much deeper national consensus on population control than there is on U.S. involvement in improving the status of women.

Repeated studies, however, have failed to prove a consistently reliable relationship between "women's status"
variables and fewer births. Nancy Birdsall (1976, p. 705) concludes that female employment, for example, is "neither a
necessary nor sufficient condition for fertility reduction,"
noting that "studies in Puerto Rico, Chile, Costa Rica, and
Taiwan indicated that female employment did appear to

result in lowered fertility; but in the Phillippines and Thailand, female working status actually appeared to increase fertility." Some studies have argued that cultural or ethnic values surrounding reproduction may be more significant than status variables.[10] Ultimately, it is not whether women work, but whether they leave their homes to work, that seems to make the difference—but who knows how long that "social law" will hold (Birdsall, 1976).[11] Similar complications exist with other variables that might logically be thought to be at the heart of the decision on family size, including infant mortality rates and various approaches to "cost/benefit" household calculations on the economic worth of children. As a result, policymakers have contracted a series of studies using multivariate analysis to sort through what is clearly a complex set of factors.

The conventional feminist critique of social scientific studies in support of modernization efforts is that they have systematically excluded women. For example, census definitions defining work as paid, full-time, and outside the home exclude women from labor force statistics and thus discount the significance of their labor in programs designed to increase productivity or provide training, credit, or social services (e.g., Dixon, 1982). Similarly, women's contributions in agriculture have been invisible and their potential role in ameliorating a global food crisis underestimated.

Women's roles in reproduction cannot be so easily dismissed. The way they are included in population research, however, illustrates the flaws in the social scientific approach. First, both the aggregate data analyses of demography and the "rational household" assumptions of the new home economics distance the policy-oriented "observers" from the "observed"—the women whose fertility behavior they are attempting to predict. Second, researchers do not always bother to figure in variables relating to women. As a review of AID-commissioned studies on fertility concludes:

The seven socioeconomic variables which they ultimately identified as being most powerfully associated with fertility decline are: adult literacy, primary and secondary school enrollment, life expectancy, infant mortality, percentage of males in the nonagricultural labor force, GNP per capita, and percent population in cities of 100,000 and above. They are quick to point out that improvements in the role and status of women are missing from this list because of the difficulty of finding appropriate data. (Sinding, 1979, p. 6)

A U.N. representative testified at the Population and Development hearings that we know little about the status of women because it is linked with culture and is not a quantitative variable, unlike infant mortality (U.S. Congress, 1978).[12]

Third, although Ravenholt recognized that women's literacy, employment, and income influence fertility, such recognition played little part in his Office's funding priorities. A GAO-commissioned study reported that only 4 percent of the Population Office's research budget from 1965 to 1976 went to research on fertility determinants (General Accounting Office, 1978, p. 51).

The fourth criticism is more radical. Demographic models view the fertility behavior of individuals as a consequence of biology conditioned by the interplay of social "variables." An alternative, "women-centered" model would work with families or with women directly to understand a series of such decisions from the inside out.

Most population experts begin with "logical hypotheses" about fertility decisions based on their Western experience rather than by immersing themselves in the real life decision environments of women—much less Third World women. By one account, 75 percent of the studies have used women as the unit of analysis, though couples and "households" have been credited with the decisions, thus ignoring the conflict between men and women on such issues. Male pronatal values have been dismissed as machismo—those irrational (and inferior) attitudes that wiser *gringos,* of course, have long overcome.

Theories and aggregate data, not the complexities of female experience, are the starting point of such studies. Social engineering attempts to manipulate them into having fewer children: "independent variables" are the social engineer's props—few in number and amenable to government "interventions." Politically, it is easier to promise "development" than to invest scarce resources in women. And, like Jane Gilsinger in Ehrlich's scenario, women are seen as objects of policy manipulation, incapable of direct understanding or direct action.

This image of female passivity is further reinforced by the single-minded definition of women in this literature as reproducers, a modern echo of the Aristotelean view that women are mere receptacles of the male life-force, and not full citizens of the polis. Occasionally, the arbitrariness of particular policy prescriptions reveals the tenuousness of the model, as when Edward Pohlberg advises that child-care services should not be provided for women in order to increase their "role conflict," and thus reduce their desire to have children (cited in Gray, 1974, p. 179) or when antinatalist arguments are used to rationalize failures to improve women's health.

Sandra Tangri's (1976) feminist critique finds population policies manipulative, but argues that "some degree of manipulation is almost inevitably a feature of any social intervention." Tangri (1976, p. 901) suggests that putting female personnel in charge of programs involving women lessens the degree of manipulation because women are "reciprocally vulnerable." This bold statement of the affirmative action case[13] does not hide the fact that Tangri has caved in to the social scientific rationale. By suggesting that, because females do the manipulating, "reciprocity" exists, she is providing feminist legitimacy to the top-down, social engineering approach. The fact that women manage population programs does not eliminate class, race, and other differences that distinguish the interests, experiences, and vulnerability of women with professional training from those of the women whose fertility they are "managing."

In sum, demography, like social science in general, distances the observers from the observed, rationalizes manipulation, and is used to justify the continued exclusion of most women from taking direct, knowledgeable, self-aware control over their own fertility. In extreme cases, scientific rationales can hide other agendas that would receive less political support—or might even come under attack if they were articulated. Thomas Littlewood (1977, p. 147) reports an interview in the United States with a "top lieutenant" of the family planning program in a southern state. In response to a question about whether there were "racial genocidal" motives to the program, the official replied:

> Not at the time. I must admit that now I have some reservations about the possibility there may have been some genocidal motives on the part of some people. I really don't think it was a national genocidal policy. But, as in the case with many technological and scientific advancements, there are unanticipated spinoffs.... When you look at the service design, the blacks were relatively over-served.... The primary recruiting area for patients—the catchment area, we called it—was the postpartum ward of the large teaching hospital, the charity hospital.... That kind of recruitment was not extended to the local Baptist hospitals where the medically indigent whites were delivering.

Other "spinoffs" may be more intentional. Ravenholt and Ehrlich, among many others in the population movement, have made no bones about the fact that they fear the possibility of violence between rich and poor nations if the growth rate is not brought under control. In Ehrlich's (1968, p. 9) words, overpopulation "does not normally mean too many people for the area of a country. *Overpopulation occurs when numbers threaten values,*" that is, when *their* numbers threaten *our* values.

CONCLUSION AND EPILOGUE

It would be trivial to say that U.S. population policy has been dominated by a biological definition of women—it could not have been otherwise. What we have tried to argue is that the biological image characteristics of the medical side of the population issue during Ravenholt's tenure was reinforced by bureaucratic imperatives. This view is reinforced, we believe, by the fact that Sharon Camp of the Population Crisis Committee could argue in 1979 that AID should return to full-scale support of the inundation approach backed by biomedical research to improve contraceptive techniques.

> Some would go so far as to suggest that funds appropriated for population planning could be more effectively used for health, agriculture, or women's projects, even though population funds represent only about 16 percent of bilateral assistance and less than 5 percent of our total development effort. ... Pessimistic estimates of motivation levels and family planning acceptance also lead to a strong emphasis on research—both on social science research to identify other determinants of fertility and on bio-medical research to identify methods of contraception which require lower levels of motivation. (U.S. Senate, 1979, p. 273)

She fends off the claims of other offices that would divert funds from the contraceptive program and chides AID for its internal controversies that have reduced congressional confidence and commitment.

> I have purposefully carried this argument *ad absurdum* to underline two points. First, most of the AID budget is already devoted to those things that are supposed to increase demand for family planning. We should not convert them into pseudo-population programs; neither should we rob the population program to support these other goals. Second, we should not become immersed in major social science research projects on the determinants of fertility which provide us with no useful recommendations for specific, cost-effective action. (U.S. Senate, 1979, p. 273)

She concludes: "Any effort to improve the well-being of women now in their reproductive years and to reduce population growth rates must place primary emphasis on the incremental improvement and wider distribution of all effective contraceptive methods already available," adding, "In this respect we must pay tribute to the Office of Population for moving single-mindedly toward this objective despite enormous obstacles and continuing controversy" (U.S. Senate, 1979, p. 274).

In this chapter, we have attempted to outline the way in which demographic and medical approaches to defining and solving the population problem have made women the targets of family planning policies rather than providing the opportunity for women to take control of their own fertility. It is our view that these approaches are manipulative and reinforcing of traditional patterns of female dependency, despite their liberating potential. There is considerable congruence between AID's population policies and other "modernizing" forces that undermine Third World interests and contribute to U.S. dominance. Critics of the population program have decried "U.S. imperialism," but not the scientific and "rational" underpinnings of that power, or the power of hierarchical, "policymaking" bureaucracies in general.

An exception is Kingsley Davis, who has attacked the technological fixation of population policy, and who argued, even in 1967, that the placing of population programs "in the hands of respected medical personnel" was an "evasion" of the issue:

> In viewing negative attitudes toward birth control as due to ignorance, apathy and outworn tradition, and "mass communication" as the solution to the motivation problem, family planners tend to ignore the complexity of social life. If it were admitted that the creation and care of new human beings is socially motivated, like other forms of behavior, by being a part of the system of rewards and punishments that is built into human relationships, and thus is bound up with the individual's economic and personal interests, it would be apparent that the social structure and economy must be changed before a deliberate reduction in the birth rate can be achieved. (Davis, 1967, p. 733)

The changes that would be necessary, Davis (1967, p. 734) concludes, would be "changes in the structure of the family, in the position of women, and in sexual mores."

Unfortunately, the point of Davis's article is that "family planning" is not enough. "Population control" is necessary, and the techniques advised include strong sanctions against unmarried mothers, pressures to postpone marriage, and increasing the costs of having children after marriage while making all forms of birth control, including abortion, easily available. To do this, the government must use its economic power and its control over education, combining economic rewards and punishments with a new system of social rewards and punishments taught through the schools. Taken to its ultimate conclusion this way, the new home economics would substitute coercion for the cruder manipulative approach of demography. Our case against the demographic approach is a criticism of social engineering rather than of the biological model of women, but it is equally important and, because it is never heard in policy circles, it is a more significant point to make.

On the surface, demography appears to "open up" the fertility issue and to raise broader questions: to admit that "the social structure and the economy must be changed" to achieve a reduction in fertility. Despite this virtue of analytical breadth, demography is not an empowering science—or rather, it empowers only the professional elite. We would argue that the telescope should be turned the other way. Where demography sees the woman's fertility decision as the ultimate dependent variable, conditioned by economic and social changes that have their origins in government bureaus or in the international marketplace, a woman-centered approach would begin with women themselves as they perceive the conflicting demands made on them and as they calculate options for change. This is a radical proposal for which there is yet no defined methodology. But, we are suggesting, a woman-centered, contextually rich case study approach could help us rethink the "variables" of conventional analysis and better understand their cumulative effects. Further, the individual orientation of such a methodology—especially if linked to appropriate public health delivery systems—would itself empower women, even if it only had the effect of making it possible for women to articulate and become consciously aware of the social, political, economic, and moral dimensions or constraints on their own decisions and behavior.

The tension between medical and demographic approaches to population policy and the feminist critiques of both may turn out to be moot if the United States fully adopts the new direction suggested by James Buckley at the U.N. Population Meetings in Mexico City last August. Given the fact that the United States was strongly attacked in Bucharest for its insistence on population programs on the grounds that development is the only effective means of lowering fertility, it is most ironic that the Reagan Administration has apparently adopted a position close to the "radical Third World" view.

According to Buckley, the best means to achieve lowered birth rates is through market-oriented development, not the failed efforts of Third World governments to achieve development through regulation and intervention. The goals of the two groups supporting this shift in U.S. policy, the supply-side economists and the antiabortion forces who want aid to be cut to any programs that "practice or promote abortion," may not be fully compatible. However, their cooperation is made easier by a significant erosion of the consensus that was built on *The Population Bomb* and *The Limits to Growth*. Since the publication of *The Resourceful Earth* by Julian Simon and Herman Kahn (1984), pessimism about ecological degradation and doubts about the ability of the planet to feed a much larger population are no longer in vogue.[14] In addition, recent studies have argued that declines in infant mortality will result in sharp declines in population growth rates that are not yet visible in the data.

This attempt to challenge long-held assumptions that support our historic population has not occurred without controversy, as many U.N. publications and Robert McNamara's (1984) article in *Foreign Affairs* clearly show (see Clausen, 1984). The issue for us is what effect will these changes have on population policy and on women? For those who have been appalled by the excesses of inundation, by horror stories of contraceptive misuse, and by the racism and sexism of U.S. population policy to date, a cutback in these programs and a weakening of the messianic zeal of their proponents would be a welcome change. Surely, they would argue, a reduction in the power of the population lobby will put the emphasis where it should have been all along: on women as "economic" producers, not "biological" reproducers.

Perhaps so, and we would agree that the current emphasis on programs for small-scale entrepreneurs, for example, have the potential to reach women effectively. However, there are hidden dangers here as well. The "biological" definition of women had at least assured that women could not be ignored in the distribution of resources associated with population programs, including maternal and child health and food-for-work grants. Our experience is that it is very difficult to ensure that economic delivery systems will be designed to reach women or that sex-differentiated data will even be gathered to measure the impact of credit, training, and other "economic" programs on women. Given considerable evidence to support the hypothesis that economic modernization marginalizes most women and reduces their access to economic and political resources, the switch from population to a focus on market-oriented development may not be as favorable to women as it appears at first glance.

Further, the market-oriented approach, insofar as it is "anti-welfare," may well deprive many women of resources that enable them and their families to survive now. Here we have tried to argue that the biological and demographic approaches to population policy should be altered in the direction of a "women-centered" approach in order to empower women. Delegitimizing the population issue may bring short-run gains, but the bureaucratic base for reaching women through economic programs is much less extensive, less likely to reach women, and as narrow in its approach as the population programs it will replace. The "population problem" can be solved only if we stop manipulating women and devote our resources instead to giving them power over their own lives, recognizing the power they now have over ours.

NOTES

1. Both authors worked in the Women in Development Office at AID, Jaquette from 1979-1980, and Staudt during 1979 under the Intergovernmental Personnel Exchange Act.

2. On redistribution, see Staudt (1985). Although these other programs pose interesting questions worth analyzing for their biological assumptions, they remain beyond the scope of this chapter.

3. See Staudt (1985, chaps. 3, 7) on AID structure, context, and reviews of population policy.

4. This restriction was removed in 1967.

5. For a very thoughtful critique of the positivist and Malthusian assumptions behind our policies, see Harvey (1974).

6. The literature reviewing population policy is quite extensive. Ecological critics include Hardin (1976). But see also Veatch (1977) and Bachrach and Bergman (1973).

7. See Ehrenreich, Dowi, and Menken (1979). They are joined in this critique by an unlikely ally, Mrs. Randy Engel, Director, U.S. Coalition for Life, testifying in "Population and Development: Overview of the Trends, Consequences, Perspectives, and Issues," U.S. Congress (1978).

8. Feminists are beginning to revalue "female culture," however. For a provocative study based on the population issue, see Greer (1984).

9. Judith Tendler (1975) emphasizes this in *Inside Foreign Aid*.

10. For a discussion of the problems with "status of women" studies, see Jaquette (1982).

11. For additional information see Ware (1981) and Corsa and Oakley (1979, pp. 129 ff).

12. Earlier, attention to women was altogether missing from the 17 independent variable lists of a "family planning advocate," who distinguished himself from "demographers" (Bogue, 1966), and even from comparative microfield studies. See Epstein and Jackson (1977).

13. AID's record on female professionals as policymakers in population is not good. As late as the 1978 Population and Development Hearings, when this question was raised repeatedly by members of Congress, agency executives admitted that only one in five professionals were female, better, than the 12 percent of female professionals in the rest of AID (Vol. III, p. 146). Women among those testifying at the many hearings on population ranged from one in ten at the 1967-1968 Population

and Development Hearings to the all-time high of one in five at the 1978 Population and Development Hearings. At the 1973 Apropriation Hearings, the highest ranking woman at AID, Harriet Crowley, testified only to that fact, but said nothing more (according to U.S. House of Representatives, 1876, p. 895). But which women are these, for what purpose are they testifying, and most important, in what bureaucratic context do they operate?

14. For another statement favoring population growth from a surprising source, see Ester Boserup (1981).

RESOURCES

Agency for International Development. (AID). (1971). *Population program assistance: Aid to developing countries by the U.S., other nations, and international and private agencies.* Washington, DC: AID, Technical Assistance/ Population.

Bachrach, P. & Bergman, E. (1973). *Power and choice.* Lexington, MA: D. C. Heath.

Birdsall, N. (1976). Review essay: Women and population studies. *Signs, 1,* 699-712.

Bogue, D. (1966). Family planning research: An outline of the field. In Bernard Berelson (Ed.), *Family planning and population programs: A review of world development.* Chicago: University of Chicago Press.

Boserup, E. (1981). *Population and technological change: A study of long term trends.* Chicago: University of Chicago.

Boynton, W. (1978). AID population policy. In E. Glassheim, C. Cargille, & C. Hoffman (Eds.), *Key issues in population policy.* Washington, DC: University Press of America.

Brown, E. R. (1979). *Rockefeller medicine men: Medicine and capitalism in America.* Berkeley: University of California Press.

Clausen, A. W. (1984). *Population growth and economic and social development.* Washington, DC: World Bank.

Corsa, L., & Oakley, D. (1979). *Population planning.* Ann Arbor: University of Michigan Press.

Davis, K. (1967). Population policy: Will current programs succeed? *Science,* 158.

Degler, C. (1980). *At odds: Women and the family in America, from the revolution to the present.* New York: Oxford University Press.

Delamont, S., & Duffin, L. (1978). *The nineteenth century woman: Her cultural and physical world.* London: Barnes and Noble Books.

Dixon, R. B. (1982). Women in agriculture: Counting the labor force in developing countries. *Population and Development Review,* 8.

Ehrenreich, B., Dowi, M., & Menken, S. (1979). Genocide, the accused: The U.S. government. *Mother Jones* (November).

Erhlich, P. R. (1968). *The population bomb.* New York: Ballantine.

Epstein, S., & Jackson, D. (Eds.). (1977). *The feasibility of family planning: Micro perspectives.* Oxford: Pergamon Press.

Freund, P.E.S. (1982). *The civilized body: Domination, control, and health,* Philadelphia: Temple University Press.

General Accounting Office. (1978). *Reducing population growth through social and economic change in developing countries: A new direction for U.S. assistance.* Washington, DC: Author.

Gray, V. (1974). Women: Victims or beneficiaries of U.S. population policy? In V. Gray & E. Bergman (Eds.), *Political issues in U.S. population policy.* Lexington, MA: Lexington Books.

Greer, G. (1984). *Sex and destiny: The politics and human fertility.* New York: Harper & Row.

Hardin, G. (1976). Carrying capacity as an ethical concept. In G. L. Lucas, Jr., & T. W. Ogletree (Eds.), *Lifeboat ethics* (pp. 120-140). New York: Harper & Row.

Harvey, D. (1974). Ideology and population theory. *International Journal of Health Studies, 4,* 515-537.

Jaquette, J. S. (1982). Women and modernization theory: A decade of feminist criticism. *World Politics, 34.*

Littlewood, T. B. (1977). *The politics of population control.* Notre Dame, IN: University of Notre Dame Press.

McNamara, R. S. (1984). Time bomb or myth: The population problem. *Foreign Affairs, 62,* 1107-1131.

Meadows, D. H., et al. (1972). *The limits to growth: A report for the club of Romes' project on the predicament of mankind.* New York: Universe Books.

Montgomery, J. (1979). Population policies as social experiments. In J. Montgomery, H. Lasswell, & J. Migdel (Eds.), *Patterns of policy: Comparative and longitudinal studies of population events.* New Brunswick, NJ: Transaction.

Ravenholt, R. T. (1969). The AID population and family planning programme: Goals, scope and progress. *Population and internation assistance and research.* Proceedings of the First Population Conference of the Development Centre. Paris: OECD.

Rosenberg, R. (1982). *Beyond separate spheres: Intellectual routs of modern feminism.* New Haven, CT: Yale University Press.

Sax, K. (1955). *Standing room only.* Boston: Beacon.

Sax, K. (1956). *The population explosion.* New York: Foreign Policy Association.

Segal, A. (1973). The Rich, the Poor, and the Population. In R. Clinton (Ed.), *Population and politics* (pp. 173-188). Lexington, MA: Lexington Books.

Simon, J., & Kahn, H. (1984). *The resourceful earth.* Oxford: Basil Blackwell.

Sinding, S. (1979). *Study of family planning program effectiveness.* Washington, DC: AID, Bureau for Program and Policy Coordination.

Sokolow, J. A. (1983). *Eros and modernization: Sylvester Graham, health reform, and the origins of Victorian sexuality in America.* Madison: WI: Associated University Presses.

Staudt, K. (1985). *Women, foreign assistance and advocacy administration.* New York: Praeger.

Sullivan, J. H. (1978). International population control: Alternative U.S. responses in the coming decade. In E. Glassheim, C. Cargille, & C. Hoffman (Eds.), *Key issues in population policy*. Washington, DC: University Press of America.

Tangri, S. S. (1976). A feminist perspective on some ethical issues in population programs. *Signs, 1*, 895-904.

Tendler, J. (1975). *Inside foreign aid*. Baltimore, MD: Johns Hopkins Press.

U.S. Congress. (1978). *Hearings before the select committee on population* (pp. 340-341). 95th Congress, 2nd session.

U.S. House of Representatives. (1974). A feminist perspective on some ethical issues in population programs. *Signs, 1*, 895-904.

U.S. House of Representatives (1976). *Hearings before a subcommittee of the committee on appropriations: Foreign assistance and related agencies appropriations for 1976*. 94th Congress, 1st sessions, Part 2.

U.S. Senate (1967). *Hearings before the subcommittee on foreign aid expenditures of the committee on government operations: Population crisis*. 90th Congress, 1st session, Part 1.

U.S. Senate. (1979). *Hearings before the committee on appropriations, foreign assistance and related programs, FY 1980*. 96th Congress, 1st session, HR4473.

Veatch, R. M. (Ed.). (1977). *Population policy and ethics: The American Experience*. New York: Irvington Publishers/Halstead Press.

Ware, H. (1981). *Women, demography, and development*. Canberra: Australian National University.

ABOUT THE CONTRIBUTORS

RUTH BLEIER is a neuroanatomist whose primary area of scientific interest has been the part of the brain known as the hypothalamus. She was trained as a physician and practiced medicine before becoming a postdoctoral fellow in neuroanatomy at the Johns Hopkins School of Medicine. She has been politically active since college, was one of the founders and leaders in the women's movement at the university of Wisconsin—Madison in the 1970s, and has been engaged in the feminist critique of science since then. She is currently Professor of Neurophysiology and Women's Studies at the University of Wisconsin—Madison.

JANET GALLAGHER is Director of the Civil Liberties and Public Policy Program at Hampshire College in Amherst, Massachusetts. A Rutgers-Newark Law School graduate, she has been deeply involved in federal and state cases dealing with access to abortion and contraception. She has a special interest in the interface between individual reproductive rights and technology.

JANE S. JAQUETTE is Professor of Political Science and Department Chair at Occidental College, Los Angeles. She has edited two books: *Women in Politics* in 1974 and *Women in Developing Countries: A Policy Focus* with Kathleen Staudt in 1983. She has been writing recently in the fields of women in development, feminist theory, female political participation in Latin America, and Latin American politics. She is currently working on a book on women and power.

LAURA KATZ OLSON is Associate Professor of Government at Lehigh University. She is the author of *The Political Economy of Aging: The State, Private Power and Social Welfare* (Columbia University Press) and coeditor of *Aging and Public Policy: The Politics of Growing Old in America* (Greenwood Press). She has been a Fulbright Fellow, Gerontological Fellow, and a NASPAA Fellow (serving as a policy analyst at the Social Security Administration).

BARBARA KATZ ROTHMAN, an Associate Professor of Sociology at Baruch College of the City University of New York, is author of *In Labor: Women and Power in the Birthplace* (W. W. Norton, 1982); also available in paperback is *Giving Birth: Alternatives in Childbirth* (Penguin). Her current research on women's experiences with amniocentesis, *The Products of Conception,* will be published by Viking Press in 1985.

VIRGINIA SAPIRO is Associate Professor at the University of Wisconsin—Madison, with a joint appointment in the Department of Political Science and the Women's Studies Program. Primarily interested in political psychology and feminist theory, she is author of *The Political Integration of Women: Roles, Socialization, and Politics* (University of Illinois, 1983), *Women in Contemporary America* (Mayfield, in press), and numerous articles on women and politics.

KATHLEEN A. STAUDT received her Ph.D. in political science, with a minor in African studies, from the University of Wisconsin in 1976. She is currently an Associate Professor of Political Science at the University of Texas at El Paso. In 1979, Kathleen worked in the Social Science Analyst/Program Office in the Office of Women in Development, U.S. Agency for International Development. In addition to her forthcoming book, *Women, Foreign Assistance, and Advocacy Administration* (Praeger), she has coedited with Jane

Jaquette *Women in Developing Countries: A Policy Focus* (Haworth, 1983). She has published articles in *Development & Change, Journal of Politics, Comparative Politics, Journal of Developing Areas, Western Political Quarterly,* and *Policy Studies Journal,* among others.

JUDITH HICKS STIEHM is currently Vice-Provost in charge of faculty affairs at the University of Southern California and is also a Professor in the Department of Political Science. She is a graduate of Columbia University with a Ph.D. in political theory. She has been at USC since 1970, and has been active in the Program for the Study of Women and Men in Society, serving as its director from 1977 to 1978 and Faculty Chair from 1979 to 1981. She has also served on various university committees, such as the Phi Kappa Phi Executive Committee, Provost's Promotion Committee, Faculty Senate, and Mortar Board. She has written or edited six books. Her three latest are *Women and Men's Wars* (Pergamon Press, 1982; edited); *Men, Women and State Violence: Government and the Military* (The American Political Science Association, 1983); and *Women's Views of the Political World of Men* (Transnational Publishers, 1984; edited). She has also written numerous articles and book chapters. She has received the Phi Beta Kappa Award, the Dart Award for Academic Innovation, and the Phi Kappa Phi Scholarly Book Award. She is also listed in *World's Who's Who of Women* and *Who's Who in the West.*

SUSETTE M. TALARICO is Associate Professor of Political Science and Director of the Criminal Justice Program at the University of Georgia. She is author of *Criminal Justice Research: Approaches, Problems, and Policy* (1980) and many articles on criminal justice.

MARIAMNE H. WHATLEY received her A.B. in English from Radcliffe College and her Ph.D. from Northwestern in biological sciences. She is currently an Assistant Professor at the University of Wisconsin—Madison, with a joint appointment in Women's Studies and the Department of Curriculum and Instruction. She teaches women's health and biology courses and directs the health education program.

GRAHAM K. WILSON is Associate Professor of Political Science at the University of Wisconsin—Madison. He received his Ph.D. from Oxford University and subsequently taught at the University of Essex. He is author of many books and articles on American politics, interest groups, and social policy including the forthcoming *The Politics of Safety and Health.*